PUBLIC ADDRESS
AND MORAL
JUDGMENT

RHETORIC AND PUBLIC AFFAIRS SERIES

PUBLIC ADDRESS AND MORAL JUDGMENT

CRITICAL STUDIES IN ETHICAL TENSIONS

EDITED BY

Shawn J. Parry-Giles and Trevor Parry-Giles

MICHIGAN STATE UNIVERSITY PRESS • *East Lansing*

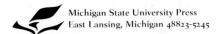
Michigan State University Press
East Lansing, Michigan 48823-5245

Printed and bound in the United States of America.

18 17 16 15 14 13 12 11 10 09   1 2 3 4 5 6 7 8 9 10

LIBRARY OF CONGRESS CATALOGING-IN-PUBLICATION DATA
Public address and moral judgment : critical studies in ethical tensions / Edited by Shawn J. Parry-Giles and Trevor Parry-Giles.
p. cm. — (Rhetoric and public affairs series)
Includes bibliographical references.
ISBN 978-0-87013-868-3 (cloth : alk. paper) 1. United States—Politics and government—1989—Moral and ethical aspects. 2. United States—Politics and government—1945–1989—Moral and ethical aspects. 3. Rhetoric—Moral and ethical aspects—United States. 4. Rhetoric—Political aspects—United States. 5. Speeches, addresses, etc., American—History and criticism. 6. English language—United States— Rhetoric. I. Parry-Giles, Shawn J., 1960– II. Parry-Giles, Trevor, 1963– III. Series.
E839.5.P827 2009
973.9—dc22
2009007070

Cover and interior design by Charlie Sharp, Sharp Des!gns, Lansing, Michigan

g green press initiative Michigan State University Press is a member of the Green Press Initiative and is committed to developing and encouraging ecologically responsible publishing practices. For more information about the Green Press Initiative and the use of recycled paper in book publishing, please visit *www.greenpressinitiative.org*.

Visit Michigan State University Press on the World Wide Web at *www.msupress.msu.edu*

To James R. Andrews

Contents

Acknowledgments

■■
■■

P ublic Address and Moral Judgment: Critical Studies in Ethical Tensions had its beginnings at the Ninth Biennial Public Address Conference, sponsored by the University of Maryland's Department
of Communication and held in Washington, D.C., in 2004. The theme
of that conference was "Constituting Political Culture," and the papers
presented there and the responses to them all focused on this theme
and its ramifications for the study of rhetoric and public address in the
twenty-first century.

As we began to gather the conference essays together for publication,
it became apparent that a critical dimension of the constitution of political culture is a concern for morality and ethical judgment. This focus
was crystallized by Marty Medhurst, a contributor to this volume and
the Rhetoric & Public Affairs series editor for Michigan State University
Press. As always, we are profoundly grateful to Marty, both for his vision

regarding this book and for his professional and personal guidance as an editor and mentor.

We are also grateful to all of the participants at the Public Address Conference, and to our colleagues at the University of Maryland—Robert Gaines, James F. Klumpp, and Mari Boor Tonn—for the hard work they put into organizing the conference. The former Department of Communication chair at the University of Maryland, Edward L. Fink, and the dean of the College of Arts and Humanities, James F. Harris, were very supportive of our hosting the conference. And many graduate students assisted in planning, organizing, and hosting the event, and we acknowledge their hard work and dedication.

Editing a volume of this kind is both rewarding and difficult, and it would not be possible without the patient and diligent support of the contributors. Each and every one of the authors in this volume deserves our endless thanks for the effort they put into revising and refining their essays and for their cheerful willingness to wait for the review process to reach its conclusion. We thank them all, and recognize the high quality of their chapters in this book.

Each Public Address Conference honors a distinguished scholar of rhetoric and public address. The Ninth Biennial Public Address Conference honored James R. Andrews, professor emeritus of Communication and Culture and Victorian Studies at Indiana University. We both were honored to study at IU when Dr. Andrews was the department chair—he served on our dissertation committees and we were lucky to take many of his courses. He was then and remains to this day a model of professional and personal kindness, a scholar of amazing insight, and a dedicated mentor. We proudly dedicate this book to James R. Andrews.

Ethical and Moral Judgment
and the Power of Public Address

Shawn J. Parry-Giles and Trevor Parry-Giles

I n his call for a rhetorical theory attending to the substance of rhetoric instead of its form or structure, Karl Wallace concluded that the basic materials of discourse were "ethical and moral values."[1] For Wallace, ethics dealt with issues of goods and values and with questions of justice and propriety, such that rhetoric fundamentally represented an art form that contributed "good reasons" to its society or statements "offered in support of an ought proposition or of a value judgment."[2]

In the decades since Wallace's call for critical attention to "good reasons," situated examples of rhetorical discourse have confirmed his theoretical conclusion; the substance of rhetoric is concerned foundationally with questions of ethics and morals. From the civil rights movement to the Vietnam War, from the struggles over the Cold War to cultural battles over women's rights and gay and lesbian rights, from defining the terrorist attacks of September 11, 2001, to understanding the emerging global economy—whatever the situation, in whichever context, the rhetoric issued to provide meaning and guide behavior often concerns the moral, the ethical, the good.

Public Address and Moral Judgment: Critical Studies in Ethical Tensions takes seriously Wallace's attention to good reasons and the critical scrutiny of the ways in which situated examples of public address enact moral codes, articulate moral judgments, and manifest ethical tensions. Each of the book's chapters carefully examines the moral dimensions of contextualized public discourse, exploring how public address functions to articulate and express the ethical tensions of its time and context. Each chapter, furthermore, highlights important and often different ways that public address works to expose problematics in ethical dilemmas— problematics of language and imagery, metaphor and character, genre and definition. Each chapter is also mindful of the tenuous relationship that exists between rhetoric and morality, between situated public address and a society's ethical foundations.

The Morality of Rhetoric

Discussing the relationships and tensions between public address and a community's morality immediately occasions a return to persistent, ancient debates about the very morality of rhetoric itself. How can a mode of human conduct (rhetoric) give expression to a community's moral code or its ethical foundations, if the activity itself is immoral? Indeed, for much of rhetoric's history, it has curried the suspicions of purists and Platonists alike who fear its power, are wary of its potential for deception, or dismiss its reliance on technique and artifice.

The ancient and lingering suspicions of rhetoric find their origins in the debates in ancient Athens between the Sophists and the Platonists. Ilham Dilman reviews the philosophical skepticism of sophistry from that period: "[Sophists] were prepared to attempt influencing people's beliefs and conduct regardless of considerations of truth and morality. This tended to undermine their pupil's regard for argument, for truth and moral considerations."[3] From the dialectician's perspective, rhetoric was at best a technique, a knack that allowed communication but that was an easily mastered, largely amoral activity. At worst, rhetoric was a danger, a diversion from the search for truth and the quest for morality. "Anxiet-ies about the possibility of deception," notes Elizabeth Markovits, "can also be seen in archaic and classical literature, beginning with Homeric poetry."[4] Such views, concludes Markovits, were so ingrained in Athenian life that "the civic ideology regarding speech was thus part of Athenian self-definition."[5]

Of course, the reason for the centrality of rhetoric in the Athenian city-state was precisely because it was rhetoric that enacted and articu-lated public life. Virtually every facet of public life for these ancients was in some way influenced by spoken language, and if such discourse gave voice to public life, its morality was open to scrutiny. So instrumental to Athenian public life was rhetoric that a situation emerged "in which the vagaries of language were linked to the success of the democracy." Not surprisingly, the community found ways to ensure the truth of the rheto-ric it heard—"Over time," Markovits notes, "the Athenians developed a set of formal, legal mechanisms in an attempt to ensure the truthfulness of speakers."[6]

These ancient tensions between morality, truth, and rhetoric do not disappear in the centuries that follow. Cicero's preoccupation with the moral character of the orator, with the creation of *virtus oratoria* through the full education of the orator in philosophy, speaks to the persistence of questions about the morality of rhetoric in the Roman world.[7] Indeed, the basis of Cicero's political theory is a belief that "the universe is governed by reason in which man has some share [and] it is only by exercise of his reasoning faculty that man can measure justice and injustice." This politi-cal theory, moreover, was intimately connected to rhetorical performance and oratorical proficiency.[8] Ultimately, this view of the community and of rhetoric's role led to Cicero's belief that "only the orator could engage in ethical instruction most effectively."[9]

Quintilian's famous definition of rhetoric as "a good man speaking well" clearly foregrounds the ethical, moral dimension of rhetoric, situat-ing this critical aspect of the oratorical art within the speaker. Arthur Walzer notes that Quintilian's belief in the role of moral philosophy in the adequate and complete training of the rhetor was as much a function of his political opportunism as anything else, but that the result of his pro-scriptions in *Institutio Oratoria* meant that rhetoric became not just a skill

but also a means for character formation.[10] As a sort of Roman bookend
to Isocrates, Quintilian envisions an educational scheme where the moral
and ethical dynamics of oratory are preeminent in the formation of a good
speaker, a good Roman citizen.

Ancient quandaries about the role of rhetoric and its capacity to function morally persisted with the tensions between philosophy and rhetoric
exacerbated by various educational and political moves in the intervening
centuries. The reconceptualization of education in the sixteenth century,
away from a Quintilian-esque model of moral and civic education rooted
in rhetoric, created a persistent situation where "rhetoric and poetry were
viewed as second-class arts designed to transmit and ornament preconceived, rational truths."[11] Designed to "correct the errors of Aristotle,
Cicero, and Quintilian," Peter Ramus's schismatic derogation of rhetoric
as only concerned with style and delivery created an intellectual environment where "rhetoric and poetry were, at once, morally neutral and
morally suspect."[12]

Ultimately, the question of rhetoric's morality remains unanswered,
with persistent concerns repeatedly raised about the dangers and possible
deceptions inherent in a culture too dependent upon communication
and symbolism. Contemporary parlance routinely denigrates political
speech as "mere rhetoric," contrasting the communicative with reality
and certainty. Ironically, the routinized critique of speech as sophistic
or baselessly rhetorical is happening precisely when academic domains,
from the sciences to the humanities, are embracing a rhetorical turn and
exploring the role of the symbolic in the formation of human reality and
meaning.

The Rhetorical Critic's Moral Role

The lengthy, often uncertain, assuredly contentious relationship between
rhetoric and morality that survived Platonic purism and Ramistic schisms
persists in contemporary studies of rhetoric and public address. The focus
has expanded, however, to include the moral and ethical responsibilities
of the rhetorical critic and further extends the deliberation over the moral
substance of rhetoric.

Rejecting the effects-based, quasi-positivistic approach of rhetorical criticism dominant at the time, critics in the 1960s and 1970s articulated the importance of an ethical stance for criticism, a meaningful assessment of the morality of rhetorical performance. In her now famous response to Forbes Hill regarding the criticism of Richard Nixon's Vietnamization speech, Karlyn Kohrs Campbell maintained the dangers of a "monistic" critical methodology that situated the critic dangerously "within the closed universe of the discourse and the ideology or point of view" of the rhetor and his or her rhetoric, all in the name of objectivity.[13] For Campbell and many others, criticism by definition required an ethical, moral judgment from the critic.

By the late 1980s, rhetorical criticism becomes, in the vision of James Klumpp and Thomas Hollihan, a form of moral action, a discourse of social change. For these authors, rhetorical criticism "obligates critics to become morally engaged," because the object of rhetorical criticism was the human use of symbols that was "fundamental to human behavior" where "social order is *performed* in language."[14] No longer, in their view, did reality and values and ethics exist prior to the rhetoric that discussed them. Instead, rhetoric's materiality was precisely its capacity to symbolically enact value and reality, necessitating that the critic operate not as a neutral observer or objective commentator, but in reaction to a "moral imperative" and a "rhetorical imperative."[15] The moral imperative, specifically, requires that the critic "recognize that a society remakes its values in responding to problems and opportunities through rhetorical choice."[16]

The concern for the moral role of the rhetorical critic has also invoked an ideological challenge to criticism, where the critic is an agent of emancipation, of freedom from oppression. In the early 1980s, Philip Wander urged rhetorical critics to examine the silences of victims rendered voiceless through domination and ideological control. Calling such a move the search for the "third persona," Wander saw a moral imperative in the critical interrogation of such rhetorics of control and domination, further extending the moral role of the cultural critic.[17] This purpose is exemplified by Charles E. Morris III, who uses Wander's vision of the third persona to argue for the queering of public address, suggesting that sexuality "stands among the last of the silent taboos, public address's shameful third persona."[18] An additional extension of Wander's critical stance is found in Raymie McKerrow's call for a "critical rhetoric" where the critic's role is to offer critiques of freedom and critiques of domination as a way of recasting "the nature of rhetoric from one grounded on Platonic, universalist conceptions of reason to one that recaptures the sense of rhetoric as contingent, of knowledge as doxastic, and of critique as a performance."[19]

On a critical level, from the ethical to the ideological, scholars for the last few decades have recognized and articulated the moral role of the rhetorical critic in the assessment of discourse. On a theoretical level, many contemporary critics embraced Wallace's redefinition of rhetoric as primarily concerned with questions of morality and ethics. For instance, in his attempt to combat the hegemony of what he labeled the "rational world paradigm," Walter Fisher articulated a competing paradigm—the narrative paradigm—for understanding the power and frequency of public moral argument. Putting aside the particularities of the narrative paradigm and what it offers to the rhetorical critic, from a theoretical standpoint, Fisher meaningfully called the attention of the rhetorical scholar away from the "rational," from the scientific, from the technical, and invited our continued scrutiny of the moral and the ethical dimensions of public argument and discourse. Fisher activated, again, a lasting focus of rhetorical inquiry, rooted in the ethical concerns of the ancient scholars and practitioners of rhetoric and emergent again in the persistent moral quandaries that confront contemporary rhetors and the audiences they address.[20]

Michael Calvin McGee took a different approach, positing a theory of ideological rhetoric that found in ideographic terms the building blocks of a society's politics, its morals and ethics, and its ideological source of public behavior and control. Still other critics have engaged more directly the role of rhetoric in the enactment of morality as expressed through situated instances of public address. Christian Spielvogel, for example, addresses the moral framing of terrorism and the Iraq war during the 2004 presidential campaign,[21] while John M. Murphy examines the ability of George W. Bush to define the September 11, 2001, attacks in such a manner as to "unify the community and amplify its values" through his almost exclusive use of epideictic, value-laden discourse.[22] And Colleen J. Shogan offers an extended discussion of the moral rhetoric of American presidents, arguing that moral rhetoric is "an instrumental tool resulting from political judgments about the costs and benefits of specific institutional environments."[23]

The essays included in *Public Address and Moral Judgment* are cognizant of the rhetorical and historical context in which they operate, a context where rhetoric is dubiously seen as morally suspect, where the critic of rhetoric occupies several, at times competing, roles, and where the object of study, the situated rhetorical address, is filled with moral and ethical meaning. In their engagement with a range of rhetorics, these critics seriously ponder how rhetoric operates to give voice to a culture's ethics, to enact a society's moral codes. In many ways, these chapters embrace Celeste Michelle Condit's call, in her programmatic statement about the relationship between rhetoric and public morality, for a recognition of "collective discourse as the source of an active public morality." Eschewing the focus on the privatization of public morality that Condit cautions against, these chapters manifest a humanly created morality that is optimistic about the capacity of human beings to "do good."[24]

Indeed, the chapters in this volume explore the very constitutive dimensions of discourse about ethics and morals for communal identity and self-definition. As James Jasinski notes, rhetoric can constitute and reconstitute individual experiences of time and space, the norms of a political culture, the experience of communal existence, and the linguistic resources of a culture.[25] Of particular concern for this project is the power of rhetoric to constitute understandings and visions of public morality. "Communal reconstitution," Jasinski points out, "can take a variety of discursive forms and rely on different textual practices as specific questions of social and political authority, power, bonds of affiliation, meaning, value, and institutional practice are confronted and negotiated."[26] Students of rhetoric and public address do well to attend to the moral dimensions of social discourse, notes Celeste Condit, because "it is possible and preferable to maintain a theory that recognizes collective discourse as the source of an active public morality."[27] In sum, these essays examine how articulations of ethics and disputes over morals can function constitutively for a community, can be at the basis of identity and nationhood, can work to give voice to essence and meaning for an entire people.

The Contexts of Active Public Morality

It is perhaps no accident, given the contemporary political environment in the United States, that war and civil rights should occasion the intense scrutiny of public address scholars interested in rhetoric's power as the articulation and enactment of public morality. As Francis A. Beer contends, "within the context of war and peace . . . is also projected the emergent pattern of human identity."[28] Similarly, Gary Gerstle argues that war is "determinative" of "nationhood" in a twentieth-century, U.S. political context, even though most "Americans do not usually think of war" in such constitutive terms.[29] War rhetoric ultimately helps create a focus "for national bonding and patriotism," while offering citizens images of themselves—"purpose, meaning, [and] a reason for living"[30]—in short, many of the moral dimensions of communal relationships.

Of course, wartime struggles can also be interwoven with contestations over civil rights; in the case of the Cold War, the civil rights abuses of African Americans in the United States exposed the moral hypocrisy of a democratic nation championing its freedoms over those countries governed by communism.[31] Such controversies over civil rights often emerge from the assumption that a "just democracy helps secure for all persons the conditions of civic equality, equal freedom, and basic opportunities,"[32] such that when these democratic values are absent, perceived disparities help create conditions for discursive political action. The prevalence of such perceived inequities gives rise to what James Arnt Aune and Enrique D. Rigsby contend is the "pervasive theme" of civil rights in American political culture.[33] Civil rights struggles required African Americans, for example, to "constitute a new conception of themselves" while also crafting a moral rhetoric that helped "overcome a system that repressed and demeaned them," Michael Leff and Ebony A. Utley contend.[34] Elaborating, Stuart Hall concludes: "Our lives have been transformed by the struggle of the margins to come into representation."[35] In turn, however, the moment of civil rights progress or "emancipation" expressed through a rhetoric of equality "opens the door to the [possibility] of freedom *and* the likelihood of massive resistance."[36]

The chapters in *Public Address and Moral Judgment* centralize the moral role of public discourse in a U.S. political context dominated by persistent concerns about war and the civil rights of its citizens. Of particular concern are the ways in which such political discourse works to (re)constitute the moral identity of the community, which in turn defines the American people and the moral imperatives accompanying such identity constructions. As Condit prophesies in her contribution to this volume: "If we have a chance of raising ourselves out of the muck of our worst potentials, it is through the tool of language . . . [T]he careful, critical study of human discourse is essential to enacting our better rather than worse potentials."[37]

A Preview of the Essays

Celeste Condit's chapter leads off the volume and asks the provocative question "Are the practices of American public address and the study of public address complicit with that moral failure [the Abu Ghraib prison abuses], or perhaps a force for amelioration?" Calling for a renewed sense of the moral dimensions of public address, Condit offers a comparative reading of George W. Bush's rhetoric in response to Abu Ghraib and Abraham Lincoln's Second Inaugural Address. Ultimately, Condit concludes that the moral has been excised from rhetorical investigation for a variety of reasons—the desire for objectivity, the tendency to demean the study of public oratory, and the failure to connect studies of culture and public address. Implicitly extending her discussion of "crafting virtue," Condit summons our continued engagement with the moral and the ethical in the criticism of rhetoric and the examination of situated public address.

Revealing the "political metaphysics" of the time in which her subject spoke, Vanessa B. Beasley in the next chapter examines the oratory of President George H. W. Bush, paying specific attention to a commencement address given by the first President Bush at West Point in June 1991. Beasley argues that Bush "subtly refutes the fundamental principles of political pluralism, the model of democracy frequently used to explain interest group politics in the United States" and thus offers a reconstitution of political culture and its conception of civil rights in the United States. Rejecting the facile conclusion that Bush was motivated largely by a sense of decency and courtesy, Beasley concludes that something more significant is happening with his rhetoric—an articulation of an emergent hyperindividualism that is fraught with moral and ethical danger for rights discourse in the twenty-first century. "How can the United States," Beasley asks, "one of the world's largest functioning diverse and culturally pluralistic democracies, survive as such without a way of talking about its own pluralities in terms of their own needs, histories, and obligations to each other?" Beasley calls our attention to the arguments, the themes, and the inventional processes at work in the articulation of an emergent moral code about diversity and civil rights in the United States.

In the third chapter, Martin J. Medhurst examines the public moral arguments advanced by both proponents and opponents of same-sex marriage. Medhurst argues that "the debate can best be understood as a battle over the place and definition of 'marriage,'" and that "this battle is enacted through public narratives that each side constructs to tell its story about married life in America." The figurative language employed by both sides also gives key insights into how the narrative appeal is structured as well as the actions that are required of auditors. Understanding how the story elements are mobilized and how the tropes and figures are deployed reveals what is at stake for each side—and, ultimately, for American society. Further demonstrating the discursive intersection of war and civil rights, Medhurst demonstrates how figurative language central to the narratives revolves around metaphors of war, images of death and destruction, and analogies to the black civil rights movement and to Nazi Germany, revealing powerfully that language use and construction are central to ethical tensions and moral judgments made in rhetorical interactions.

In the fourth chapter, James Jasinski and John M. Murphy turn to a signature figure of the civil rights movement, Martin Luther King Jr., and consider how his speech "A Time to Break Silence" is significant for expressing U.S. moral rhetoric of the late 1960s. Tracing the intersecting contexts of war and civil rights, Jasinski and Murphy identify the speech as a radical jeremiad and note how King's moral oratory exploited time, space, and genre in its articulation of a radicalized call for rethinking U.S.

political culture and the nature of civil resistance. In this way, Jasinski and Murphy reveal the singular power of civil rights rhetoric to articulate a moral code for a political culture confronting its own contradictions and hypocrisies during a time of war. At the same time, using the critical tools of form and genre, these authors call attention to the power of discourse to express via form a vision of moral rightness.

A critical moment in the constitution of U.S. political culture was World War II, and James J. Kimble's examination of the government war bonds program during this great conflagration highlights the power of discourse emanating from institutional sources to significantly shape the public's moral consciousness during wartime. Kimble highlights the anxieties felt by the government at the outset of World War II concerning the level of engagement of a relatively secure and isolated home front in the war effort, and he details how the Roosevelt administration, through the Treasury Department, sought to address such apathy. In particular, he accentuates the importance of metaphors in the creation of *communitas* or national solidarity surrounding the war effort through war bonds, which featured a militarization of such domestic contributions, transforming citizens into soldiers and providing moral meaning and power to a conflict that for many existed in distant lands across vast oceans.

Assuming a longitudinal view of presidential foreign policy rhetoric in the next chapter, Shawn J. Parry-Giles furthers the notion of the rhetorical presidency as a means of constituting the romantic ideological formations of the nation-state during times of war. More specifically, this essay situates the Bush administration's doctrine of preemption in the history of presidential constructions of war and peace, centering on the extended thematics of rhetorical presidents, who serve as some of the most powerful voices of the nation-state. This chapter assesses the influence of a nineteenth-century construction and commitment to a moral benevolence in addressing African Americans, Native Americans, and immigrants—a rhetorical legacy that reappears in twentieth-century *war* discourse. As the rhetoric of the Cold War takes shape, *benevolent war* constructions exist alongside rhetorics of an *imperial peace*. So as to combat images of an aggressor nation, a discourse of benevolence and thus morality functions to temper American commitments to militarism. Yet, because of the perceived equation of peace with weakness and war with strength, linguistic usages of peace assume an imperial and masculine focus, where commanders-in-chief accentuate U.S. supremacy and power.

The final chapter features Rebecca Gill and Marouf A. Hasian Jr.'s examination of Abu Ghraib and the vilification of Lynndie England for alleged wartime atrocities, revealing the limits of the moral and ideological formations and the potential outgrowth of hegemonic masculinity and the arrogance of power on those carrying out the public's contributions to public moral judgment about these events. Gill and Hasian suggest that the feminization of Iraq and thus the masculinization of the United States furthered the potential for atrocities. In order to lessen the international fallout over the photographs that circulated around the Internet and revealed the civil rights abuses in Iraq, the Bush administration depicted the atrocities as anti-American and worked to scapegoat the individual perpetrators of the acts, hoping to preserve the illusion of American exceptionalism. Highlighting another problematic in the relationship between rhetoric and morality, Gill and Hasian emphasize the ethical ambiguities of photography and gender as means of giving voice to moral outrage.

Each of the chapters of *Public Address and Moral Judgment* explore the power of public morality as a focus of rhetorical performance, a nexus for rhetorical enactment. Confronting a series of ethical tensions, the rhetors examined in this book invoke, define, constitute, and challenge public moral argument as they strive to craft virtue and offer rhetorical judgment for a community craving such leadership.

Early in the Cold War, in 1952, William Norwood Brigance reflected on just such questions in an address to the Southern Speech Association meeting in Jackson, Mississippi. Brigance's speech, given as it was in the throes of the Korean War, and immediately prior to the outbreak of the civil rights movement, concluded that public rhetoric (and specifically, public oratory) offers a "watering and cultivating of ideas." "We live in a world that confronts us with many sorts of problems," Brigance argued. In that world, he said, "We are beset by temptations. We are haunted by fears. We are uncertain of the future." One solution, he maintained, was to listen to oratory: "We listen to speeches because we hope the speakers will give us new ideas, or new information, or will simply water and cultivate old ideas. We listen because we want to be given encouragement, to renew our faith, to strengthen our determination."[38]

The essays collected here consider this powerful role of public discourse, about various topics and coming from a variety of sources, in the constitution of a moral code for the American people. They indicate how the close examination of rhetorical discourse contributes to the ongoing scholarly conversation about public morality and public ethical judgment, a conversation critical to the constitution of public life in a contemporary, democratic community.

NOTES

1. Karl Wallace, "The Substance of Rhetoric: Good Reasons," *Quarterly Journal of Speech* 49 (1963): 240.

2. Ibid., 247.

3. Ilham Dilman, *Morality and the Inner Life: A Study in Plato's Gorgias* (New York: Barnes and Noble Books, 1979), 9.

4. Elizabeth Markovits, *The Politics of Sincerity: Plato, Frank Speech, and Democratic Judgment* (University Park: Pennsylvania State University Press, 2008), 63.

5. Ibid.

6. Ibid., 64.

7. See W. Leonard Grant, "Cicero on the Moral Character of the Orator," *Classical Journal* 38 (1943): 473.

8. S. E. Smethurst, "Politics and Morality in Cicero," *The Phoenix* 9 (1955): 116.

9. E. Armstrong, *A Ciceronian Sunburn: A Tudor Dialogue on Humanistic Rhetoric and Civic Poetics* (Columbia: University of South Carolina Press, 2006), 32.

10. Arthur Walzer, "Moral Philosophy and Rhetoric in the *Institutes*: Quintilian on Honor and Expediency," *Rhetoric Society Quarterly* 36 (2006): 263–280.

11. Armstrong, *Ciceronian Sunburn*, 19. See also Walter J. Ong, *Ramus, Method, and the Decay of Dialogue: From the Art of Discourse to the Art of Reason* (Cambridge: Harvard University Press, 1958).

12. Armstrong, *Ciceronian Sunburn*, 18. See also Peter Levine, *Living without Philosophy: On Narrative, Rhetoric, and Morality* (Albany: State University of New York Press, 1998), 47.

13. Karlyn Kohrs Campbell, "'Conventional Wisdom—Traditional Form': A Rejoinder,"

Quarterly Journal of Speech 58 (1972): 453–454.

14. James F. Klumpp and Thomas A. Hollihan, "Rhetorical Criticism as Moral Action," *Quarterly Journal of Speech* 75 (1989): 87–88, emphasis in original. See also Philip C. Wander and Steven Jenkins, "Rhetoric, Society, and the Critical Response," *Quarterly Journal of Speech* 58 (1972): 441–451.

15. Klumpp and Hollihan, "Rhetorical Criticism," 90.

16. Ibid.

17. Philip C. Wander, "The Third Persona: An Ideological Turn in Rhetorical Theory," *Central States Speech Journal* 35 (1984): 197–216.

18. Charles E. Morris III, "Introduction: Portrait of a Queer Rhetorical/Historical Critic," in *Queering Public Address: Sexualities in American Historical Discourse*, ed. Charles E. Morris III (Columbia: University of South Carolina Press, 2008), 4.

19. Raymie E. McKerrow, "Critical Rhetoric: Theory and Praxis," *Communication Monographs* 56 (1989): 92.

20. Walter R. Fisher, "Narration as a Human Communication Paradigm: The Case of Public Moral Argument," *Communication Monographs* 51 (1984): 1–21.

21. Christian Spielvogel, "'You Know Where I Stand': Moral Framing of the War on Terrorism and the Iraq War in the 2004 Presidential Campaign," *Rhetoric & Public Affairs* 8 (2005): 549–569.

22. John M. Murphy, "'Our Mission and Our Moment': George W. Bush and September 11," *Rhetoric & Public Affairs* 6 (2003): 602. See also Michael J. Hyde, "The Rhetor as Hero and the Pursuit of Truth: The Case of 9/11," *Rhetoric & Public Affairs* 8 (2005): 1–30.

23. Colleen J. Shogan, *The Moral Rhetoric of American Presidents* (College Station: Texas A&M University Press, 2006), 11.

24. Celeste Michelle Condit, "Crafting Virtue: The Rhetorical Construction of Public Morality," *Quarterly Journal of Speech* 73 (1987): 79.

25. Jasinski, "A Constitutive Framework," 75.

26. Ibid., 77.

27. Condit, "Crafting Virtue," 79.

28. Francis A. Beer, ed., "Language and the Meaning of War and Peace," in *Meanings of War and Peace* (College Station: Texas A&M University Press, 2001), 177.

29. Gary Gerstle, *American Crucible: Race and Nation in the Twentieth Century* (Princeton, N.J.: Princeton University Press, 2001), 9.

30. See Nira Yuval-Davis, *Gender and Nation* (London: Sage, 1997), 97; and Chris Hedges, *War Is a Force That Gives Us Meaning* (New York: Public Affairs, 2002), 3.

31. See Mary L. Dudziak, *Cold War Civil Rights: Race and the Image of American Democracy* (Princeton, N.J.: Princeton University Press, 2000), 14–15.

32. Amy Gutmann, *Identity in Democracy* (Princeton, N.J.: Princeton University Press, 2003), 29.

33. James Arnt Aune and Enrique D. Rigsby, eds., "Rhetorical Constitutions and Reconstitutions of the Meaning of Civil Rights," in *Civil Rights Rhetoric and the American Presidency* (College Station: Texas A&M University Press, 2005), 10.

34. Michael Leff and Ebony A. Utley, "Instrumental and Constitutive Rhetoric in Martin Luther King Jr.'s 'Letter from Birmingham Jail,'" *Rhetoric and Public Affairs* 7 (2004): 38.

35. Stuart Hall, "The Local and the Global: Globalization and Ethnicity," in *Dangerous Liaisons: Gender, Nation, and Postcolonial Perspectives* (Minneapolis: University of Minnesota Press, 1997), 183.

36. Kirt H. Wilson, *The Reconstruction Desegregation Debate: The Politics of Equality and the Rhetoric of Place, 1870–1875* (East Lansing: Michigan State University Press, 2002), 183.

37. Celeste Michelle Condit, "Where Is Public Address? George W. Bush, Abu Ghraib, and Contemporary Moral Discourse," in this volume.

38. William Norwood Brigance, "Demagogues, 'Good' People, and Teachers of Speech," *Speech Teacher* 1 (1952): 159.

Where Is Public Address?
George W. Bush, Abu Ghraib, and
Contemporary Moral Discourse

Celeste Michelle Condit

I t is time for us to take stock of where public address study is today, in order to think about where we might want to push it in future years. To do that, we need a measuring stick, and the one that I have chosen is the rhetoric surrounding the humiliation of prisoners at Abu Ghraib and related facilities by U.S. soldiers and our government's other employees.

I choose Abu Ghraib because I believe that it provides a clear demonstration of serious moral failure by the United States of America acting on the world stage. While there are many good arguments that the invasion of Iraq itself was a moral failure of the nation, that claim is at least contestable. In contrast, only the most extreme of commentators—such as Rush Limbaugh, who repeatedly compared the goings-on in Abu Ghraib to a typical Madonna or Britney Spears concert—fail to understand that the behaviors at Abu Ghraib represent significant moral failure.[1] Even President Bush, though he denied the representativeness of the event, portrayed the behavior of American personnel at Abu Ghraib as morally reprehensible, describing them as "disgraceful" and "abhorrent."[2] So Abu Ghraib can be reasonably taken as standing for the failure of American will to prevent morally impermissible actions by the purveyors of our power.

Where, then, does the practice and study of public address in the United States stand in relationship to such a measuring stick? To answer this question, I will first briefly describe public morality as a set of codes constituted by rhetorical processes. I will next overview a series of fragments of (im)moral discourse pervasive in American culture that provided the fodder for the performance of the behaviors of Abu Ghraib. I will then move to establish an oratorical criterion for Bush's response to this public moral debasement by highlighting rhetorical scholarship about Lincoln's Second Inaugural Address as a touchstone for comparison. After examining Bush's speech in light of that touchstone, I will return to American values and contrast them to those of the Iraqis to illuminate some substantive differences in the moral value systems at stake in the "conflict" or "war" between the two national cultures. I will conclude by charting a series of failures of public address scholarship, which stand simultaneously as a chart for future opportunities for public address scholarship and pedagogy.

Rhetoric Constitutes Morality

To question the culpability of public address scholars in Abu Ghraib, given the prominence of particular academic theories today, I need to defend using a *moral* measuring stick. Many politically well-meaning scholars eschew the term *morality* in favor of the term *ideology* on political and epistemological grounds. Those political grounds need to be historicized. Yes, there has been a historical proclivity for the right wing to claim that its social codes are "moral," when in fact they are merely ideological. Despite this history, however, there are a few moral codes that transcend culture and class. Moreover, while ideology arguably consists of masking self-interest as general interest,[3] one only knows that there is a masking to the extent that one has a conception of the moral.

In philosophical and theological traditions, morality or ethics has been defined variously in terms of duty, rules, or virtues.[4] However, I have previously argued that adopting a rhetorical frame reveals morality to be constituted by a set of codes created by the processes of public discussion over the long term.[5] On this account, the distinctively moral component of such codes is the specification of behavior that requires taking account of the needs and value of the "Other," rather than acting solely on self-interest. The behavior at Abu Ghraib provides a relatively clear example of immoral behavior. Such behavior is not only unconscionable in our culture; it appears so according to the overlapping moral codes of other cultures on the globe. The behaviors are readily recognizable as demeaning humiliation, even when not precisely conceived as torture. If these behaviors took place in other contexts—other countries or times—there might well be situational efforts to defend such behavior, but it is very difficult to defend the world's superpower taking advantage of the helpless. Such behavior smacks self-evidently of narrow self-interest of the most brutish sort.

So a *moral* measuring stick might be said to be appropriate, even, I would argue, required.[6] And, I would suggest, Abu Ghraib is one of the low-water marks that indicates the moral failure of the American empire. So the question is, "Are the practices of American public address and the study of public address complicit with that moral failure, or perhaps a force for amelioration?" Another way to put this is to ask whether, in order to make a contribution toward improving the moral caliber of the national character we need to fundamentally alter how others practice public address and how we study and teach it, or whether we just need a lot more of what we do, to counter other global factors. I ask this question not because I believe that we can, like superwoman, sweep in and save the day if we only get right what we are doing, but because I believe we have an obligation to align our actions with forces that would ameliorate such wrongs, even if we ultimately might not have the requisite force to achieve our ends.

The Fragments of Public Address That Form the Fodder for Constituting Abu Ghraib

A brief inspection of the contemporary practice of public address with regard to Abu Ghraib is not encouraging. As my former colleague Kevin

DeLuca argues, one of the dominant arenas for public address today is the public screen,[7] and our television serials and movies are filled with valorizations of behavior that model analogues of the actions at Abu Ghraib, or visual fragments that are easily assembled into those actions. The best analogues for the Abu Ghraib photos are in the X-rated magazines and movies. Before dismissing the significance of these images in our culture, remember that pornographic videos represent one out of every five movie rentals in the United States.[8] I do not expect anyone to recognize, or at least admit to having seen, these movies, but the photos of Abu Ghraib are clearly pornographic. They include photos of laughing male and female soldiers mocking the prisoners whose heads they have covered with bags and whom they have forced into the postures of group sex. If one wants to know where our soldiers got their ideas for their Abu Ghraib photos, she should check out X-rated magazines and movies. This is an area we don't talk about in communication criticism much, but given their popularity, and now apparent influence on behavior, perhaps rhetorical scholars need to work up the strength to deal with them more directly.

Even in more visible, "public" media, however, there is fodder for Abu Ghraib–like action. In *Raiders of the Lost Ark* we mocked the Arabs who fight with swords, brandishing our superior weapons. This theme was reprised in *Hidalgo*, where the redneck American cowboy shows how crass, ill-mannered American strength and power can outshine the ancient traditions of the Arab world. More common, and therefore perhaps of greater impact, is the "brutal interrogation" scene that appears in almost every crime drama on television. In these scenes, a righteous and wrathful interrogator grabs the suspect by the throat, or shoves him into a wall or table, trying to physically wring out the truth. In such scenes we are generally positioned to side with the interrogator. Disrespect for the humanity of people being interrogated is normalized by these portrayals.

American comedy provides another component at this image bazaar. In American comedy today, everything is funny. There are no longer any bounds of what used to be called "good taste." You can make fun of any racialized group, any gender, even handicapped people, and people who are dying are considered fair game.[9] Whether it's slapstick video in cheap movies or stand-up comic routines in expensive Las Vegas venues, we have indulged ourselves in mocking everything. Why should our soldiers think that prisoners were off limits? What's wrong, don't you have a sense of humor?

One final piece of the cultural input is our news media. Shortly after the invasion of Afghanistan, I was watching television news coverage of the entry of prisoners to Guantánamo Bay prison camp. Prisoners were hooded, isolated, handcuffed, shoved along at rifle-point, through barbed-wire runs. The inhumane treatment sickened me. I re-upped with the ACLU. The country registered only a ripple of concern about these prisoners' rights. Our reaction was subdued because the pictures manifested our fear, still fresh from the assault of 9/11. The guards were treating each prisoner as an unpredictable bomb that might go off at the slightest opportunity. The ease with which Americans discarded the rules of law and feelings of common humanity in the face of this fear accurately foretold the ease with which we would discard basic moral behavior once we reassured ourselves that our overwhelming power allowed us to "shock and awe" others (rather than the other way around). In other words, the behaviors in the later set of photos—those at Abu Ghraib—are the same set of behaviors in the earlier set of photos—news pictures at Guantánamo Bay. The only difference is the felt confidence of the person enacting the behaviors. When we are afraid, we dehumanize and control the other, but cautiously. When we are confident, we dehumanize and control the other, but we are happier about it; we can joke and laugh. Because our news media today feed on shocking visual images, but eschew any liberalizing commentary, even provide normalizing commentary, our news too is part of the culture that produces an Abu Ghraib.

This media culture dominates our political and social *actions* in the absence of a voice of loyal opposition in the political arenas of the nation. In the first year after the photos were revealed, where there was political debate, the focus was not on the need to assess or improve our character, or even to understand why Americans might have behaved in such a fashion. Rather, the voice was merely the whining attack of political partisanship, seeking to influence the nearest election. Hence, the debate over Abu Ghraib devolved into a debate over whether the Bush administration directly ordered soldiers to behave in an atrocious manner. Given that the administration probably did not directly do so, they, and presumably we, all stand absolved. Only a few individual soldiers with inadequate legal counsel have been found to be wanting in moral responsibility at Abu Ghraib.

But of course that is not a sufficient standard. We are guilty, as a nation, either for encouraging or for not adequately restraining the soldiers at Abu Ghraib (or both). If you believe that human behavior is entirely cultural, our culture is guilty for encouraging such behavior. If you believe that human behavior is inherently predisposed to such depravity, then we are guilty for failing to restrain such behavior. In either case, our public address is implicated—first, by fomenting such behavior through our culture industry, and then by targeting Iraqis supportive of Saddam Hussein through our presidential proclamation of a "crusade" against them as an alien force of inherent evil.[10] Our cultural and political discourse together made those people fitting scapegoats for September 11, to apply Kenneth Burke's still very apt reading of the nature of scapegoating discourse.[11]

Lincoln's Second Inaugural as a Touchstone

I will return to give more detail to the reading of President Bush's rhetoric, but first, what about us, the students of public address? What about our possible relationship to American atrocities at Abu Ghraib? I want to begin an answer to that question at some distance from the immediate case by recalling one of the best moments in the history of public address scholarship. At the combined Southern-Central Convention in 1987 a panel of scholars, introduced by David Zarefsky, explored Abraham Lincoln's Second Inaugural Address. The talks of all the panelists were subsequently published in volume 1 of *Communication Reports*. At that panel, Michael Leff gave a brilliant reading of Lincoln's speech that cemented his recently developed version of close textual analysis, which highlights the temporality of texts. Martha Solomon Watson responded with a pointed counter-reading based on the interaction of the text with different audience sensitivities. James Arnt Aune then provided a sinuous analysis interweaving the tropes of the text and the moral model it made available, while Ronald Carpenter presented the results of combing the historical archives to show how key parts of the text emerged from circulating fragments of discourse. This was a key moment in public address studies because it brought together people who were experts in mining public address with different tools and to different ends, and who analyzed a single text on a single shared stage. This revealed the potential richness of public address study, the depth of its development as an academic practice, the range of insight it could provide, as well as the synergy of the different approaches, even at the moments of their greatest disagreement. However, this moment was possible only because Lincoln's text itself had the depth, intensity, and scope to engage this breadth of exploration.

Lincoln's Second Inaugural was significant not simply because it had excellent tropes. Lincoln's address had unique power because it was a nexus point in which a centrally positioned, skilled source funneled, in a higher moral direction, powerful forces at large in the nation. It was, as the collection of analyses revealed, a speech in which the art of language was skillfully used to guide the ideological forces of the historical context in a particular direction. The speech was not particularly successful in its historical moment. The telling fragments it artfully deployed might not have been highly successful at channeling the roaring forces of Northern retribution even if Lincoln had lived out his presidential term. But of course, rhetoricians have long understood the need to judge a rhetorical act by its deployment of the available means of persuasion rather than by its ability to overcome barriers that may be too large for any effort. The speech lives on in our memories because of the combination of the skill of the effort and because of its moral appropriateness. As Aune rightly pointed out, what Lincoln gave the nation was a model for moral behavior that surpassed the moral models of the era.

I have previously maintained that the constitutive power of rhetoric to produce novel and more elevated moral codes is a unique value of human discourse.[12] The symbol-using capacities of human beings not only create the possibility of morality, they create the possibility of innovation to provide new moral codes, as well as ways of understanding new situations in relationship to moral codes. Furthermore, these human capacities allow us to create new types of situations to enable moral codes, and the ability to hold ourselves and others accountable to those codes that we endorse. This prodigious capacity of discourse is counterbalanced by the relatively unrestrained potential for innovation that is also a hallmark of the symbolic realm. Not all innovations are good, especially with regard to their moral contents, and this makes judgment of those innovations imperative. In art, we value and judge symbolic innovations for their simple novelty or for the specific ways in which they fit different components together. In public address, we value innovations for how they direct us to live together. This is why rhetoric always is more than a *techne* separated from moral issues and social contexts. This understanding allows us to see an alternative to Plato's representation of rhetoric as either devoid of morals or subordinate to a moral code learned elsewhere. *Rhetorical activity creates moral codes, and the judgment of action is intrinsic to the code.*

This is why we should attend more carefully to Michael Leff's argument that public address scholarship serves humanity by providing an accumulation of well-understood touchstones.[13] Such touchstones provide us with a repertoire that reveals the modes of rhetorical action that have so far been invented by human beings. To be sure, to provide a truly human scope, such models must be multicultural. Moreover, I would argue that they can profitably include examples of morally debauched rhetoric in order to chart the shadow side of human potential. However, when we accumulate a sufficiently broad and diverse group of such touchstones, and when we understand each from multiple perspectives, we gain a guidebook to human potentials. Such a guide allows us not simply to predict human behavior, success, and failure (though it may make us somewhat better at those things), but to gauge our existing human limits. It thereby allows us to set expectations for ourselves that exceed not only our animal capacities, but also our own histories.

The Constitution of Public Morality in Lincoln's Second Inaugural

So let us use Lincoln's Second Inaugural as a touchstone for comparison to our own moment, specifically the rhetoric of Abu Ghraib. This leap in time, from our own moment to March 4 of 1865, is not so long a stretch as it might seem. On that day, Abraham Lincoln stood in a position that was in important ways analogous to our own. He had won a war, but now he faced the challenge of winning the peace. Then, as now, it was, as Henry Ward Beecher observed, "more dangerous to make peace than to make war." Lincoln's Northern troops and Northern citizenry had shed much blood and treasure in the horrific fighting. They had dehumanized Southerners in order to be able to kill them. They would be tempted to torture, to bully, to disregard the humanity of their conquered foes.

Lincoln recognized this state of his Northern audience. But he also recognized that people always live with multiple tendencies. They can be led to hatred and murder, but they can also be led to forgiveness and neighborliness. Lincoln's speech crafted a rhetorical bridge for moving the Northern audience from enemies to neighbors (rather than to bullies). This is the speech that ends with a powerful vision that is a call to moral action. Lincoln says,

> With malice toward none, with charity for all, with firmness in the right as God gives us to see the right, let us strive on to finish the work we are in, to bind up the nation's wounds, to care for him who shall have borne the battle and for his widow and his orphan, to do all which may achieve and cherish a just and lasting peace among ourselves and with all nations.[14]

The readings of this speech provided us by Aune and Leff in 1987 revealed the tools Lincoln used to make this vision compelling. Stated oversimply for present purposes, Leff's argument was that Lincoln's speech created an artistic whole that moved from secular to sacred time and thereby moved his audience toward the "elemental virtues of Christianity." Aune's analysis focused on the tropes in the speech, and showed how the progression of tropes allowed Lincoln to craft a reconstruction of American individualism into a national self-definition of suffering servanthood. Both Leff and Aune noted how prior temporal conditions and attitudes were worked upon by rhetorical elements to allow the production of another alternative motivational set, one based in Christianity, but drawing on the fundamental virtues of human caring.

Bush's Apologia/Nonapology for Abu Ghraib

How then, does our contemporary presidential address regarding an at least somewhat similar situation measure up to this touchstone? President Bush gave planned interviews to Arab-language news outlets that were designed to position America in response to the atrocities. These interviews are interesting in their own right, and are quite different from the speech he gave to the American people on May 24, 2004.[15] But it is the speech to the American people that must carry the freight in this situation, for a call to moral accountability must be made to the perpetrators, not to the victims.

Much has been made of the fact that Bush himself offered no apologies about Abu Ghraib in any of his discourses. Explicit apologies were left to lower-ranking individuals on the ground in Iraq, rather than on the U.S. public screen.[16] Although Bush did not apologize, this speech should nonetheless be read as an apologia, because it was the only speech addressed to the U.S. public that responded to the charges against the nation and the administration regarding the evil actions at Abu Ghraib. The speech also can be located in that genre, because of the visibility of typical apologic strategies, including transcendence and differentiation, and some bolstering.[17] Explicitly and most obviously, Bush differentiated America, the nation, from the Americans who committed the acts. America did not commit these war crimes, he asserted—rogue individuals did so.

Bush's larger strategy may not be so obvious. It requires familiarity with genre theory to identify clearly. Bush used the strategy genre theorists have labeled *transcendence* to imply that the actions at Abu Ghraib were insignificant, not worth worrying about really, given the context of larger goals. Although the occasion, the press, and the opposition called for Bush to explain, even defend, the occurrence of the mistreatment or torture of prisoners at Abu Ghraib, Bush downplayed the event, constituting it not as a major moral crisis requiring sustained attention, but rather as a minor error by a few soldiers, one that was reasonably subsumed within the larger war effort and best addressed by replacing the building where the event occurred. To execute this strategy, the address is dominated by the war goals and contexts, and the issue of Abu Ghraib is subordinated to a small subsection.

This usage of the strategy of transcendence was so powerful that the speech does not immediately appear on its surface to be an apologia at all. The transcendent causes Bush emphasizes loom so large that they obscure the actions of Abu Ghraib and thereby justify Bush's cursory treatment of them. Nonetheless, though this use of transcendence proves to be a distressingly effective strategy for deflecting attention from the events at Abu Ghraib, a comparison to Lincoln's rhetorical choices highlights its inadequacy.

Given my larger objectives, I am only going to attend to some central features of Bush's speech, though there are several mutually reinforcing points that could be made. The speech begins with an ode to warfare, for it is delivered at the Army War College, surely an interesting location and beginning for an apologia on war crimes. The president begins with an active and confident declaration: "I've come here tonight to report to all Americans, and to the Iraqi people." The speech is framed as a report on the progress of the war; it is not framed as an apologia. Any need for national apology, let alone introspection, is thereby downplayed if it is not outright denied. What is needed in the face of the exposure of the images of Abu Ghraib, Bush indicates instead, is a report on our goals and our plans for completing our "agenda."

From the beginning, Bush positions himself as the central agent in the global drama, an approach that contrasts dramatically with Lincoln's address. As Leff has noted, the inaugural address began in an oddly passive, self-abnegating fashion (Lincoln says: "at this second appearing to take the oath of the presidential office there is less occasion for an extended address than there was at the first").[18] Moreover, throughout Lincoln's speech, it is not individuals, but larger forces that shape the world—history, God, and large geographic regions. Only at the end of the speech does Lincoln prescribe activity for less abstract agents—Lincoln and the people are described as "we" who must act with charity to bind up the nation's wounds. In contrast, President Bush's speech is bristling with active agents, and though the agent is often "we" or "they," the president himself is the commanding actor. "I sent American troops to Iraq to defend our security," he says. "At my direction," the efforts in Iraq are being accelerated, he indicates. "I asked," "I directed," "I thank them," he repeats. The only place where Bush eschews personal direction of American actions is in the passage on Abu Ghraib. There other individuals are the source of agency.

Though Bush portrays himself as an active agent in the speech, this is not a simple Agent-Act ratio.[19] The actions Bush takes are those justified by and appropriate to the context. He is the agent who does what the scene calls for, but he is not commanded by scene; rather his actions are directed to conquering that scene. This set of ratios explains why the speech must spend so much of its space describing the actions of evil enemies.

The first four paragraphs detail the brutality of the enemies of the United States and imagine the putative future of a free Iraq. Bush does not say he is addressing the images from Abu Ghraib, but they are clearly motivating when he tries to reconstitute the historical moment by offering alternative visual images:

> We've also seen images of a young American facing decapitation. This vile display shows a contempt for all the rules of warfare and all the bounds of civilized behavior. It reveals a fanaticism that was not caused by any action of ours and would not be appeased by any concession.

Though the notorious photographs are not explicitly addressed as such, when the speech is understood, because of its timing and latent contents, as the apologia for Abu Ghraib, this opening provides the grounds that justify the president's choice to transcend the moral quagmire of the prison scandal and focus instead on the war. The context of the war justifies the occurrence of torture or mistreatment of prisoners. The war is a context in which U.S. soldiers are daily threatened with decapitation, and where our enemies have contempt for "civilized behavior." Subtly, the president suggests that the enemy does not, perhaps, deserve civilized treatment. Because decency is not reciprocated, it appears that we may be absolved of the obligation to act decently. At the least, this context suggests that one might understand how U.S. soldiers would respond in uncivilized ways to uncivilized people. We are thereby urged, as a nation, to see the behaviors of Abu Ghraib in a context that downplays their seriousness and makes them perhaps expected or excusable, if not precisely normal.

This is a moral code diametrically opposed to that suggested by Lincoln's inaugural. Lincoln suggested that the chaos of war was not caused by a single agent, and that the causes did not remove the responsibility for humane, even charitable actions. Perhaps a key part of what enabled Lincoln to maintain such a moral code was that he did not box his audience and himself in by assigning the cause of the war to specific human agents, nor did he assign himself the central responsibility for ameliorating the scene (as Bush does). Instead, Lincoln transcended the limitations of individuals and called on collective and higher forces to drive the constitution and implementation of a higher moral code. Lincoln eschewed a harsh, dichotomizing style, and instead employed pentadic ratios and a style that wove agents, scenes, and temporal domains together.[20] In contrast, by placing Bush as the central agent of a battle in which the opposition was pure evil, Bush's rhetorical strategy made it impossible to vest moral culpability in the United States without vesting it primarily in himself. He also made it impossible to condemn any actions of the United States without thereby lauding or absolving the enemy. Not only was he unwilling to do these things politically, but as I will later argue, such a description of the causes of Abu Ghraib would have been inadequate, if my description of the U.S. moral terrain is at all correct.

The next several paragraphs of Bush's speech therefore can merely continue to emphasize that the situation—caused by the enemy—explains the soldiers' behavior, and by implication absolves us of moral responsibilities. Bush notes that "our work has been hard," the situation "chaotic." The president also bolsters the morality of the nation's actions by suggesting that we are building hospitals and inspiring people to live in hope. Bush says, "Our enemies in Iraq are good at filling hospitals, but they don't build any. They can incite men to murder and suicide, but they cannot inspire men to live in hope and add to the progress of their country." Thus, any moral lapses are more than paid back in an alternative moral coin. The centerpiece of this currency are the five steps the United States is enacting to achieve "democracy and freedom" in Iraq. The third step addresses the need for rebuilding the nation's infrastructure. It is here that Abu Ghraib makes its only explicit appearance. Bush says:

A new Iraq will also need a humane, well-supervised prison system. Under the dictator, prisons like Abu Ghraib were symbols of death and torture. That same prison became a symbol of disgraceful conduct by a few American troops who dishonored our country and disregarded our values.

America will fund the construction of a modern maximum security prison. When that prison is completed, detainees at Abu Ghraib will be relocated. Then with the approval of the Iraqi government, we will demolish the Abu Ghraib prison as a fitting symbol of Iraq's new beginning.

Burkean critics will easily recognize the use of scene as the controlling pentadic element in this section of the speech.[21] The prison is literally a symbol of death and torture. As such the prison building is a structure that somehow brings out such behavior. Eliminate the symbolic structure and you have effaced the problem. The moral chill is enormous here, as all that is required to redress the problem is for a "modern maximum security prison" to replace the old building. The contrast to Lincoln's call for charity and benevolence could not be starker. For Lincoln, fate was responsible for bringing about the horrors of war, but the nation is collectively responsible for a better future. For Bush only the enemy and individual American soldiers bear responsibility, and the chart for the future is vested in bricks and mortar—a new kind of prison in place of a reinvigorated moral code.

President Bush portrays himself as the master agent who acts to control a scene made chaotic by an evil enemy. Having diminished the significance of Abu Ghraib in the context of a war scene that he has constituted as larger than the almost-unspoken moral lapses at Abu Ghraib, he positions himself to be able to obliterate the moral stain by obliterating the scenic token. There is obviously much left unsaid in this treatment of Abu Ghraib by our president. Throughout the speech, Bush's discussion represses those moments when the behaviors of our "enemies" and our own behaviors are identical—those moments contained inside the walls of Abu Ghraib, as well as those many moments when innocents have been killed in Iraq, by all sides, since our invasion. Bush also does not articulate why the troops' actions dishonored our nation or what the values that were disregarded might be. The moral code that should guide behavior is left virtually unarticulated (and this unwillingness to articulate a truly moral code with regard to torture would continue to dominate and bedevil the Bush administration's policies across the next several years). Moreover, the guilt is individual, not collective, and there is no moral responsibility on the part of the nation or the military or the administration for having failed to prevent such dishonorable behavior. There is almost no *moral* address of the issue whatsoever. The five sentences I have cited constitute the entire explicit treatment our president gives to the Abu Ghraib incident for the American public.[22]

The speech seems to have been effective at deflecting attention from Abu Ghraib. While partisan political opponents attacked the speech and Bush's broader response,[23] Bush suffered no apparent loss of national credibility (either personal or institutional) as a consequence of Abu Ghraib in the months immediately after its occurrence. If we are using Lincoln's Second Inaugural as our touchstone, however, we are not satisfied with questions of immediate success. We recognize the significance of a speech as having, at least in part, some larger horizon. If we wish to assess Bush's speech on any larger horizon, then we must ask about the moral impact of this way of addressing the rhetorical context. To do that requires exploring the moral values that ground it.

Bush's Constitution of the American Moral Code

In this speech, Bush is quite explicit, and quite limited, in the repertoire of values that he offers as the purpose terms and guiding abstract commitments of our nation—values to which we hold other nations accountable. The most contentious set of values he offers is condemnation of the killing and violence by his enemies. This is a difficult set of values to cope with in time of war, and it is obvious that Bush holds different standards for American use of killing and violence and torture, but enough has been written on such contradictions. Instead, I propose to focus on the values that the speech recommends for Iraq. Bush is explicit about which values are international and cross-cultural, and about specifying that outside of those transcendent values, different nations can enact what values they will. He specifies the transcendent values that must be enabled in Iraq as "freedom and independence, security and prosperity," but he insists, "I sent American troops to Iraq to defend our security, not to stay as an occupying power. I sent American troops to Iraq to make its people free, not to make them American." He repeats and emphasizes the difference between the international values (especially freedom) and more local, cultural values, saying, "Like every nation that has made the journey to democracy, Iraqis will raise up a government that reflects their own culture and values."

Bush's list of mandatory, international values is not a list of moral values. Freedom, independence, security, and prosperity are a wish list of personal rights and power, not moral values. Indeed, human beings, whether as nations or as individuals, cherish freedom, security, prosperity, and independence. And these are good values. One might even suggest that Bush's fundamental contrast, the one that drives his entire mission and virtually every speech—the contrast of freedom and dictatorship— has merit. But these are not values that transcend the interest of the individual and reach out to concerns with regard to others. Even when Bush does consider the Other, it is only to the extent that the Other is a "friend." One goal of the war he describes as "to give strength to a friend." But it is also clear that for Bush, a friend is someone who helps one achieve one's goals; it is only a free Iraq, one that provides security for the United States, that Bush insists will always find a "friend" in the United States. Specifically, he says, "Iraqis can be certain a free Iraq will always have a friend in the United States of America."

In contrast to Lincoln, there is little room for caring for the widow and orphan in Bush's speech. In the value structure the president promotes, the widow and orphan are responsible for taking advantage of their freedom and independence to make themselves prosperous and secure. More important for the purposes of this speech as an apologia, the values of freedom, independence, security, and prosperity provide no backstops against brutality and the humiliation of those who are one's wards. I would even go so far as to suggest that this kind of value structure creates bullies. If you are free, independent, prosperous, and secure you can do whatever you want, including entertain yourself with visions of sexual objectification and violence, or even participation in such activities. It is precisely moral values that are needed to restrain these personal rights. If one is free, rich, secure, and independent, from what source could constraints upon one's behavior arise? This is the moral vision our situation calls for, but in contrast to President Lincoln, President Bush does not close his speech by offering such a vision.

Bush closes by reemphasizing the global context, in his words "the world as we find it." This world is one of good versus evil, where evil is defined as terrorists (those who kill us and oppose freedom) and good is defined as those who defend freedom with "measured force or overwhelming force." This context is one where the enemy is fighting "to impose Taliban-like rule country by country across the greater Middle East. They seek the total control of every person in mind and soul. . . . They commit dramatic acts of murder to shock, frighten and demoralize civilized nations." In such a context, are not the actions of a few American soldiers at Abu Ghraib trivial, if not to be expected—one of those unfortunate excesses of war? Perhaps this is even a world where limited ends justify unlimited means.

With such a moral vision, are not such actions to be expected?

American and Iraqi Values

Let us leave Bush's speech now, and return to the broader cultural arena, for one of the major foci of the past thirty years in rhetorical studies has been to emphasize that speeches do not arise from the independent, isolated, autonomous brains of single powerful men. Individuals and their speeches are also representations of a broader social discourse. So, let us assume that George Bush's mouth is simply a floodgate through which the U.S. national culture is being deployed to Iraq. In that case, we need to consider the values that shape the cultures of Iraq and the United States.

Despite Bush's belief that freedom is a transcultural value, there are restraints on freedom that operate in Arab cultures that do not operate in ours, and it is in part the meaning of those restraints over which we are fighting. In the United States, there is an enormous disjunction between the claim that something is "just entertainment" and the application of any moral standards. Freedom of speech and the marketplace are taken to be the only values that may operate in the realm of entertainment. Consequently, our network television has come to be filled by low-grade pornography, and our movie screens are dripping in violence. Arab cultures do not accept freedom of speech and the marketplace as their only values. Consequently, they do not accept the disjunction between media products and cultural values. On this ground I think the Arab culture may have a grain of virtue that we have lost. That is, other values may provide necessary restraints to the value of "freedom."

I am not advocating implementing a theocracy in the United States. Moral codes can be products of culture that are not dependent on church institutionalization. Indeed, I would suggest that the mass media representation of the church in the United States has become almost completely separate from morality. If you watch the telepreachers, you will find that the dominant message is not "be good," but rather that one will get personal advantage from being a Christian. This includes believing in Christ in order to be saved regardless of your sins, but also taking care of your health, prospering in your work life, and generally being happy.[24] Though organized religion does not need to be the source of moral codes, there do need to be some sources. The academy might offer such a resource, but the dominance of the scientific worldview in the academy has led even the humanities to be uncomfortable with moral discussion as a component of academic production. Academics are supposed to offer information, perhaps understanding, but not judgment. And indeed, as poststructuralists have highlighted, there are dangers in academics taking up the goal of moral judgment.[25] We risk becoming no different from daily politics if we simply judge. *Academic judgment has to be a deferred judgment built on understanding and an openness to novelty, rather than simply on the rote implementation of motive preferences or rules.*[26] We do not have a vision for that today in the academy.

Americans thus lack any vocabulary and any source for espousing restraints on freedom. We conflate *permitting* everything with *approving and practicing* everything. This is driven by the fact that the dominant source of discourse in our society is the entertainment industry, which is driven by individual pleasure and the profit motive, whereas morality requires an accounting for that which stands beyond immediate individual pleasure or profit. I would suggest, therefore, that when President Bush indicates in his interviews with the Iraqi media that "what took place in that prison does not represent the America that I know,"[27] he is wrong. Our behavior at Abu Ghraib exactly reproduces the American zeitgeist: be the winner, and the winner's prize is to taunt and humiliate the loser, and have fun doing it (in the model words for which Governor Schwarzenegger was elected, "Hasta la vista, baby"). It's just shock and awe, on the personal scale. As Rush Limbaugh's suggested, some American fraternity boys view this behavior as normative, and they practice it on each other as part of their rituals of status and bonding.[28] The soldiers themselves have indicated that they were taking pictures because they were just having fun.

I am not, of course, denying that Americans do indeed have and recognize moral codes that prohibit the behavior at Abu Ghraib. But we have repressed the applicability of such codes in the rush of more entertaining visions that put us in the powerful and amusing position of the humiliator. Indeed, our military structure obviously lacks the presence of moral leadership that would have prevented or immediately disciplined this behavior, rather than allowing it to spread. But if we did not still have such codes available to us, we would not have recognized the pictures at Abu Ghraib as manifestations of repugnant, immoral, disgraceful behavior. In the right context—where others are performing the behaviors in a context explicitly labeled "political" or "social"—we can be induced to call up our moral codes and put them to work. But they are not the discourse codes we apply in our daily life, and they are increasingly enfeebled.

Bush's speech takes him, and us along with him, further toward unconstrained freedom and away from moral codes. It is so natural and easy to use the apologic strategy of differentiation to do this, because we live in a culture of disassociation: entertainment and politics are supposed to be different realms. We deny that what we, as a people, watch on our screens day in and day out actually affects our behavior. We separate the personal from the political, and pay as little attention to the political as possible. But, of course, the personal is political, because the personal and the political are both products of the same culture. The individual nonetheless has the potential to overcome that culture, and any president has the responsibility to overcome those elements of the culture and to insist on a higher moral standard.

That marks a clear difference between President Bush's speech on Iraq and Lincoln's Second Inaugural. Lincoln crafted a model of the self in service to the other, and urged that as the national course of action. He did so by moving the audience's imagination from an almost-guiltless past, through a transcendent judgment, to a higher future purpose. Bush just floats along on the cultural imbrications. He calls for punishment of individuals as a solution, but turns no mirror on American behavior, reflects no light into our national soul. This is a speech that Americans—as products of an immoral culture—might easily buy, but as Martha Solomon Watson and Philip Wander have taught us, it is important to think about all the audiences of a speech,[29] and the mirror on the meaning of America offered by the Arab world is less distorted with self-satisfaction. It reveals the shallowness, the childishness even, of Bush's response. Arab culture recognizes the fight over "freedom" as precisely a fight over the ability to restrict individual behavior within the bounds of a shared moral compass. Whether we agree with the Arabs on the specific features of a moral code or not, they are right to identify individual freedom on the American model as a threat to their moral values. And they might also therefore see the actions of the American soldiers at Abu Ghraib as precisely a manifestation of what the promise of American freedom may bring.

President Bush's apologia will never be a model for the future of leadership or moral perspicuity, or calling a nation to greatness. It does not seek to marshal the historical flows of discourse and direct them to higher ends. It employs the mentality of "I didn't take it, Mom, Tommy did." This judgment arises not from my own political commitments (though surely those commitments led me to ask these questions), but from a comparison to a touchstone that achieved that higher level of rhetorical performance—Lincoln's Second Inaugural Address. Sadly, I believe that few members of the American public would recognize the differences between the two speeches. Moreover, they would likely chalk up my analysis of Bush's speech as partisan, if not verging on the unpatriotic or even traitorous.

"Failures" (or Future Opportunities) for Public Address Studies

The passive response to Bush's apologia on Abu Ghraib arguably marks a series of failures of the public address community. We have failed in part because we do not reach a very broad audience. How many people take a rhetorical criticism course anyway? But that is simply a matter of needing to do more PR for our endeavor, and we are ultimately not accountable for the success or failure of that PR effort, because there are, indeed, larger forces at work than our poor voices. There are, however, some internal failures, for which I believe we are accountable. Speaking of failures, however, is a framework of condemnation, rather than one of opportunity, so let us consider trends in public address studies and how they might be revised.

The study of public address over the past few decades has featured three problematic trends: (1) among those who do public address, weak connections between the artistic and the ethical and between the present and the past, (2) a tendency for those who want to appear avant-garde to demean the significance of the study of political speech, on the mistaken grounds that since all discourse is political, that to pay special attention to speeches by powerful individuals is some kind of elitist plot, and (3) insufficient connections between studies of cultural discourses and studies of political discourses. I will address each of these trends briefly in turn.

The weakness of the connections between the artistic and the ethical derives from multiple sources. First, for some, it derives from the desire to appear objective, either for the sake of seeming more academic or for the sake of avoiding the shallow analysis that can result from a rush to judgment. As I suggested earlier, it might also result from the mistaken sense that the term *ideology* subsumes the term *morality*. For others, the separation of the artistic and the ethical derives from the mistaken notion, first suggested by Plato, and later forwarded by Ramus, among others, that the artistic is the unique province of rhetoric. Wichelns was a key figure in arguing that in public address studies, art is only half the game, but he did not reconcile art with ethics but rather with history, and so avoided

a direct address of the issue.[30] As I've suggested, and as the work of Leff
and Aune and of many others indicates, this is not a tenable separation.
Although questions of public ethics are damnably difficult, and taking
up the issue of the ethical runs the risk of reducing scholarship to moral
propagandizing, the risk is inevitable if public address scholarship is to
do its job of helping humans become more than they have been on the
collective level.

A similar reluctance exists with the linking of past and present. I
have explicitly compared a discourse from the nineteenth century to
one from the twenty-first century. I could likewise profitably compare
Bush's speech announcing war with Iraq (March 19, 2003) to several of
Churchill's war addresses, especially the one sometimes called "The War
Situation I."[31] I do not mean to suggest that every time a public address
scholar studies a speech in the nineteenth century she has to compare
it to a contemporary issue. That would be an excessive doctrine of relevance. But in our classrooms and in our shared discussions, we need
to do more with actually using the touchstones we are accumulating to
make richer judgments of contemporary speeches. Such efforts require
sensitivity to cultural and temporal issues, but in my judgment, better
to start off doing them badly than not at all. Without a more pervasive
sense of how noncontemporary speeches might inform our contemporary
and future deliberations, we risk stifling public address studies with the
stamp of "old, done, irrelevant."

The second problematic trend in our community is the tendency,
especially but not exclusively, among younger scholars, to demean the
significance of the study of political speech. When the story of the history
of rhetorical criticism is recounted by most people today, it goes something
like this: we used to study single speeches, then this cool postmodern
stuff came along and we learned to study fragments. Having come of age
as a scholar in the eighties, I recognize that as a false account. The skilled
study of single speeches qua speeches congealed, largely in the 1980s,
largely as a product of a few scholars led by Michael Leff, who was also
the driving force behind the Biennial Public Address Conference, but also
Stephen Lucas and others. This was exactly the same time that Michael
McGee, along with Raymie McKerrow, Barry Brummett, and others, was
leading the charge for studies of cultural discourses at large. The study of

single texts and the move to study cultural discourses qua fragments of discourses congealed at the same time out of an older mass of scholarship that often privileged single speakers and frequently attended to historical events, but did not generally provide close analysis of single texts. So this is not a question of an "old" tradition of single-speech studies being supplanted by a "new" tradition of cultural studies.

A second rationale for the preference for attending to cultural discourses comes from the notion of elite versus popular discourse. McGee, among others, frequently argued that fourteen-year-old boys listened to pop music, not political speeches. And this is right. Insofar as it stands as a justification for studying cultural discourses, it is absolutely appropriate. As I've already indicated, entertainment discourse is the biggest source of shared discourse in the United States today. The converse is not true, however. The rise of entertainment discourse does not mean that the speeches of governance have become irrelevant and inconsequential. The fact that fourteen-year-old boys (or girls) do not currently attend much to political speeches does not mean those discourses lack importance to their lives. Political speeches, to which the lad or lass never attends, may send him or her one day to the Middle East to fight and die. On a more mundane level, political speeches determine where and to whom her or his tax money goes, and in what quantities.

We need to think of public speeches as nexus points where popular discourses are amplified, reworked, redirected, and deployed to produce concentrated collective action or change. This redirection draws on the cultural discourses, and so mapping cultural discourse is part of the process of understanding politics. However, a television sitcom or even a news broadcast, though both are political, does not play the same role as a speech or other discourse of governance. When a president announces an invasion or a ban on stem cell research, or a tax cut, he (someday she) is exercising levers that are not available to others and that redeploy discourse on a scale not generally available to other sources. Similar kinds of levers are available to the Supreme Court, some governors, Congress collectively, government bureaucracies, and some other agents situated inside institutions. This is not to assert that these sources are autonomous or unchecked, and it is not to deny that entertainment and other discourses shape individual lives in enduring and important ways. It is rather to suggest that we need to understand the discourse of governance and other cultural discourses as operating in a shared system with different roles.

Some feminist and ethnic studies have also contributed to the dismissal of attention to the discourses of governance. Since white men have so often been in power, the study of texts that lie at the nexus points of power often constitute the study of white men's discourse. While it is important to broaden the scope of public address studies beyond the voices of white men if we are to truly have touchstones that represent the full range of human possibility, it is inevitable that we are going to continue to study a lot of white men's texts if we are to understand the distribution of power. The lesson of feminism and ethnic studies should, therefore, be both to broaden our understanding of nexus points of power and also to use a rigorous skepticism about race and gender issues when doing such analyses. It should not, however, be to disvalue the study of those texts that wield leveraged power, for that is to encourage blindness in an area where we should not want to be blind.

As we have begun to study cultural discourse more, we have tended to study political speech less. The republican answer here is the only good one: we need to expand the pie. Rather than fighting over limited resources, we need to guard the study of both cultural texts and the texts of governance very carefully within our discipline and promote that study outside the discipline as well. If we stop thinking of cultural texts and the texts of governance as separate slices of a pie and start thinking of cultural texts as filling and governance texts as crust, then doing away with either component seems less desirable.

This leads me to the last "failure" of public address. We have not yet sufficiently connected our studies of culture and public address. I have tried in this chapter to provide a hint at what such a connection might look like in at least one case. The late and great Janice Hocker Rushing provided such a connection in her study of the linkages between President Reagan's "Star Wars" address and the evolution of models of the new frontier in cultural models of space exploration.[32] The work of Bonnie Dow approaches the nexus from another angle, tying her analyses of cultural artifacts such as prime-time television to specific political events, such as the development of feminism as a political force.[33] The new work in visual rhetoric by younger scholars such as Cara Finnegan and older scholars such as Robert Hariman and John Louis Lucaites also is doing more to link up culture and governance. But there is far too little of such cross-linkages in the discipline.[34]

I want to close my chart for the future by extending these research issues into the realm of teaching. One of the most powerful means by which we lay the ground for future human potentials, and the means by which we help call our culture to those models that are, to date, the best available, is through our teaching. Young people indeed learn in part by imitation (and hence the cultural trauma we inflict upon ourselves through a mass media permeated by violence and apelike dominance behavior). Young people also learn, however, by examining exemplars and what makes them exemplary. Teaching undergraduates the rhetorical touchstones of governance is no easy task. For the most part, students are happier studying *Sex and the City* (even when instructors engage some ire by pointing out that it is sexist, classist, racist, ablest, and homophobic) than they are studying Lincoln's Second Inaugural, Frederick Douglass's Fourth of July Oration, or even something more contemporary like Mary Fisher's address on AIDS to the Republican Convention. But the belief that teaching is primarily entertainment is a bad one, and even the idea that connecting to what students find immediately relevant is the best way to teach is flawed. Part of our job is to expand what students find to be relevant and meaningful. Forwarding the idea that we are only responsible for our personal relationship to the products of consumer culture is not pardonable. It is important, in other words, that we continue to teach speeches.

This does not mean that we have to teach only speeches. The now well-developed line of pedagogy that helps students be critical consumers of cultural texts is also valuable. But in teaching as in research, the sum can be far more than the individual parts. Cultural texts can lead students into an issue, and speeches can show them how power gets deployed in a focused context on a collective scale.

I am distraught over the national discourse that led us to behave in a shameful fashion at Abu Ghraib, and I am at least equally distraught at our national response to those images and the events they witnessed. I occasionally become despondent over our national behavior more generally and even the behavior of human beings at large. But I do believe that if we have a chance of raising ourselves out of the muck of our worst potentials, it is through the tool of language, and that the careful, critical study of human discourse is essential to enacting our better rather than worse potentials. Thus, if there is cause for concern in the failures of presidential discourse on Abu Ghraib, there remains cause for hope in the touchstones that we have and can bring to bear upon those failings.

NOTES

1. Media Matters for America, "The Rush Limbaugh Show 5/03/04," available at http://mediamatters.org/static/pdf/limbaugh-20040503.pdf, accessed January 16, 2009.

2. The description of the events as "intolerable" came in the president's speech of May 25, 2004, at the U.S. Army War College, available at http://www.whitehouse.gov/news/releases/2004/05/20040524-10.html, accessed January 16, 2009. The description of the events as "abhorrent" came in the interview with Al Arabiya Television, published in a White House press release, May 5, 2004, "President Bush Meets with Al Arabiya Television on Wednesday," available at http://www.whitehouse.gov/news/releases/2004/05/20040505-2.htm, accessed January 16, 2009.

3. Anthony Giddens, *Central Problems in Social Theory: Action, Structure, and Contradiction in Social Analysis* (Berkeley and Los Angeles: University of California Press, 1979).

4. Renford Bambrough, *Moral Scepticism and Moral Knowledge* (Atlantic Highlands, N.J.: Humanities Press, 1979); Alasdair MacIntyre, *After Virtue: A Study in Moral Theory* (Notre Dame, Ind.: University of Notre Dame Press, 1981).

5. Celeste Michelle Condit, "Crafting Virtue: The Rhetorical Construction of Public Morality," *Quarterly Journal of Speech* 73 (1987): 79–87; and Celeste Michelle Condit, "Democracy and Civil Rights: The Universalizing Influence of Public Argumentation," *Communication Monographs* 54 (1987): 1–18.

6. Some scholars distinguish between "ethical" and "moral" systems, in an effort to abjure the problematic political associations of the promoters of "morality." I believe that the argument I am making here could be made in essentially the same form if one substituted the term *ethical* for *moral*, but I choose to use the term *moral* because it is the less academic term, and since what is true of *ethical* is also

true in this case of *moral*, the more general, less nuanced term is more correct.

7. Kevin Michael DeLuca and Jennifer Peeples, "From Public Sphere to Public Screen: Democracy, Activism, and the 'Violence' of Seattle," *Critical Studies in Media Communication* 19 (2002): 125–151.

8. Patricia Corrigan, "Pornography Is Harmful, Author Asserts with Statistics," *St. Louis Post-Dispatch,* September 21, 2005, E3.

9. For plentiful examples, watch a few episodes of *Family Guy* or *South Park.*

10. George W. Bush, "Remarks by the President Upon Arrival 9/16/01," available at http://www.whitehouse.gov/news/releases/2001/09/print/20010916-2.html, accessed January 16, 2009. Two days later at the White House daily press briefing, press secretary Ari Fleischer reported that Mr. Bush regretted using the term but meant it "in the traditional English sense of the word. It's a broad cause." See Ari Fleischer, "Press Briefing by Ari Fleischer," September 18, 2001, available at http://www.whitehouse.gov/news/releases/2001/09/20010918-5.html, accessed January 16, 2009.

11. Kenneth Burke, "The Rhetoric of Hitler's Battle," in *The Philosophy of Literary Form,* 3rd ed. (Berkeley and Los Angeles: University of California Press, 1973), 191–220.

12. Condit, "Crafting Virtue."

13. Michael Leff, "Textual Criticism: The Legacy of G. P. Mohrmann," *Quarterly Journal of Speech* 72 (1986): 377–389.

14. Abraham Lincoln, "Second Inaugural Address," March 4, 1865, *The Abraham Lincoln Papers at the Library of Congress,* available at http://memory.loc.gov/cgi-bin/query/r?ammem/mal:@field(DOCID+@lit(d4361300)), accessed January 16, 2009.

15. See Bush, "Interview with Al Arabiya Television," and George W. Bush, "President Bush's Interview with Al Hurra TV," *Washington Post* (online), FDCH E-Media, Wednesday, May 5, 2004; 12:08 PM, http://www.washingtonpost.com/, accessed June 18, 2004.

16. "Brig. Gen. Mark Kimmitt, the top U.S. military spokesman in Iraq, profusely apologized on Arabic television, as did Maj. Gen. Geoffrey Miller, the commander in charge of detainee operations," according to Fred Kaplan, "Why Bush Didn't Apologize," *Slate,* May 5, 2004, available at http://slate.msn.com/id/2100015/, accessed June 18, 2004.

17. B. Ware Harrell and W. Linkugel, "Failure of Apology in American Politics: Nixon on Watergate," *Communication Monographs* 42 (1975): 245–261.

18. Lincoln, "Second Inaugural Address."

19. Kenneth Burke, *A Grammar of Motives* (Berkeley and Los Angeles: University of California Press, 1969).

20. In responding to this essay at a public address conference, Leff pointed out that Lincoln's style is consonant with his charitable rhetoric and that Bush's either-or, absolutist style contrasts with Lincoln's and likewise is integral to Bush's worldview and persuasive purpose.

21. Burke, *A Grammar of Motives.*

22. As I mentioned before, the two interviews to Arabic-language media were more complicated, but not much more morally forthcoming.

23. Richard Ronconi Berne, "Bush's Apology Needed to Be Made to Iraqis," *Times Union,* May 14, 2004, A8.

24. The best way to get support for this claim is simply to spend a few hours watching a variety of on-line ministries. However, a representative list of one of the most prominent televangelism's topics is available at http://www.cbn.com/700club/Guests/, accessed January 16, 2009. Topics in order of their frequency include (1) making the church stronger/defense of the church/giving money to the church; (2) celebrity models of conversion and other media gossip; (3) personal health, succeeding at work, other ways you'll increase personal happiness if you live as a Christian; (4) censure of others for their immoral behavior (especially gays); and (5) miscellaneous other topics, including a few focused on others such as one program on civil rights and one on poverty.

25. Raymie McKerrow, "Critical Rhetoric: Theory and Praxis," *Communication Monographs* 56 (1989): 91–111.

26. Marco Abel, "Don DeLillo's 'In the Ruins of the Future': Literature, Images, and the Rhetoric of *Seeing* 9/11," *PMLA* 118 (2003): 1236–1250.

27. See Bush, "President Bush's Interview with Al Hurra TV."

28. Media Matters for America, "Rush Limbaugh Show 5/03/04."

29. Martha Solomon [Watson], "'With Firmness in the Right': The Creation of Moral Hegemony in Lincoln's Second Inaugural," *Communication Reports* 1 (1988):32–37; and Philip Wander, "The Third Persona: An Ideological Turn in Rhetorical Theory," *Communication Studies* 33 (1984): 197–216.

30. Herbert A. Wichelns, "The Literary Criticism of Oratory," in *Readings in Rhetorical Criticism,* ed. Carl Burgchardt (State College, Penn.: Strata, 1995), 3–17.

31. Celeste M. Condit and April M. Greer, "The Particular Aesthetics of Winston Churchill's 'War Situation I,'" in *Rhetoric and Community: Studies in Unity and Fragmentation,* ed. J. Michael Hogan (Columbia: University of South Carolina Press, 1998), 167–203.

32. Janice Hocker Rushing, "Ronald Reagan's 'Star Wars' Address: Mythic Containment

of Technical Reasoning," *Quarterly Journal of Speech* 72 (1986): 415–434.

33. Bonnie J. Dow, "Fixing Feminism: Women's Liberation and the Rhetoric of Television Documentary," *Quarterly Journal of Speech* 90 (2004): 53–80.

34. Part of the problem is that such projects are highly demanding. You have to master at least twice as much material as a study focused solely on the political discourse or solely on the cultural discourse. The current academic economy—which favors rapid publication of shallow work—discourages such efforts. Consequently, this challenge is one mature scholars may be best placed to undertake. It is also, however, a place for collaboration, and I would encourage the organizers of the next public address conference to plan a session or two in which participants worked together to explore a common event or issue combining political texts and social discourses, to enable the development of models of this kind of work and encourage its flowering.

George H. W. Bush and the Strange Disappearance of Groups from Civil Rights Talk

Vanessa B. Beasley

In her opening chapter, Celeste M. Condit once again asks public address scholars to reconsider the relationship between rhetoric and public morality.[1] More specifically, she asks readers to view "public morality as a set of codes constituted by rhetorical processes."[2] The "moral component of such codes," she writes, "is the specification of behavior that requires taking account of the needs and value of the 'Other,' rather than acting solely on self-interest."[3] The idea that rhetoric constitutes a shared sense of morality is obviously closely related to the idea that rhetoric constitutes identity.[4] Put differently, who we are called to be via discourse also has implications for how we morally act toward each other.

Sometimes these implications are obvious and troublesome. Condit, for example, sees that the discourse surrounding Abu Ghraib demands scholarly attention because the precipitating events represent a "clear demonstration of serious moral failure by the United States," and we can look to language for clues to how and why such atrocities could have happened.[5] At other times, however, the precipitating events are not as obvious. Indeed, sometimes there may be no one focal event at all, but instead a series of events or even a more generalized sense that something within the political culture is changing, with this change itself begging questions about the relationship between rhetoric, identity, and morality.

We can look back to the 1990s to see evidence of such a potentiality within presidential rhetoric about civil rights and national identity. If a hallmark of morality is the mitigation of self-interest, as Condit suggests, rhetoric about civil rights in general and race relations in particular remains a fruitful place to look for how such calls show up in public discourse, as members of a so-called majority must be persuaded to look outside of their own perceived self-interests in order to support the advancement of the rights of others. In the United States at the end of the twentieth century, however, the civil rights movement of the 1950s and 1960s was starting to feel more and more like a distant memory; its arguments for equality, especially those made on explicitly religious and moral grounds, were less prominent within the public sphere. What other arguments were being made about civil rights in the 1990s? How was the president, for example, instructing the American people to think about such matters?

In this chapter I answer these questions through a reading of examples of President George H. W. Bush's public discourse in response to a legislative battle surrounding the Civil Rights Acts of 1990 and 1991. On more than one occasion, President Bush explained his opposition to proposed civil rights legislation in very specific terms. As straightforward as the president was, however, we can also view his discourse as being complex in at least two senses, both of which have implications for our understanding of rhetoric's constitutive functions.

First, President Bush repeatedly asked his listeners to think of themselves as individuals rather than members of groups. From a historical perspective, this position may reflect vestiges of Reaganesque thinking or the ascent of neoliberalism within the United States' political culture during the 1990s. From a rhetorical perspective, however, such discourse can tip U.S. democracy's cultural balance between individualism and more pluralistic commitments into one direction at the expense of the other. In terms of national identity, then, Bush's discourse asked his listeners to think of themselves and their democratic responsibilities to each other in a particular way. Second, the question of how Bush's discourse constituted a sense of morality is even more complicated. As we will see, Bush himself explicitly aligned his position with the cause of morality, and it is not my goal here to suggest that he was being disingenuous in that characterization. Rather, the explicitly moral tone of his highly individualistic rhetoric raises questions about the grounds for his claim, especially to the extent that standards of morality can be assumed to reside within questions of relational obligations to others.[6]

In order to explore these questions, I first describe both the social context and the legislative environment that prompted Bush to discuss civil rights within his public speeches, with particular emphasis on his stated opposition to the Civil Rights Act of 1990. Then I discuss a series of textual moments to bring attention to a particular set of themes within the discourse that emerged as he positioned himself relative to his veto of the 1990 legislation as well as its emerging successor, the Civil Rights Act of 1991. To conclude the chapter, I return to questions of what this case may reveal about the constitutive functions of rhetoric for both identity and morality in the United States.

U.S. Racial Politics in the Early 1990s: Context and Exigencies

Shawn Parry-Giles and Trevor Parry-Giles have noted that "the 1990s were a time of considerable angst in the United States."[7] Within my analysis, what matters most is the opening years of this decade, when many cultural anxieties were already obvious, especially on matters of race, including its perceived significance within employment law.

As the decade began, for example, it became increasingly clear that black-white race relations were still difficult, complicated, and contentious in the United States. In March of 1991, for example, television viewers watched the repeated broadcast of the videotaped recording of a brutal beating of Rodney King, an African American man, by four Los Angeles police officers. One year later, when three of the police officers were found not guilty of police brutality by a jury in largely white Ventura

County, California, an intense and violent "race riot" broke out in Los Angeles. Today, the 1992 Los Angeles riots are remembered as one of the most violent domestic uprisings in U.S. history.

It was not just the potential for civil unrest that troubled some Americans; also worrisome was the potential for change within the Supreme Court. In June of 1991, Justice Thurgood Marshall, the first and only African American on the Court, announced that he was retiring, fueling widespread speculation about his replacement and its implications for the future of civil rights law enforcement. Later that summer, after President Bush named a potential replacement for Marshall, civil and women's rights groups voiced outrage over his choice of Clarence Thomas, an African American judge and former civil servant known for his conservative views. But before Thomas could be confirmed, he faced allegations of sexual harassment from former employee Anita Hill, and in early October, the Senate held televised hearings in which these accusations were discussed in lurid detail. Over and over again, speakers at the Thomas-Hill hearings acknowledged the persistence of racial and gender discrimination in their everyday lives.

The poor state of the U.S. economy was also salient to citizens because the decade began under conditions of recession.[8] During the late 1980s, the United States experienced turbulent economic conditions, including a severe stock market crash in October of 1987. By the beginning of the 1990s, relatively high unemployment rates were among the signs that the economy was not recovering quickly. In fact, it was a series of court cases alleging employment discrimination that would lead to the drafting of the Civil Rights Act of 1990.

David Zarefsky has pointed out that the "civil rights controversy of the Bush administration did not arise, as had been the case in the 1960s, from dramatic evidence of systematic denial of basic rights, nor from an organized movement demanding action . . . Rather, the controversy of 1990 and 1991 would be fought on narrower ground."[9] Zarefsky is referring to a group of cases, most notably *Wards Cove v. Antonio* in 1989.[10] Zarefsky has summarized the legal intricacies of these cases elsewhere, so I will not go into deep detail here.[11] For my purposes it is sufficient to note, as he already has, that their "practical effect . . . was to make it harder for plaintiffs to win employment discrimination suits."[12] Importantly, then, if the defining argumentative topoi for the civil rights era of the midcentury had been philosophical and moral in nature, with "We shall overcome" being a banner not only for collective action but also for the fulfillment of a certain democratic telos, the civil rights battles of the 1980s and 1990s would be fought in the courts, with far more emphasis on the quotidian details of individual cases.

Nevertheless, some of these cases were decided by a close vote on the Supreme Court. As a result, Zarefsky writes, "a number of civil rights organizations . . . sought congressional legislation to reverse these decisions," thus placing the burden of proof on employers rather than plaintiffs; "Sen. Edward M. Kennedy (D-MA) and Rep. Augustus F. Hawkins (D-CA) sponsored such a bill."[13] The Kennedy-Hawkins bill would later evolve into the Civil Rights Act of 1990, or S.2104.[14] Importantly, the press soon reported that Bush's attorney general, Richard Thornburgh, had interpreted this legislation's primary impact as introducing "quotas by stealth."[15] This description was inaccurate and intentionally controversial, according to supporters of the bill.[16] Yet regardless of the actual content of the legislation, the label caught on. A little over a month after Thornburgh's public comments, President Bush made it clear that he also viewed the bill as a "quota bill," and this was the main reason he opposed it in spite of his career-long commitment to civil rights. In remarks in the Rose Garden on May 17, 1990, Bush stated that while he and his administration would remain "committed" to "action that is truly affirmative . . . to strike down all barriers to advancement of every kind for all people," he simply could not sign this bill. "No one here today would want me to sign a bill whose unintended consequences are quotas because quotas are wrong and they violate the most basic principles of our civil rights tradition and the most basic principles of the promise of democracy," the president argued.[17]

Zarefsky notes that Bush used the Rose Garden speech to differentiate "'true' affirmative action and some other kind," an "unacceptable" form that would violate the very principles that it purports to uphold, presumably by using quotas.[18] Such a distinction—that there was a right way and a wrong way to protect civil rights—is clearly part of the rationale that accompanied Bush's use of *quotas* as a devil term both before and after his veto. Yet there was another devil term in much of Bush's rhetoric as well, one that was far less obvious and yet compelling nonetheless: the word *groups*. When this word appeared in Bush's rhetoric, listeners often heard the president suggesting that there is a right way and a wrong way to be an American, too.

Rhetoric and Philosophy: Bush's Positions on Groups and Why They Matter

Following his veto of the Civil Rights Act of 1990, President Bush made several public speeches in which he explained his fundamental philosophy on civil rights. The veto itself had placed Bush in the unfortunate rhetorical position of appearing indifferent or perhaps even hostile to civil rights—a dangerous state of affairs for an incumbent president preparing for another election—and thus he had to be careful about how to reposition himself on the issue. This need was especially acute because both congressional Democrats and the Bush administration were advocating specific features within a reintroduced version of the law that would eventually become the Civil Rights Act of 1991, thus putting the president in a position to signal which legislative changes he would and would not support.[19]

At a commencement address at U.S. Military Academy at West Point on June 1, 1991, for example, Bush made remarks that would amount to one of his most concise explanations of his own beliefs. Bush used his role as West Point's commencement speaker to deliver a "major policy speech" in which he discussed the types of reforms he favored.[20] As Zarefsky has noted, "Celebrating that successful integration of the military on a color-blind basis provided the backdrop against which he would set out his views on affirmative action."[21]

Indeed, at West Point the president lamented the fact that racial discrimination still existed within the United States. "Regrettably, racism and bigotry still exist in this great country of ours," Bush said. "But let there be no doubt, this President and this administration will strike at discrimination wherever it exists. Because, you see, prejudice and hate have no place in this country, period."[22] Having suggested his administration's willingness to further the cause of civil rights, the president then alluded to the problems with previous approaches, pointedly referring to the Civil Rights Act of 1990:

> Today, some talk not of opportunity but of redistributing rights. They'd pit one group against another, encourage people to think of others as competitors, not colleagues. That's not the way to achieve justice and equality here in America. We need to adopt a more unifying, moral, and noble approach.[23]

As even this short quotation makes clear, Bush was concerned not only with whom quotas would force employers to hire and colleges to admit, but also with how a quota system might cause them to think about and act towards each other. By his own account, the nation needed a more "moral" approach, one more "unifying" and "noble" than that which would "pit one group against another," as a quota system presumably would. Seeing other citizens as "competitors, not colleagues" was "not the way to achieve justice and equality" in the United States, and, by implication, such an approach was also immoral in Bush's estimation.

Whatever arguments he was putting forth about affirmative action in this speech, then, President Bush was also making constitutive claims about both American identity and American morality. Despite the fact that both groups and competition have played central if not crucial roles in the history of justice and equality in the United States, Bush wanted his listeners to see themselves as individuals first and foremost, a view consistent with the rise of neoliberal economic policies at century's end.[24] Yet this constitutive rhetoric has potentially serious consequences—we might even label them moral consequences—for the state of race relations in the United States. Given that no one would argue that civil rights victories have historically been won in the United States through individualism and collegiality, the rhetorical move to disassociate the *means* of group affiliation from the *end* of eliminating discrimination is a curious one in which collectivity itself seems dubious.

Yet the June 1 speech, with its telling reference to the dangers of placing "one group against another," provides just one example of an anti-group logic that also appears in other pieces of Bush's rhetoric during the 1990–91 civil rights controversy as well. Such moments of suspicious talk about "groups" are worthy of our attention, I will argue. For one thing, they can reveal a great deal about a particular orientation to civil rights within the political culture of Bush's day. In the West Point speech, for example, Bush seems to be taking a very specific position about the relationship between equality and individualism: that individualism itself is both the means and the end of equality. In other words, this view states that a heightened sense of individualism will both promote equality and also be evidence of its achievement within civil rights law. Once the American people started viewing each other as individuals, according to this logic, the nation would move even closer to meeting the philosophical goals of the civil rights era.

Yet this position itself also reveals the conflicting moral themes at play within post-civil-rights-era assessments of U.S. race relations as well as within legislative attempts to remedy these tensions. Bush presents his antigroup position as the "moral" and "unified" way to protect civil rights and promote social justice, presumably because once citizens see each other as individuals first and foremost, they will also recognize each other's humanity and equality. Such compassionate fellow-feeling is noble, to be sure. Yet this model does not have history or theory on its side. More specifically, it refutes both the descriptive and the normative principles of political pluralism, the theory that puts interactions between and among interest groups as a leading factor within both democratic stability and social justice in the United States. To put it differently, when Bush's rhetoric suggests that identification with "groups" is problematic, his discourse also repudiates some of the theoretical foundations of U.S. democracy.

Furthermore, this repudiation is also problematic in light of another tendency within this sample of Bush's rhetoric. Within his civil rights discourse, there are a few occasions in which he suggests that group affiliation is primarily–and pejoratively—associated with race, as I will demonstrate shortly. The negative connotations of such a linkage speak volumes to one of the major challenges still present in U.S. race relations: namely, the persistent public denial of systemic causes of inequality in the United States as well as the moral implications of such a stance. Given that my argument that Bush's civil rights rhetoric is overly individualistic at the expense of more pluralistic approaches, it is worth reviewing the ways in which previous scholars have discussed the role of groups within U.S. democracy.

The Centrality of Groups to U.S. Politics

Clearly the terms *quotas* and *groups* were linked within Bush's June 1 speech. Ethnic, minority, and other historically disadvantaged groups have been frequently presumed to be the beneficiaries of "quotas," and as Zarefsky's research has shown, several of Bush's executive predecessors, going back at least to Nixon, have also defined quotas as being inherently discriminatory, and therefore, in Nixon's words, "totally alien to the American tradition."[25] But groups themselves are certainly not alien to this tradition. To the contrary, groups have always been viewed as both a sociological and a political reality within U.S. democracy, even as this reality has existed as the counterpart of an equally hearty, if often romanticized, tradition of individualism.[26]

The inevitability of group conflict in the United States was a concern for the founders, for example, with James Madison arguing in Federalist No. 10 that the prospect of factionalism was one reason for a republican government.[27] For Madison, the dominance of any partial view—even the majority one—could lead to tyranny, and therefore he argued that a "scheme of representation" of multiple interests had to be part of the republican system.[28] Alexis de Tocqueville was more optimistic about the role of groups in American life; he confessed surprise at the extent to which Americans used "associations" to address both political and civic problems:

> Among democratic peoples associations must take the place of the powerful private persons whom equality of conditions has eliminated. As soon as several Americans have conceived a sentiment or an idea that they want to produce before the world, they seek each other out, and when found, they unite. Thenceforth they are no longer isolated individuals, but a power conspicuous from the distance whose actions serve as an example; when it speaks, men listen.[29]

If Tocqueville was correct that freedom of association is one of the necessary conditions for democracy, and especially if people are more likely to
listen when groups rather than "isolated individuals" speak, then perhaps
it is no surprise that we now view groups as a political fact of life in the
United States.

Indeed, many observers consider the "reigning paradigm in [U.S.]
political science" to be pluralism, in which "power is, or should be, dis-
tributed among many groups and interests in society."[30] Such an arrangement is one of the defining characteristics of Robert Dahl's influential
characterization of the United States as a "polyarchal democracy," in
which both universal suffrage and "rights to form political organizations
to influence or oppose the existing government" differentiate this model
from other forms of democracy.[31] In addition, pluralism is closely related
to group theory, which holds that "societies consist of a large number
of social, ethnic, and economic groups, more or less well-organized, in
political competition with each other to put pressure on the government
into producing policies favorable to the relevant group."[32] As Samuel
Huntington has noted, this competition itself is presumed to promote
the common good. Pluralism's promise in the United States, according
to Huntington, has been that a "rough approximation of the public interest [could] emerge out of the open, competitive struggle in the political
free market."[33] Ideally, as Avagail Eisenberg has noted, pluralism would
therefore ensure that "power [is] shared by a plurality of groups."[34]

In a sense, then, pluralism is assumed to promote and maintain both
a moral and a social order within U.S. democracy, at least to the extent
that a common good is assumed to be maintained via both public and private negotiations among groups and their representatives. To wit, when
scholars such as Robert Putnam have lamented the decrease in membership in civic and volunteer groups in the United States, they often have
associated this trend with an attendant decline in civic engagement and
even the overall health of U.S. democracy.[35]

Whatever its current iterations, however, the pluralist paradigm has
clearly not been enough to eliminate inequality in the United States.[36] In
the most obvious sense, this problem stems from the fact that Tocqueville
was wrong: "equality of conditions" has not been attained (nor was it attained in his own time) and it has obviously not eliminated "the powerful

private persons" that he assumed "associations" would replace. To put it differently, if a key assumption within pluralism is that "many centers of power exist and that different groups have access to a variety of power centers," U.S. history has frequently revealed that some groups have had better access than others.[37]

The limits of U.S. pluralism have been especially evident in the areas of class and race. Paula McClain and Joseph Stewart argue that "despite pluralism's contention that political resources are counterbalanced, with one group's financial resources being neutralized by another group's population base, pluralism tilts political outcomes in favor of those with economic and political resources."[38] As E. E. Schattschneider observes, 'The flaw in the pluralist heaven is that the heavenly chorus sings with an upper class accent.'"[39] Herbert J. Gans puts it more bluntly: "Pluralism, the doctrine with which America handles the representation of a multiplicity of interest groups . . . is regressive, enabling those groups already politically and economically powerful to become more so."[40]

Likewise, McClain and Stewart also maintain that pluralism has not offered sufficient explanations of how racial and ethnic groups gain, lose, or maintain political influence. To the extent that pluralism assumes that "once groups realize their subjective interests, they will become incorporated into the political system," it ignores the "fact that racial minorities are treated as groups; no individual achievement improves the status of the individual or changes the position of the group."[41] If traditional pluralistic theory assumes that individuals are bound together as members of interest groups—in which individual membership is largely a matter of choice—with the goal of influencing specific policy outcomes, it has not fully come to terms with the post-civil rights rise of identity politics and, more specifically, attendant notions of group identity or cohesion, defined as the "extent of feelings of solidarity with other members of the group—*and perceptions of discrimination.*"[42] In other words, we might assume that there is a qualitative difference between being a member of the Parent Teacher Association and being a member of the NAACP. Even though both groups are interest-driven, membership in the latter is arguably less a matter of perceived choice or self-identification—that is, one may have a choice to join a group or not, but one does not have a choice to be born into one racial or ethnic group and not another. Recalling McClain and

Stewart's wording, "racial minorities are treated as groups" whether they want to be or not.[43]

However lacking the pluralist paradigm might seem in this regard, it is important to note that even these critiques of pluralism underscore the influential role of groups and group affiliation in American history. Neither of these critiques asserts that groups do not matter in U.S. politics; in fact, both critiques suggest that observers ought to pay _more_ attention to the types of groups that have historically been left out of the pluralist competition for resources. In fact, much of the history of the civil rights movement in the United States—along with the histories of women's rights, labor activism, gay rights, and other progressive social movements—can be read as the study of this competition itself, with every success and failure providing lessons for future generations.

Indeed, this view of U.S. democracy is so compelling that Bush himself invoked it, at least before he became president. In his nomination acceptance speech at the Republican National Convention in 1988, Bush-the-candidate spoke explicitly about his views on the role of groups in the United States, painting a picture of himself as an enlightened pluralist indeed:

> Liberal democrats . . . see "community" as a limited cluster of interest groups, locked in odd conformity. In this view, the country waits passive while Washington sets the rules. But that's not what community means—not to me. For we are a nation of communities, of thousands and tens of thousands of ethnic, religious, social, business, labor union, neighborhood, regional, and other organizations, all of them varied, voluntary, and unique.[44]

Read in the context of the previous discussion of pluralist theory, Bush's comments are interesting. Here Bush seems to suggest that his opponents have an old-fashioned, elitist, and even undemocratic model of pluralism, in which "interest groups" working in a "limited cluster" try to influence how "Washington sets the rules." Although candidate (and Vice President) Bush uses this negative reference to an "inside the Beltway" form of politics to set up arguments he will make later in the speech, he is also endorsing a normative theory of democratic pluralism, in which all kinds of people are part of the Tocquevillian associations whose influence and interactions promote a common good.

Lest Bush's multiculturalism go unrecognized, he immediately amplifies his point by using specific examples:

> This is America: the Knights of Columbus, the Grange, Hadassah, the Disabled American Veterans, the Order of Ahepa, the Business and Professional Women of America, the union hall, the Bible study group, LULAC, "Holy Name"—a brilliant diversity spread like stars, like a thousand points of light in a broad and peaceful sky.[45]

Although it is the last few words that have received the most attention, Bush's choices in the first part of this passage merit our attention, too, because his list is so inclusive as to be telling. It features organizations that are proudly ethnic (e.g., the Order of Ahepa, which stands for American Hellenic Educational Progressive Association, and LULAC, the League of Latin American Citizens), religious (the Knights of Columbus, the "Bible study group" presumably of various Protestant traditions, and Holy Name, or the National Association of the Holy Name Society), or both (Hadassah). Bush's selections also foreground gender (the Business and Professional Women of America and, again, Hadassah), military service (the Disabled America Veterans), and trade (the Grange and the union hall).

Notice, too, however, that these groups are also voluntary associations, even if they are largely homogeneous in terms of majority ethnicity, religious beliefs, or gender. Just as his famous image of the "thousand points of light" assumes that this constellation of engaged groups can promote a more engaged polis, his mention of these specific groups suggests that they comprise the types of pluralities that make the United States' democracy so healthy and ripe with opportunities for all of its citizens. These specific clusters of "stars," in which group identity results from the conscious blending of chosen and not-chosen characteristics of individual identity, can presumably play the role of the nation's moral North Star, guiding the United States on its true path toward good at home and abroad.

Given that these are the "safe" types of groups that a self-professed conservative presidential candidate could champion in 1988, it is also worth asking which types of groups are missing from the list. Where, for example, are African American and gay rights groups? From an ideological perspective, it would have been surprising if the latter sort of rights group had made Bush's list of potential points of light. As a member of the Reagan administration in particular, he would not have considered it advisable, strategic, or even, yes, "prudent" to acknowledge this group's political power or seek its vote in 1988. But why no African American groups? Why no Alpha Kappa Alpha, Jack and Jill, or Urban League? For an analysis of Bush's civil rights rhetoric, the omission of historically African American groups may be especially important, for it may tell us something about the political culture Bush was interested in both navigating and influencing from the Oval Office.

A Different Kind of "Group Talk": Bush in 1990 and 1991

Even if candidate Bush in 1988 was not as inclusive a pluralist as he might have been, at least he sounded like a pluralist. By 1990 and 1991, however, President Bush seemed considerably less supportive of the idea of pluralism. As I have already suggested, his suspicion of "groups" was especially pronounced in his June 1 commencement speech at West Point, in which he made explicit reference to the need for a more "moral" approach to civil rights than one that pitted people against each other. In this section I will discuss additional examples of his antigroup rhetoric and its iterations within various contexts.

Consider first his public remarks on October 20, 1990, just two days before the actual veto. After referring to Kennedy-Hawkins explicitly as a "quota bill" no less than three times within the seven opening sentences, Bush provided one of the most concise and specific objections against quotas he had yet offered: "Instead of solving problems, quotas foster divisiveness and litigation, set group against group, minority against minority, and in so doing, do more to promote legal fees than civil rights."[46] Missing here, of course, is the vision of pluralistic "community" Bush spoke of in 1988 as his party's nominee, the nation created by "organizations" cooperatively working together "like a thousand points of light in a broad and peaceful sky."[47] To the contrary, here groups are pitted against each other—"minority against minority"—with only lawyers reaping the rewards of such contests. In other words, if the American people view each other as members of groups, and especially as members of minority groups, such recognition will only create more problems, rather than further the nation's march towards full equality. In fact, Bush makes the latter point explicitly when he states that the proposed legislation "turns back the clock on progress that has occurred since the Civil Rights Act of 1964."[48]

In his actual veto message, dated October 22, 1990, President Bush made the point once more. This time, however, his rhetoric suggested that he might have been trying to reach two different types of audiences. First, for the specialized audiences who may have the most to lose or gain from this legislation (including lawyers and business owners, for example), Bush explains:

Despite the use of the term "civil rights" in the title of S.2104, the bill actually employs a maze of highly legalistic language to introduce the destructive force of quotas into our Nation's employment system. Primarily through provisions governing cases in which employment practices are alleged to have unintentionally caused the disproportionate exclusion of members of certain groups, S.2104 creates powerful incentives for employers to adopt hiring and promotion quotas. These incentives are created by the bill's new and very technical rules of litigation, which will make it difficult for employers to defend legitimate employment practices.[49]

The president's tone here is strikingly legalistic, which is probably appropriate given that he is foreshadowing the bureaucratic nightmare that will result from the "maze" of "very technical rules of litigation" in S.2104. Note too that there are no real people in this passage. The agents here are instead "employment systems," "governing cases," and "employment practices." Their results of their practices were not premeditated, but instead were "unintentional"; their offenses caused not discrimination or inequality, but rather "disproportionate exclusion."

Contrast this specialized, jargonistic, and depersonalized tone with the more individualized and vivid language the president used at the conclusion of this same veto message. Referring to "his" civil rights bill as a more attractive alternative, Bush concludes:

> Again, I urge the Congress to act on my legislation before adjournment. In order to enhance equal opportunity, however, the Congress must also take action in several related areas. The elimination of employment discrimination is a vital element in achieving the American dream, but it is not enough. The absence of discrimination will have little concrete meaning unless jobs are available and the members of all groups have the skills and education needed to qualify for those jobs. Nor can we expect that our young people will work hard to prepare for the future if they grow up in a climate of violence, drugs, and hopelessness.[50]

Bush is obviously no longer talking only to lawyers and other enforcement-oriented professionals here. Instead his comments seem to be geared also toward voters and especially to those citizens, including fellow politicians, who would accuse him of being indifferent to civil rights. After aligning the clumsy and syllable-ridden phrasing "the elimination of employment discrimination" with the more eloquent and crisp "American dream," Bush attempts to transform a legal memorandum into something more akin to a campaign speech. There are real people with real problems in this part of the passage, as Bush talks about the need for more jobs and better education for "members of all groups." Yet even as this sentence is winding its way into the next, it becomes even clearer who Bush's subject is, or more to the point, which groups are his concern: those whose "young people" may be growing up "in a climate of violence, drugs, and hopelessness." Their problem is not the "Nation's employment system," according to Bush; their problems stem from the systemic barriers some people face before they can enter this system.

Who, exactly, is Bush's "they"? The next and final sentences of the veto message, presumably crafted in order to show the depths of the president's genuine concern for civil rights, also reveal a great deal about the president's sense of the true moral imperative facing the nation at century's end:

In order to address these problems, attention must be given to measures that promote accountability and parental choice in the schools; that strengthen the fight against violent criminals and drug dealers in inner cities; that help to combat poverty and inadequate housing. We need initiatives that will empower individual Americans and enable them to reclaim control of their lives, thus helping to make our country's promise of opportunity a reality for all. Enactment of such initiatives, along with my Administration's civil rights bill, will achieve real advances for the cause of equal opportunity.[51]

In this passage, Bush does in fact give "concrete meaning" to his vision for civil rights through the noteworthy types of actors and problems his rhetoric features. When he first mentions schools, for example, he could be talking to and about all Americans. But as his references progress, he is clearly speaking about—if not to—poor black Americans, at least those who stereotypically populate the "inner cities" terrorized by "violent criminals and drug dealers," where people struggle to "combat poverty and inadequate housing." These African Americans belong to the "group" whose name cannot be spoken outright; theirs are the real civil rights problems that demand attention, even though there is no mention of any specific policies of Bush's that would address such issues, no actual "measures" to which "attention must be given." Appearing as these images do at the emotional end of an otherwise technical veto message, it is almost as if Bush seeks to highlight the total irrelevance of S.2104 to contemporary racial problems of violence, drug abuse, poverty, and hopelessness—the real moral crises of his times.

Neither Bush's alternative legislation, which Congress would reject, nor the law that would ultimately be passed (with the president's signature) as the Civil Rights Act of 1991 would explicitly address any of these problems.[52] Yet perhaps Bush's veto message may offer insight into why he had such difficulty crafting effective responses to civil rights issues. As mentioned, even though he was ostensibly speaking about problems that had the most negative impact on African American citizens, Bush never once used the terms *black* or *African American* in his veto. When he did use the term *group*, it was to refer to persisting inequalities ("The absence of discrimination will have little concrete meaning unless jobs are available and the members of all *groups* have the skills and education needed to qualify for those jobs") that have historically been associated with the civil rights movement. Was *groups* being used here as a short-hand for racial groups, or possibly even just for African Americans alone? And was the segmentation of the American people into "groups," in fact, part of the problem?

It is easy to get that sense when one reads the commencement speeches that Bush made the following spring. The president discussed civil rights explicitly in five of the eight commencement speeches he gave in 1991, including the June 1 address I have already mentioned.[53] For the purposes of this chapter, I will provide an extended discussion of only one other address: Bush's May 4, 1991, commencement speech at the University of Michigan at Ann Arbor.

President Bush did not use the word *groups* at all in this speech. Instead, he employed other language to warn against "the tyranny of 'they,'" potentially placing collectivity itself as a chief enemy of U.S. democracy. In this speech, the president laid out his personal philosophy of civil rights. He also revealed the depths of his philosophical opposition to pluralism and the previous cures for civil rights problems that had been attempted in its name.

Relatively early in the speech, for example, President Bush spoke about speech codes, an issue that would have been timely and sensitive on the Ann Arbor campus, and also an issue commonly associated with insensitivity to diversity, broadly defined. "What began as a crusade for civility has soured into a cause of conflict and even censorship." Bush noted:

> Throughout history, attempts to micro-manage casual conversation have only incited distrust. They have invited people to look for an insult in every word, gesture, action. And in their own Orwellian way, crusades that demand correct behavior crush diversity in the name of diversity. We should all be alarmed at the rise of intolerance in our land and by the growing tendency to use intimidation rather than reason in settling disputes. Neighbors who disagree no longer settle matters over a cup of coffee. They hire lawyers, and they go to court. And political extremists roam the land, abusing the privilege of free speech, setting citizens against one another on the basis of their class and race.[54]

Even though Bush is directly attacking the "Orwellian" "political extremists" who "roam the land, abusing the power of free speech," there is also a familiar motif here: the notion that citizens are being "[set] against one another on the basis of their class and race." This sounds remarkably similar to the phrase from the October 20, 1990, statement, in which Bush alleged that Kennedy-Hawkins would "set group against group, minority against minority, and in so doing, do more to promote legal fees than civil rights."[55] It is interesting to note that citizens are portrayed as being relatively passive in such phrasings; they are subject to "intimidation," for example, and their diversity can be "crushed." Furthermore, within the logic of the president's rhetoric, citizens do not choose such identifications and the associations that follow; they are instead almost unwittingly forced or into such groupings.

And who is doing this forcing? Bush's rhetoric names "activists," to be sure, but it also suggests that the culprits are lawyers. In fact, in Ann Arbor as in the October 20 statement and the actual veto message, Bush seems eager to note the inevitable fingerprints of "the lawyers" when such pernicious group affiliations are invoked. The American people must resist such agitation, the president urges:

> But, you see, such bullying is outrageous. It's not worthy of a great nation grounded in the values of tolerance and respect. So, let us fight back against the boring politics of division and derision. Let's trust our friends and colleagues to respond to reason. As Americans we must use our persuasive powers to conquer bigotry once and for all.[56]

Here Bush's finger-pointing is obvious. The activists and lawyers are "bullies" who would chip away at the nation's foundational values of "tolerance and respect." What's more, their "politics of division and derision" are "boring" and possibly even unreasonable. To conquer bigotry, Bush asserts, we must not turn to lawyers or activists, but instead "use our persuasive powers" and presumably talk other citizens out of their prejudices and fears.

However much Bush might have liked to use his bully pulpit to meet such ends, the president makes clear later in the Michigan speech that such attitudinal change is not the government's job any more than it is the lawyers' province. "If we learned anything in the past quarter century,"

Bush suggests, "it is that we cannot federalize virtue. Indeed, as we pile law upon law, program upon program, rule upon rule, we actually weaken people's moral sensitivity."[57] As evidence for his claim, Bush turns to history, and more specifically, to a famous commencement speech given by one of his predecessors on this same Michigan soil:

> When Lyndon Johnson—President Johnson—spoke here in 1964, he addressed issues that remain with us. He proposed revitalizing cities, rejuvenating schools, trampling down the hoary harvest of racism, and protecting the environment—back in 1964. He applied the wisdom of his time to these challenges. He believed cadres of experts really could care for the millions. And they would calculate ideal tax rates, ideal rates of expenditures on social programs, ideal distributions of wealth and privilege. And in many ways, theirs was an America by the numbers: If the numbers were right, America was right. And gradually, we got to the point of equating dollars with commitment. And when programs failed to produce progress, we demanded more money. And in time, this crusade backfired. Programs designed to ensure racial harmony generated animosity. Programs intended to help people out of poverty invited dependency.[58]

Perhaps this characterization of LBJ's policies is exactly what we might expect from a Republican president with a different ideological agenda. Yet if we read Bush's comments through the critical lens suggested thus far in this essay, we may notice two especially interesting features of this passage.

First, Bush says that the thinking LBJ used, the "wisdom of his time," was in fact the product of another group: the "cadres of experts" who would "calculate ideal tax rates . . . ideal rates of expenditures . . . [and] ideal distributions of wealth and privilege." When Bush refers to this misguided approach as "an America by the numbers," it is probably not too much of a stretch to suppose that he could use the same language to describe his objection to quotas. Quantitative solutions to civil rights problems only cause more problems, Bush seems to suggest, and the groups that endorse them hurt the very cause they seek to further.

Second, in this passage we again see Bush linking problems of race with problems of economics, even without naming any specific groups of alleged victims or perpetrators of such problems. Johnson's crusade backfired, according to Bush, when "programs designed to ensure racial harmony" instead "generated animosity," just as "programs designed to help people out of poverty" paradoxically "invited dependency." Missing in Bush's history lesson, however, are specific characters. Against whom did racial programs backfire? Why? Did these efforts provide insufficient help to African Americans and other people of color, for example, or did they instead backfire because they were too taxing for white people, both literally and metaphorically?

If Johnson's calculated solutions to help calculated groups of Americans did not work, Bush offers one that could: individual Americans need to change the way they each think about civil rights problems.

> We need to rethink our approach. Let's tell our people: We don't want an America by the numbers. We don't want a land of loopholes. We want a community of commitment and trust. When I talked of a kinder, gentler nation, I wasn't just trying to create a slogan. I was issuing a challenge. An effective government must know its limitations and respect its people's capabilities. In return, people must assume the final burden of freedom, and that's responsibility.[59]

In these last few words, Bush's approach to civil rights—and the most important reason, perhaps, why he is suspicious of groups themselves—becomes clear: he sees the solution to the dilemmas posed by inequality coming through greater identification with one's self and one's personal responsibility, not group affiliation. Although he speaks of wanting a "community of commitment and trust," his discourse suggests that the "final burden of freedom" is placed upon individuals. In fact, as the speech begins to end, when he turns his attention directly to the new graduates, it is to make exactly this point: "Once your commencement ends, you'll have to rely on the sternest stuff of all: yourself."[60]

In the event that the contrast between Bush's philosophy of individualism and LBJ's philosophy of "numbers" does not seem clear enough to his listeners, Bush then uses his final moments at the podium to draw even sharper distinctions:

> My vision for America depends heavily on you. You must protect the freedoms of enterprise, speech, and spirit. You must strengthen the family. You must build a peaceful and prosperous future. We don't need another Great Society with huge and ambitious programs administered by the incumbent few. We need a Good Society built upon the deeds of the many, a society that promotes service, selflessness, and action.[61]

In Bush's formulation, then, it is the strong individual who will ultimately protect civil rights and, indeed, public morality in the United States. The only group the United States needs is a "many" comprised of multiple "you's," with each one protecting, strengthening, and building a society of "service, selflessness, and action." Every individual has an important role to play in this mission, regardless of his or her own circumstances, according to President Bush:

> The Good Society poses a challenge: It dares you to explore the full promise of citizenship, to join in partnership with family, friends, government to make our world better. The Good Society does not demand agonizing sacrifice. It requires something within everyone's reach: common decency—common decency and commitment. Know your neighbors. Builds bonds of trust at home, at work, wherever you go. Don't just talk about the principles—live them.[62]

If you must think about "the theys" in your life, suggests the president, let them be the right kinds of "theys": your family, your friends, your coworkers, and even your government. This identification is not only the morally right thing to do, according to this logic, but it is also relatively easy; it "does not demand agonizing sacrifice." Likewise, this type of thinking is free and available to everyone, regardless of race, creed, gender, or ethnicity. "Common decency" is "within everyone's reach," and if everyone would just live according to it, no lawyers, experts, or activists would be required.

It is not my intent to suggest that Bush was disingenuous in these remarks. In fact, there is reason to believe that Bush spoke exactly as he felt. Mary Stuckey has argued persuasively that "decency" was a guiding principle behind Bush's approach to issues of diversity throughout his presidency. On such occasions, she writes, he would typically argue that "courtesy was more important than policy . . . that good people could not knowingly damage others . . . [and] that while governments, democratic or not, could forget this principle, the American people, *en masse,* could not."[63] Furthermore, Stuckey has also suggested that Bush was a strong believer in the need for "fair play" and thus may have read policy questions about affirmative action as having deeply moral dimensions as well.[64]

But even if we can view Bush's rhetoric as an indication of his personal feelings, I have argued that it can also be read as something more: a refutation of the pluralist paradigm of U.S. politics in the name of an allegedly more moral position championing individualism. In the concluding section, I will suggest that Bush's antigroups approach to civil rights can also be read as a sign of his own political times. Additionally, this discourse also raises questions about the prospect of public morality within a "hyperindividualized" political culture.

Groups, Then and Now: Bush's Rhetoric in His Own Time and Beyond

Mary Ann Glendon's research would suggest that no one should be surprised that George H. W. Bush's civil rights rhetoric in 1990 and 1991 had little use for groups. Glendon has shown that, since as early as the 1950s and 1960s, public discourse in the United States has become increasingly dominated by a particular kind of "rights talk." She argues that this "rights dialect" is uniquely American in several respects, one of which is strikingly relevant to Bush's rhetoric: "hyperindividualism."[65]

In general, American "rights talk" has become "hyperindividualized," according to Glendon, because of two features: it "promot[es] an image of the rights-bearer as a radically autonomous individual" while it also "neglect[s] the social dimensions of human personhood."[66] When Americans talk about civil rights, they are likely to be talking about *their* rights, and thus more likely still to be talking about individual rights rather than group rights. If this is true, then perhaps George Bush was no more than a vessel for his era. To speak about rights at all, and especially to speak about civil rights, in the 1990s, was to speak within a cultural context that valued radical individualism.

And yet it is worth remembering that individualism has limits, too, and these limits themselves beg at least two sets of questions about the relationship between rhetoric and public morality. First, recall Glendon's characterization of this discourse as ignoring the "social dimensions of human personhood." If we are to follow Condit's suggestion to view "the distinctively moral component of such codes" as those with "the specification of behavior that requires taking account of the needs and value of the 'Other,'"[67] then the problem becomes obvious. Highly individualistic discourses do not necessarily promote prescriptions for moral behavior. Even if they do—and here I recall Bush's earnest call in Ann Arbor for "a society that promotes service, selflessness, and action"— there is potentially an internal contradiction between taking a view of one's self as an individual agent, a strong self, if you will, and then also feeling obligated to act with selflessness. To put it differently, there is potentially a tension between the constitutive rhetoric of hyperindividualized identity and the constitutive rhetoric of morality calling for service to others. Which part matters more? Which is the a priori commitment? Exactly how are these two characteristics interdependent?

Robert Bellah and his colleagues once wrote that U.S. democracy required concerted efforts at balance between individualism and community commitments.[68] "Individualism alone does not allow persons to understand certain basic realities of their lives, especially their interdependence with others," they wrote.[69] It is possible—indeed, I suspect that it is even likely—that Bush assumed that strong individuals would in fact be motivated by traditions of service and common decency within their communities. Yet in the arena of U.S. race relations in particular, with its deep history of violence and mistrust, leaders may have to take care to be explicit in their calls for such balance between individualism and community-mindedness. They may also need to spell out the reasons why citizens need both characteristics.

Therefore the second set of questions raised by this analysis concerns the implications such a loss of balance between individualism and community may have within U.S. racial politics. As other scholars have noted, excessive focus on individualism may have contributed to the valorization of a "colorblind" telos within arguments about contemporary civil rights issues—one that suggests, for example, that since no less an authority than Dr. Martin Luther King, Jr., aimed for a day when individual character would count for more than skin color, we are somehow closer to achieving his dream when we ignore race altogether.[70] Yet there is evidence that the completely "colorblind" position may actually be more conservative on civil rights than a majority of Americans believe is appropriate.[71] When analyzing political rhetorics that either explicitly or implicitly argue for such color-blindness, rhetorical critics are obligated to point out the dangers of the very language.

For example, while our language can sometimes seem to force us into absolute "either/or" constructions—us versus them, black versus white, groups versus individuals—our lived experience takes place more often in the "both/and," *especially* if we are involved in creating and maintaining the "community of trust" so lauded by Bush when he spoke in Ann Arbor. To the extent that language championing individualism in the name of color-blindness ignores distinctions related to privilege, it also promotes both symbolic and material forms of insularity between members of racial groups. In the words of Robert Staples, "The 'color-blind theory' ignores the reality of . . . America: that race determines everyone's life chances in this country. In any area where there is a significant racial diversity, race impacts on where people live and go to school, whom they vote for, date, and marry, with whom they do business, whom they buy from and sell to, how much they pay and so on. This does not sound like the racial utopia Martin Luther King dreamed of."[72]

In short, radical individualism does not translate easily into positions that are inherently morally tenable. Here I have shown that in seeking to find a "more unifying, moral, and noble approach to civil rights," President Bush deployed a discourse of individualism that repudiated a pluralist commitment to those same goals. In addition to turning *quotas* into a devil term within affirmative action debates, as Zarefsky's research has shown, I have argued that Bush's civil rights rhetoric also deployed constitutive themes that were far more subtle. This discourse made group identification seem suspicious as a potential threat to both collegiality and equality among citizens and argued that individualism was the only moral way to approach civil rights. If public morality is constituted through discourse, as Condit has argued, and individualism is able to trump pluralism within U.S. civil rights talk, then we may be left with a curious predicament regarding the future. How can the United States, one of the world's largest functioning diverse and culturally pluralistic democracies, survive as such without a way of talking about its own pluralities in terms of their own needs, histories, and obligations to each other? Both democratic stability and common decency require that we seek answers to these questions. Both of these goals require that we attend to each other, both as individuals and as members of various communities.

NOTES

1. See also Celeste M. Condit, "Crafting Virtue: The Rhetorical Construction of Public Morality," *Quarterly Journal of Speech* 73 (1987): 79–87, and Celeste M. Condit, "Democracy and Civil Rights: The Universalizing Influence of Public Argumentation," *Communication Monographs* 54 (1987): 1–18.

2. Celeste M. Condit, "Where Is Public Address? George W. Bush, Abu Ghraib, and Contemporary Moral Discourse," in this volume.

3. Ibid.

4. Maurice Charland, "Constitutive Rhetoric: The Case of the Peuple Québécois," *Quarterly Journal of Speech* 73 (1987): 133–141.

5. Condit, "Where Is Public Address?"

6. As I have mentioned, Condit uses such a standard within her definition of morality. For an influential account of this standard, see John Rawls, *A Theory of Justice* (Cambridge: Belknap Press of Harvard University Press, 1971).

7. Shawn Parry-Giles and Trevor Parry-Giles, *Constructing Clinton: Hyperreality and Presidential Image-Making in Postmodern Politics* (New York: Peter Lang, 2002).

8. See Joseph Stiglitz, *The Roaring Nineties: A New History of the World's Most Prosperous Decade* (New York: W. W. Norton, 2004).

9. David Zarefsky, "George Bush and the Transformation of Civil Rights Discourse, 1965–1990," in *Civil Rights Rhetoric and the American Presidency*, ed. James A. Aune and Enrique D. Rigsby (College Station: Texas A&M University Press, 2005), 238–239.

10. *Wards Cove v. Antonio*, 490 U.S. 651 (1989).

11. See Zarefsky, "George Bush," 239–241.

12. Ibid., 240.

13. Ibid., 241.

14. This legislation restored the Uniform Guidelines on Employee Selection Practices created as a result of *Griggs v. Duke Power Company* in 1971. Among other features, these guidelines placed the burden of proof within workplace discrimination lawsuits on the employer—who had to show that any discrimination arose from "business necessity"—rather than the employee. *Griggs*, and thus the Uniform Guidelines, were struck down by the Supreme Court as part of the *Ward's Cove v. Antonio* ruling in 1989. For a full discussion, see Zarefsky, "George Bush," 238–242.

15. Zarefsky, "George Bush," 241.

16. Ibid., 244.

17. George H. W. Bush, "Remarks at a Meeting with the Commission on Civil Rights, May 17, 1990," *Public Papers of the Presidents: George Bush, 1990* (Washington, D.C.: Government Printing Office, 1991), 1:677.

18. Zarefsky, "George Bush," 242.

19. Ibid., 249.

20. Ibid., 250.

21. Ibid.

22. George H. W. Bush, "Remarks at the United States Military Academy Commencement Ceremony in West Point, New York, June 1, 1991," *Public Papers of the Presidents: George Bush, 1991* (Washington, D.C.: Government Printing Office), 1:591.

23. Ibid.

24. See David Harvey, *A Brief History of Neoliberalism* (Oxford: Oxford University Press, 2005).

25. Zarefsky, "George Bush," 235; Richard M. Nixon, "Remarks on Accepting the Presidential Nomination of the Republican National Convention," *Public Papers of the Presidents: Richard Nixon, 1972* (Washington, D.C.: Government Printing Office), 2:788.

26. See Robert Bellah et al., *Habits of the Heart: Individualism and Commitment in American Life*, updated edition with new introduction (Berkeley and Los Angeles: University of California Press, 1996).

27. James Madison, "Federalist Paper No. 10," in *100 Milestone Documents from the National Archives* (New York: Oxford University Press, 2003), 36–38.

28. Quoted in Robert A. Dahl, *On Democracy* (New Haven: Yale University Press, 2000), 17.

29. Alexis de Tocqueville, *Democracy in America*, 12th ed., ed. J. P. Meyer, trans. George Lawrence (New York: Harper Perennial, 1988), 516.

30. For the quote about the "reigning paradigm," see Paula D. McClain and Joseph Stewart Jr., *Can We All Get Along? Racial and Ethnic Minorities in American Politics* (Boulder, Colo.: Westview, 1999), 61. For the definition of pluralism, see Geoffrey K. Roberts, *A Dictionary of Political Analysis* (London: Longman, 1971), 151.

31. Dahl, *On Democracy*, 90.

32. David Robertson, *A Dictionary of Modern Politics*, 3rd ed. (London: Europa Publications, 2002), 215.

33. Samuel P. Huntington, *American Politics: The Promise of Disharmony* (Cambridge: Belknap Press of Harvard University Press, 1981), 7.

34. Avagail Eisenberg, *Reconstructing Political Pluralism* (Albany: State University Press of New York, 1995), 4.

35. Robert D. Putnam, *Bowling Alone: The Collapse and Revival of American Community* (New York: Simon and Schuster, 2000).

36. See James Arnt Aune, *Selling the Free Market: The Rhetoric of Economic Correctness* (New York: Guilford, 2001).

37. McClain and Stewart, *Can We All Get Along?* 61.

38. Ibid., 62.

39. Ibid., 62; Schattsneider cited in McClain and Stewart, *Can We All Get Along?* 62.

40. Herbert J. Gans, *Middle American Individualism: Political Participation and Liberal Democracy* (Oxford: Oxford University Press, 1988), 121.

41. McClain and Stewart, *Can We All Get Along?* 61.

42. Ibid., 62; emphasis added.

43. Ibid., 61.

44. George H. W. Bush, "Nomination Acceptance Speech, Republican National Convention, August 18, 1988," accessed at http://www.americanrhetoric.com/speeches/georgehbush1988rnc.htm.

45. Ibid.

46. George H. W. Bush, "Statement on Civil Rights Legislation, October 20, 1990," accessed at http://bushlibrary.tamu.edu/research/public_papers.php?i=2343&year=1990&month=10.

47. Bush, "Nomination Acceptance Speech."

48. Bush, "Statement on Civil Rights Legislation," accessed at http://bushlibrary.tamu.edu/research/public_papers.php?id=2343&year=1990&month=10.

49. Http://bushlibrary.tamu.edu/research/public_papers.php?id=2345&year=1990&month=10.

50. Ibid.
51. Ibid.
52. The closest it came was in the educational arena, where it banned "race norming" or the adjustment of test scores according to race. Otherwise, the Civil Rights Act of 1991 is widely viewed as primarily only changing employment laws, including an increase in the upper limit for damages from discrimination claims and provisions for punitive damages in cases where intentional discrimination is proved.
53. The five commencement speeches that contain explicit comments on quotas, equal opportunity, and other topics related to race relations took place at the following locations on the following dates: University of Michigan, May 4, 1991; Hampton University, May 12, 1991; United States Air Force Academy, May 29, 1991; FBI Academy, May 30, 1991; and United States Military Academy, June 1, 1991. The three speeches where the president did not make such remarks were Yale University, May 27, 1991; James H. Groves Adult High School, Seaford, Delaware, June 11, 1991; and California Institute of Technology, Pasadena, June 14, 1991.
54. George H. W. Bush, "Remarks at the University of Michigan Commencement Ceremony in Ann Arbor, May 4, 1991," *Public Papers of the Presidents: George Bush, 1991*, 1:471.
55. "Statement on Civil Rights Legislation," 2:1435–1436.
56. Bush, "Remarks at the University of Michigan Commencement," 471.
57. Ibid.
58. Ibid.
59. Ibid., 472.
60. Ibid.
61. Ibid.
62. Ibid.
63. See Mary E. Stuckey, *Defining Americans: The Presidency and National Identity* (Lawrence: University Press of Kansas, 2004), 302. See also John R. Greene, *The Presidency of George Bush* (Lawrence: University Press of Kansas, 2000), 144.
64. Stuckey, *Defining Americans*, 303.
65. Mary Ann Glendon, *Rights Talk: The Impoverishment of Civil Discourse* (New York: Free Press, 1991), x.
66. Ibid., 109.
67. Condit, "Where Is Public Address?"
68. Bellah et al., *Habits of the Heart*.
69. Ibid., ix.
70. Edward G. Carmines and Paul M. Sniderman, "The Structure of Racial Attitudes:

Issue Pluralism and the Changing American Dilemma," in *Understanding Public Opinion*, ed. Barbara Norrander and Clyde Wilcox, 2nd ed. (Washington, D.C.: Congressional Quarterly Press, 2002), 105–119.

71. Ibid., 107.
72. Robert Staples, "The Illusion of Racial Equality: The Black American Dilemma," in *Lure and Loathing: Essays on Race, Identity, and the Ambivalence of Assimilation*, ed. Gerald Early (New York: Viking Penguin, 1993), 231.

Public Moral Argument on Same-Sex Marriage, 2000–2005: A Narrative Approach

Martin J. Medhurst

On every subject there are two speeches that oppose one another.

—Protagoras

On May 17, 2004, Massachusetts became the first of the fifty "united" states of America to offer legal same-sex marriage. The event drew reporters from around the world, and within the first week 2,468 same-sex couples had taken out marriage applications. It was considered by many observers to be the greatest victory for the gay liberation movement in its thirty-five-year history.[1] Yet even as gay activists celebrated from coast to coast, the movement was confronted with a set of formidable obstacles: a federal law called the Defense of Marriage Act (DOMA), thirty-seven states that had passed state-level defense of marriage acts, four states that had passed constitutional amendments banning same-sex marriage, a president of the United States who had endorsed an amendment to the federal Constitution that would limit marriage to the union of one man and one woman, and national polls that consistently found that 59 percent of the voting public opposed legalizing same-sex marriages.[2]

For some gay activists the subject of same-sex marriage had been an issue of concern since the early 1970s;[3] for most straight Americans the subject was virtually unheard of until the 1990s, culminating in December 1999, when a court ruling in Vermont resulted in the state legislature passing a law to establish "civil unions" as an alternative to same-sex marriage.[4] The civil union bill was signed into law by Governor Howard Dean and took effect on July 1, 2000. From that moment to the present, the debate over same-sex marriage has been joined in the public arena.[5] The debate is an almost perfect example of what Walter Fisher and others have called public moral argument. According to Fisher, "*Public* moral argument is a form of controversy that inherently crosses fields. It is not contained in the way that legal, scientific, or theological arguments are by subject matter, particular conceptions of argumentative competence, and well recognized rules of advocacy." Further, "Public *moral* argument is moral in the sense that it is founded on ultimate questions—of life and death, of how persons should be defined and treated, of preferred patterns of living." Such questions involve "status issues," according to Joseph Gusfield, and their resolution indicates "the group, culture, or style of life to which the government and society are publicly committed." Finally, public moral *argument* refers to "public controversies—disputes and debates—about moral issues." Such debates are carried on in the public realm through narrative structures based on "good reasons" adduced by each side in the debate.[6]

In this chapter I want to examine the public moral arguments advanced by both proponents and opponents of same-sex marriage as those arguments appeared in the mainstream media between 2000 and 2005. My argument is that the debate can best be understood as a battle over the place and definition of "marriage," and that this battle is enacted through public narratives that each side constructs to tell its story about married life in America. I shall argue that each side paints a narrative picture using eight basic story elements. In the case of the pro-gay marriage rhetors, those elements are rights, discrimination, freedom, equality, love, family, protection, and the common good. In the case of anti-gay marriage advocates, those elements are nature, tradition, sacredness, morality, children, family, protection, and the common good. Note that the last three elements are shared by both narratives. It is through the skillful combination of these eight terms that each side weaves its story about what constitutes "marriage."[7] Further, I contend that the figurative language employed by both sides gives key insights into how the narrative appeal is structured as well as the actions that are required of auditors. Understanding how the story elements are mobilized and how the tropes and figures are deployed reveals what is at stake for each side—and, ultimately, for American society. Figurative language central to the narratives revolves around metaphors of war, images of death and destruction, and analogies to the black civil rights movement and to Nazi Germany.

I turn first to the story on behalf of same-sex marriage, then examine the narrative against same-sex marriage, and end with an overview of the figurative language used by both sides to try to structure audience thought and action. I will examine the unique elements of each narrative first, then turn to the three elements that they share—family, protection, and the common good. Since the complete narratives cannot be found in any single text, I have used rhetorical fragments from mainstream media accounts to reconstruct each narrative, using the story elements that repeat themselves in the rhetoric of such advocates of same-sex marriage as the Human Rights Campaign (HRC), Freedom to Marry, the National Gay and Lesbian Task Force (NGLTF), and Gay and Lesbian Advocates and Defenders (GLAD). I have reconstructed the narrative in opposition to same-sex marriage by examining the rhetoric of Focus on the Family, the Family Research Council (FRC), the American Family Association (AFA), the Alliance for Marriage, and the Traditional Values Coalition (TVC).[8]

The Narrative on Behalf of Same-Sex Marriage

The story told by advocates of same-sex marriage takes a familiar form: citizens denied their legitimate rights under the Constitution petition their fellow countrymen and the courts for redress of grievances. As the central element in the story, the term *rights* plays an organizing role. Winnie

Stachelberg, head of the Human Rights Campaign, observes: "You know, marriage is about a thousand rights and benefits and responsibilities that are accorded to committed couples in this country today. . . . Things like Social Security survivor's benefits, hospital visitation, and ability to make funeral arrangements for a loved one." For many advocates, same-sex marriage is nothing less than a bedrock human and civil right. As Representative Dennis Kucinich (D-Ohio) put it, this is a "fundamental civil rights issue . . . that shouldn't even be a close question. . . . We have to be courageous in protecting people's rights." San Francisco mayor Gavin Newsom agreed: "I can't believe people of good conscience, from any ideological perspective, can honestly say that the Constitution should be used to take rights away from people when the Constitution was conceived to advance the rights of people in this country." Even Senator John Kerry, the 2004 Democratic nominee for president, whose support stopped short of marriage, underscored the centrality of rights to the debate when he said: "I'm for civil union, I'm for partnership rights, I think what ought to condition this debate is not the term marriage, as much as the rights that people are afforded. . . . I'm for rights—not for terminology or status—rights."[9]

If rights is the central god term of the narrative, then *discrimination* is the chief devil term. Armed with the language of the judicial opinions in both the *Lawrence v. Texas* and *Hillary Goodridge et al. v. Department of Public Health* cases, which held that laws against sodomy were "an invitation to subject homosexual persons to discrimination both in the public and in the private spheres" and that laws barring same-sex marriage denied "the dignity and equality of all individuals," making them into "second-class citizens," advocates attacked discrimination as the central evil of the narrative. "Discrimination is as wrong in civil marriage as in any other public institution," claimed Kenneth Roth, executive director of Human Rights Watch. In preparation for issuing marriage licenses to same-sex couples in San Francisco, Mayor Gavin Newsom opined: "California's Constitution leaves no doubts. It leaves no room for any form of discrimination." Dorothy Erlich, executive director of the American Civil Liberties Union of Northern California, agreed: "Just as we told the state in 1974 when they passed a statue limiting marriage to a man and a woman, that kind of discrimination against same-sex couples violates the

California Constitution's promise of equality. Discrimination in marriage was wrong then and it's wrong now." Noting John Kerry's willingness to amend the Massachusetts state constitution to prevent same-sex marriage, the *Washington Blade* editorialized: "Writing discrimination into the constitution—any constitution—is wrong." After President Bush endorsed an amendment to the federal Constitution on February 24, 2004, same-sex marriage advocates adopted a common refrain. "He wants to move America backwards," claimed Peter Schuman, executive director of MoveOn.org, "by enshrining discrimination in the U.S. Constitution." The idea of "writing discrimination into the constitution" became a standard argumentative topos by advocates of same-sex marriage.[10]

Also central to the narrative is an expansive notion of individual *freedom* and liberty. As, perhaps, the central god term of the American experience, freedom carries a presumption in its favor. That presumption was underscored in *Lawrence* when Justice Kennedy, writing for the majority, held: "Liberty presumes an autonomy of self that includes freedom of thought, belief, expression, and certain intimate conduct." Advocates of same-sex marriage argue that they should be "free" to be who they are.

As Reverend Troy Perry puts it: "Marriage involves the most fundamental civil right: the freedom of individual choice." Rebecca Mead sees that freedom of individual choice as a release from social mores. "The *Times* same-sex wedding announcements," she writes, "will be the supreme expression of the contemporary ideal of marriage as a grand, individualistic romance detached from society's strictures. . . . Gay marriage is the ultimate celebration of individualism." When Massachusetts governor Mitt Romney acted to restrict same-sex marriage licenses to residents of that state, Bobbi Cote-Whitacre responded: "I just think it's a shame the he doesn't believe in freedom for everyone."[11]

If freedom is the philosophical grounding of the same-sex marriage narrative, then *equality* is the practical goal. "We only ask that the government and President Bush provide all people the same standing and extend to them their constitutional right to equality under the law," says David Tseng, executive director of PFLAG (Parents, Families and Friends of Lesbians and Gays). Same-sex marriage advocates find the warrant for equality in the founding documents of the nation. "In a country where all people are created equal," claims Cheryl Jacques, president of the

Human Rights Campaign, "it is intellectually dishonest and deeply unfair that some people cannot have the legal rights and protections for their relationships that most others take for granted, and that all families need." In this narrative, equality—and only equality—will satisfy the needs of same-sex partners. As Perry notes:

> Anything less than full marriage equality is second-class status for gays and lesbians. I know the argument: "Can't we get most of our rights through civil unions? Or domestic partnerships? Can't we settle for something less than full marriage equality and still make progress?"
>
> Those weren't acceptable answers to women who worked for full legal equality at the turn of the 19th century. Those weren't acceptable answers to African-Americans who worked for full legal equality in the 1950s and 1960s. And they aren't acceptable answers to the lesbian, gay, bisexual and transgender communities who are working for legal equality—including marriage equality—at the dawn of this new millennium.[12]

While the term *equality* is clearly related to "rights," it transcends rights alone. Those committed to full equality reject civil unions, even though Howard Dean has repeatedly argued that "with civil unions . . . everybody is equal." But for advocates of same-sex marriage equality goes beyond specific rights to encompass status, both personal and social. *Marriage* is the term that connotes that status; thus the narrative rejects all arrangements short of marriage. As Jonathan Rauch puts it: "For gay people, civil unions and the like are a seat at the back of the bus, a badge of inferiority pinned on every same-sex union." Advocates of same-sex marriage intend to "hold America to its commitment to be a country where everyone has the right to be both different and equal—and where no one has to give up her or his difference to be treated equally."[13]

Finally, advocates of same-sex marriage feature *love* as a major element of their narrative of same-sex marriage. Evan Wolfson, executive director of Freedom to Marry, notes: "Marriage is many things in our society. It is an important choice that belongs to couples in love." Here the key is not whether the couples are gay or straight, but that they share love one for another. As one placard at a protest in Athens, Ohio put it:

"Love Knows No Gender." To Stachelberg, "Love and commitment makes a wonderful family." What counts, according to Wolfson, "is not family structure, but the quality of dedication, commitment, self-sacrifice, and love in the household." It is, in fact, "the prospect of a love which is complete" that motivates advocates of same-sex marriage. Echoing the sentiment from the 1955 song "Love and Marriage" ("Love and marriage, love and marriage, go together like a horse and carriage"), Wolfson holds that "marriage is the vocabulary in which nongay people talk of love, family, dedication, self-sacrifice, and stages of life. It is the vocabulary of love, equality, and inclusion."[14]

These five elements—rights, discrimination, freedom, equality, and love—form the core of the same-sex marriage narrative. Still to be added to that narrative are the elements of family, protection, and the common good. But before turning to those elements shared with the opponents of same-sex marriage, let us first turn to the opponents' narrative.

The Narrative Opposed to Same-Sex Marriage

The narrative told by opponents of same-sex marriage is grounded in the world of *nature*. According to this story heterosexual marriage is normative because it is the only kind of marriage that has natural, biological, and physiological warrants. The very structure of the human body and the biological necessities of sperm and egg commingling to produce life argue, in this narrative, against homosexual unions. As Dr. James Dobson, clinical psychologist and founder of Focus on the Family, notes, men and women "are designed to 'fit' together, both physically and emotionally." "True freedom and genuine fulfillment can be found," he goes on to argue, "only when we live in harmony with our design." Wilton Gregory, president of the United States Conference of Catholic Bishops, agrees. "A same-sex union is not equivalent to marriage," notes Bishop Gregory, because "it is not based on the natural complementarity of male and female." Such complementarity, according to Monsignor William Fay, cannot be found outside of "the order of nature." Because nature itself is understood as a creation of Almighty God, its testimony is not only self-revealing, but partakes of the divine. In the words of the Hebrew scriptures: "So God created man in his own image, in the image of God he created him; male and female he created them. God blessed them and said to them: 'Be fruitful and increase in number.'" Nature is the way it is because that's the way God the Creator intended it to be. As Bishop Gregory argues, "Marriage is a basic human and social institution. Though it is regulated by civil laws and by church laws, it did not originate from either the church or state, but from God." Or, in the words of Jerry Falwell, "The issue of marriage is simply an eternal one—that is, one man married to one woman."[15]

Because marriage dates from time immemorial, it has become *traditional*. In the words of George W. Bush, "The union of a man and woman is the most enduring human institution, honored and encouraged in all cultures and by every religious faith. Ages of experience have taught humanity that the commitment of a husband and wife to love and to serve one another promotes the welfare of children and the stability of society." Indeed, marriage is so ancient that it even predates the law, according to Peter Sprigg of the Family Research Council, who holds that "marriage is not a creation of the law. Marriage is a fundamental human institution that predates the law and the Constitution. At its heart, it is an anthropological and sociological reality, not a legal one. Laws relating to marriage merely recognize and regulate an institution that already exists." According to D. James Kennedy, senior minister of the Coral Ridge Presbyterian Church, marriage is, in fact, "the first institution. It precedes, both in primacy and in the order of creation, the institutions of civil government, the Church, and the school." As an institution, marriage, according to Kennedy, "is the keystone in the arch of civilization." Therefore, we should not tamper with marriage as traditionally understood.[16]

Because of its grounding in nature, in creation, and in tradition, marriage is *sacred*. Along with the related terms *sanctity* and *sacrament*, the sacredness of marriage is featured repeatedly in the narrative of those opposed to same-sex marriage. According to President Bush, "If our laws teach that marriage is a sacred commitment of a man and a woman, the basis of an orderly society and the defining promise of a life, that strengthens the institution of marriage. If courts create their own arbitrary definition of marriage as a mere legal contract, and cut marriage off from its cultural, religious, and natural roots, then the meaning of marriage is lost, and the institution is weakened." While opponents use terms like sacred, sanctity, and sacrament freely, like Bush they appear to connote something more than just "holy" or "set apart," the standard dictionary definitions of sacred. Kenneth Burke seems closer to their meaning when he writes:

> The Latin *sacer*, we may recall, did not correspond simply to our word "sacred." The criminal was *sacer* (an ambiguity that was at least retained in the vocabulary of action if not that of explicit linguistic usage, as we see it in the "rite of sanctuary" whereby a fugitive from the law could not be molested while under the protection of the altar, or perhaps in the design of the Crucifixion, with Christ surrounded by thieves). *Sacer* might thus be more accurately translated as "untouchable," since the extremely good, the extremely bad, and the extremely powerful are equally "untouchable."[17]

This seems to be the sense in which Bush and others use the term *sacred*. To them marriage is untouchable. Hence, the comment from Miriam Guardado, a housewife from Oakland: "Homosexuals are free to live their lives, but marriage is not for them. Marriage is sacred."[18]

It is this "untouchableness" of marriage that allows it to function as a *moral* norm. As Maggie Gallagher notes: "Marriage is inherently normative: It is about holding out a certain kind of relationship as a social ideal." Since it is grounded in nature, creation, and tradition, marriage is, by definition, a good. Arrangements opposed to traditional marriage must, therefore, be evil and as such cannot partake in the moral norm. Hence, the comment by Tom Minnery of Focus on the Family following the decision in *Lawrence*: "With today's decision the court continues pillaging its way through the moral norms of our country. If the people have no right to regulate sexuality then ultimately the institution of marriage is in peril." Minnery was, of course, echoing the minority opinion in *Lawrence*, written by Justice Scalia. For opponents of same-sex marriage, the marriage of one man to one woman is "part of the common moral heritage of humanity." Since it is an ideal of the whole of humanity, it cannot be overturned by any subset of the whole, especially by a handful of unelected judges. Hence, following the *Lawrence* ruling, Gary Lavy, an attorney with the

Alliance Defense Fund, charged that "the U.S. Supreme Court rejected the moral judgment of the Texas Legislature and imposed the moral views of six justices on the entire country." The logic here is that the legislative branch represents the moral consensus of the community, whether city, state, or nation. The legislature is the repository of social, cultural, and moral ideals. To usurp its role is to overthrow the moral consensus. Hence Dobson's comment that same-sex marriage could mean "the end of morality," for if courts can no longer consider community norms and judges continue to usurp legislative authority, then the prevailing ideal will effectively have been destroyed.[19]

By destroying the moral norm, opponents hold, not only will traditional marriage be undermined, but in the process of undermining marriage, *children*, too, will be harmed. Senator Sam Brownback of Kansas states the case succinctly: "The government registers and endorses marriage between a man and a woman to ensure a stable environment for the raising and nurturing of children." Such an environment is, in this narrative, the ideal. "Children do need a male and a female role model," says Ron Crews, spokesperson for the Coalition for Marriage. "Children do best when they have a mom and a dad in the home. Public policy is about what is ideal, what is the best." President Bush, too, links the debate over marriage to the welfare of children: "I am committed to supporting strong families and strong marriages to help ensure that every child grows up in a safe, loving family. Statistics show that children from two-parent families are less likely to end up in poverty, drop out of school, become addicted to drugs, have a child out of wedlock, suffer abuse, or become a violent criminal." In short, "children without a married mom and dad suffer significantly." According to this narrative, "Gay marriage would cut the final cord that ties marriage to the well-being of children."[20]

Dueling Narratives: Family, Protection, and the Common Good

The narratives for and against same-sex marriage contend for adherents in the public realm. One speaks the language of rights and equality, while the other speaks the language of nature and morality. Yet both appeal to a trinity of terms that seems to be elastic enough to serve either narrative: family, protection, and the common good.

For opponents of same-sex marriage the traditional *family* is seen as the bedrock of society. According to Matt Daniels, president of the Alliance for Marriage, "We all rise or fall collectively with the health of our social infrastructure—built upon the foundation of the family. This is why healthy marriages are—in a sense—everyone's business." Opponents of same-sex marriage hold that "we simply cannot survive without the fundamental institution of civil society; the family formed uniquely and essentially by the union of the two genders to parent the next generation." But proponents of same-sex marriage insist that they have families, too. "This is a struggle about the real lives of real people who are being told their lives don't exist," charged Beth Robinson, cocounsel to GLAD. "They experience daily assaults on the integrity of their families." "For all the president's rhetoric about the sanctity of marriage, he staunchly refuses to make a commitment to protecting the pursuit of happiness for all American families," says Tseng. "Those families and children deserve the rights and protections of marriage," claims Jacques, "and we are deeply disappointed that the President used the [2004] State of the Union address to attack our families and divide the country." To underscore this perspective, proponents of same-sex marriage ran a million-dollar ad campaign in major newspapers around the country using the headline "Why Are 'Pro-Family' Groups Attacking This Family?" One such ad features a same-sex couple from Maryland and their three children. The ad reads: "Between 'skinned knees' and 'soccer practice . . . they face all the same joys and frustrations as other parents—but without the same protections.'" The ad campaign sounded a theme often repeated by proponents of same-sex marriage. In the words of Andrew Sullivan, "When people talk about gay marriage, they miss the point. This isn't about gay marriage. It's about marriage. It's about family. It's about love."[21]

Opponents reject such reasoning. As Ed Vitagliano, news editor of the *American Family Association Journal*, argues: "This strategy of legitimacy by association involves a classic fallacy. Just because all dogs are mammals doesn't mean that all mammals are dogs; likewise, just because families love each other doesn't mean that all people who love each other are families." He goes on to note, "If by family we mean nothing really specific—or if we define it in the most malleable of terms—then family really comes to mean nothing at all. It is like a formless, intangible vapor that can enter and fill a jar of any shape." Charles Colson links this effort to redefine family to the moral breakdown in society: "The authority of the family to teach and reinforce moral standards is undermined by the insistence that it can take any form we choose. Like religion, the family's power to teach is rooted in the belief that it is the individual who must conform to its requirements and not the other way around. . . . A future in which the traditional family and religion play less of a role is a future where moral commonality is less, not more, likely."[22]

Proponents respond that "the nuclear family as we know it is evolving. The emphasis should not be on it being a father and a mother, but on loving, nurturing parents, whether that be a single mother or a gay couple living in a committed relationship." California legislator Sheila Kuehl charges that the "defense [of the traditional concept of the family] inevitably takes the form of drawing a tight circle around one form of an otherwise flexible word. Then that circle is fixed into law, demonizing all those who don't fit its narrow definition." To Lou Sheldon, chairman of the Traditional Values Coalition, the rhetoric advocating same-sex marriage is "all part of a carefully calculated campaign to provide the appearance of normalcy to homosexual behavior," while to the Reverend Karen Oliveto, a United Methodist pastor in San Francisco, same-sex marriage is "a good and holy thing. It's traditional family values at their best." The duel over the term *family* is at the heart of the struggle for same-sex marriage. Both sides realize that if they are to prevail, then their definition—specific in the case of opponents, general in the case of proponents—must carry the day. To cede the definition of family is to surrender to the other side.[23]

Closely related to the narrative element of family is the term *protection*. While both sides employ the term frequently, they do so in different ways and to different ends. For proponents of same-sex marriage, "protection" usually refers to the safeguarding of their persons and property. It is protection of individuals. For opponents of same-sex marriage, "protection" usually refers to traditional marriage. It is protection of the institution and, by extension, of society at large. For Colin Stewart of the Family Research Council, "Marriage must be protected." "We absolutely agree with the president," says Stewart, "that marriage must be defended. Not just the word, but also the institution." But for the Human Rights Campaign, the debate is about "the civil responsibilities and protections afforded through a government issued civil marriage license." For public proponents of same-sex marriage the term *protection* echoes the legal rulings in both *Romer v. Evans* ("We find nothing special in the protections Amendment 2 withholds. These protections . . . constitute ordinary civil life in a free society") and *Goodridge v. Department of Public Health* ("We declare that barring an individual from the protections, benefits, and obligations of civil marriage solely because that person would marry a person of the same sex violates the Massachusetts Constitution"). Hence, in the public discourse, protection is often preceded by the adjective *legal*. To Wolfson, opponents of same-sex marriage are out "to deny gay people any measure of legal protection and human dignity." Closely related is the adjective *equal*, as when Jacques praises San Francisco mayor Newsom for helping the "many families who sought and received the equal protection he made possible for them through a civil marriage license." At times the two terms are joined in phrases such as *equal protection under law*.[24]

To opponents of same-sex marriage, however, it is the institution and the society or culture that are in need of protection. Dobson charges: "Homosexual activists are determined to ignore existing laws that protect the institution of marriage and to co-opt the family for their own purposes." Yet it is not only the institution, but the culture itself that is under attack. "We need to protect the lifeblood of culture," asserts Focus on the Family vice president Bill Maier. To protect the institution and the culture, opponents of same-sex marriage started a campaign to ask "state lawmakers and members of Congress to sign 'protect marriage' pledges" affirming that "marriage should be defined as a union between one man and one woman." And President Bush pledged that he would "support law to protect marriage between a man and a woman." In so doing, Bush pointed a finger at what he called "activist judges" who "legislate from the bench," thus affirming opponents' views that the institution was in need of "protection from renegade liberal judges." In this view, the social organization of the entire culture, "the very foundation of human social order," is under attack. "Western civilization itself," Dobson warns, "appears to hang in the balance."[25]

Commingled with the debate over what constitutes a family and who or what is in need of protection is the discussion of what the *common good* requires. For advocates of same-sex marriage the common good requires strict equality grounded in the autonomy of the individual, what Justice Kennedy, writing in the *Lawrence* case, called the "liberty of the person both in its spatial and more transcendent dimensions." For opponents of same-sex marriage the common good requires a moral standard that transcends any one individual or group of individuals to encompass the culture as a whole. While both sides appeal to communal standards, their understandings of what constitutes community is radically different. For one side, community is like a rainbow—composed of many different colors, joining together to form a whole, with each equally valued and equally important. For the other side, community is like a pyramid, with heavy foundation stones at the base and lighter stones composing the upper layers. All are part of the pyramid, but not all are equally valu-able to the integrity of the structure. Indeed, if one removes one of the foundation blocks, the whole will weaken and eventually crumble. Thus, Fay can argue that marriage is "the center and foundation of our human community." Building on this understanding, Cardinal Ratzinger (now Pope Benedict XVI) holds that "the common good requires that laws recognize, promote, and protect marriage as the basis of the family, the primary unit of society." Failure to support traditional marriage, he claims, "would result in changes to the entire organization of society, contrary to the common good."[26]

As if in response to Ratzinger, Jonathan Rauch agrees that mar-riage is a primary good and that, as such, it is not only good for straight people, but good for gays as well. He titles his book *Gay Marriage: Why It Is Good for Gays, Good for Straights, and Good for America.* "Far from decoupling marriage from its core mission," Rauch writes, "same-sex marriage clarifies and strengthens that mission. Far from hastening the social decline of marriage, same-sex marriage shores up the key values and commitments on which couples and families and society depend. Far from dividing America and weakening communities, same-sex marriage, if properly implemented, can make the country both better unified and truer to its ideals." In this view, that which is held in common is the com-mitment to marriage as an institution, but not as an institution defined in

a particular way. For Rauch the common good is to be found in the act of
marriage itself. For opponents of same-sex marriage the common good is
what follows from the marriage of one man and one woman. Such a marriage, according to Bishop Gregory, "makes a unique and irreplaceable
contribution to the common good of society when it fulfills its natural,
God-given purposes, namely, to bring children into the world and care for
them and to provide a way for a man and a woman to seek each other's
good in a committed, lifetime relationship." While both sides are committed to the common good, each interprets that phrase in a different way.[27]

Metaphor, Image, and Analogy: The Battle Joined

Since the debate over same-sex marriage is widely understood to be the
latest skirmish in an ongoing culture war, it is not surprising that images of battle dominate the public discourse. The language of war has
been a constant part of the public debate at least since the moment Pat
Buchanan declared at the 1992 Republican National Convention: "There
is a religious war going on in our country for the soul of America. It is a
cultural war, as critical to the kind of nation we will one day be as was the
Cold War itself."[28] What may be surprising—and a bit disconcerting—is
the extent to which the metaphor of war and its related entailments have
been literalized in the debate over same-sex marriage.

Proponents of same-sex marriage declare their court victories in *Lawrence* and *Goodridge* to be a "powerful new weapon in our legal battles"
for gay marriage. They remind their allies that "the war's ground zero" is
"in bedrooms and in streets, in bars and parking lots." They charge opponents with having launched an "attack" on gay families. When President
Bush announced his support for a constitutional amendment banning
same-sex marriage, Matt Foreman, executive director of the National Gay
and Lesbian Task Force, proclaimed: "We consider this a declaration of
war on gay America. . . . We did not ask for this fight, but if the President
wants one, he will have one." When the Massachusetts legislature voted
to approve a state constitutional amendment to ban same-sex marriage,
Arline Issacson of the Massachusetts Gay and Lesbian Political Caucus
said: "Today, fear and prejudice won out over courage and decency. Do

not be discouraged. Today is a loss, but it's only the beginning of the battle." And Wolfson promised: "We do the groundwork in order to build up ammo and allies for eventual legislative battles."[29]

Opponents of same-sex marriage take the metaphor of war to an even higher level of intensity. As early as 1999, B. K. Eakman wrote: "If we are to save our way of life in the coming century, individuals of principle will have to don the mentality of the resistance fighter." Chuck Colson speaks of a "great sleeping army" that will be aroused to fight "the mother of all culture war battles." Opponents view themselves as fighting against "a cultural timebomb, one which will have devastating and long term effects." According to the Reverend Chuck McIlhenny, same-sex marriage is what happens "when the wicked seize the city. . . . Anyone who speaks out against homosexuality is discriminated against. Churches are firebombed. It happens in San Francisco." The imagery of bombs and explosives permeates the rhetoric of same-sex opponents. Gary Bauer warns that the advocates of same-sex marriage are "sitting on a political powder keg." Former Boston mayor Ray Flynn speaks of gay marriage as "a ticking time bomb in America," while Family Research Council president Tony Perkins speaks of a "cultural time bomb" and criticizes President Bush for waiting to speak out until "after the bomb goes off and the damage is done."[30]

Writing in 2003 about the potential of same-sex marriage in Massachusetts, John Aman of the Center for Reclaiming America warns that "marriage in Massachusetts will have been hit by the cultural equivalent of a nuclear blast. The fallout will reach every other state and, in the view of some marriage defenders, effectively destroy marriage in America." Richard Land, head of the Southern Baptist Convention's Ethics and Religious Liberty Commission, promises: "Politicians who don't know the radioactive nature of this issue now will by November of 2004." With the war escalating to nuclear exchanges, John Aravosis could write in the *Washington Blade* that the FMA [Federal Marriage Amendment] is the legislative equivalent of a nuclear bomb." With both sides now in possession of nuclear weaponry, it is not surprising that images of death and destruction permeate the discourse.[31]

Dr. Dobson states the cases succinctly: "The traditional family is dying." Daniels agrees that we are on "a path to destroying marriage" and advises that "we cannot survive as a nation if marriage is destroyed by a handful of activist lawyers and judges." U.S. senator Rick Santorum of Pennsylvania claims to hear "the death knell of our society" and warns that as we move further from the ideal "children suffer and cultures die." And the Reverend Dr. D. James Kennedy opines: "If homosexual, or same-sex 'marriage,' is forced on this nation by judicial decree, we will either mend that legal atrocity through a constitutional amendment or witness the destruction of marriage in America." Dobson agrees, pointing out the devastating impact that same-sex marriage has had in Scandinavia: "In Norway, Denmark, and Sweden, the family is destroyed."[32]

For advocates of same-sex marriage, it is efforts to restrict marriage to one man and one woman that are harbingers of disaster. Referring to the House of Representatives' vote to prevent federal judges from requiring one state to recognize a same-sex marriage licensed in another, U.S. Representative Jerrold Nadler warned: "We are playing with fire with this bill, and that fire could destroy the nation we love." Referring to the same House vote, George Bakan, publisher of the *Seattle Gay News*, declared: "We must all work to take these bigoted, demonic theocrats out of public office before they destroy the Constitution and democracy itself." But first and foremost, it was the proposed federal amendment itself that drew the fire of same-sex marriage advocates. To the American Civil Liberties Union (ACLU), the Federal Marriage Amendment was "'a neutron bomb' with the potential to destroy all basic protections for gay and lesbian couples and families." In a letter to the editor of the *Las Vegas Mercury*, the Reverend Ian Brumberger pleaded: "Don't destroy the Constitution in a short-sighted attempt to lash out in the dark against those you fear. Love thy Constitution as thyself."[33]

In addition to metaphors of war and images of death and destruction, two analogies figure prominently in the debate. One is the analogy of the fight for same-sex marriage to the battle for racial equality generally, and the fight to secure interracial marriage specifically. The other is a series of analogies, used by both sides, to the Nazis.

Proponents of same-sex marriage argue that their struggle is analogous to that waged by African Americans to secure their basic civil rights. Activists Naomi Fine claims that "the fact that we are denied this basic right, a marriage that is protected by law, seems as preposterous as

denying marriage rights based on skin color." Veteran civil rights activists
and U.S. Congressman John Lewis agrees: "We cannot keep turning our
backs on gay and lesbian Americans. I have fought too hard and too long
against discrimination based on race and color not to stand up against
discrimination based on sexual orientation. I've heard the reasons for opposing civil marriage for same-sex couples. Cut through the distractions,
and they stink of the same fear, hatred, and intolerance I have known in
racism and in bigotry." Wolfson makes the comparison explicit:

> It took from 1776 until 1948 before any court in the country had the cour-
> age to strike down the ban on interracial marriage. When the California
> Supreme Court became the first to strike down race discrimination
> in marriage (by a 4–3 vote, much like the 2003 Massachusetts ruling
> ending sex discrimination in marriage), polls showed 90% of the public
> opposed marriage equality for interracial couples. As late as 1967, when
> the U.S. Supreme Court finally made the same ruling nationwide, the
> polls showed 70% opposed. . . . That is the history of our country, and
> history is on our side.[34]

Interestingly, both the majority opinion and the minority opinion in *Goodridge* cited *Brown v. Board of Education* to buttress their arguments—
"the dissent for the proposition that state-sanctioned racial differences
are unique," and therefore not analogous to the current debate, "and the
majority for the proposition that any separate legal system for gay relationships is 'separate and unequal.'" So, too, in the public argumentation
do we find both sides speaking to the civil rights analogy, an analogy that
would seem, at least on the surface, to advance the case for same-sex
marriage. Yet not all agree.[35]

One African American pastor put the case succinctly: "To equate a
lifestyle choice to racism demeans the work of the entire civil rights movement." In Atlanta, more than two dozen black ministers signed a statement
declaring, "We utterly reject the notion that same-sex marriage is a civil
right." Even Jesse Jackson observed that gay Americans had never been
counted as only three-fifths of a person, indicating a perceived disconti-
nuity in the analogy. Summing the differences in perception, Daniel de
Leon, Sr., testifying before the Senate Judiciary Subcommittee, argued:

"Laws forbidding interracial marriage are about racism. Laws protecting traditional marriage are about children." And if the polls are to be believed, most African Americans appear to be rejecting the analogy, with opposition to same-sex marriage running several percentage points higher in the black community (62–65 percent) than in the country at large.[36]

In addition to the civil rights analogy, both sides make frequent reference to Adolf Hitler and the Nazis. Dobson opens chapter 2 of his book *Marriage under Fire: Why We Must Win This Battle* with the story of Hitler's annexation of Austria and Czechoslovakia. He then writes:

> Today, more than six decades later and on the other side of the Atlantic Ocean, we find ourselves in a terrible battle of a different sort, but one that also threatens the very existence of our society. This struggle is not being fought with guns and bombs, but with ideas, with creative uses of the law, and with methods of intimidation. It is a battle for the very soul of the nation. . . .
>
> Like Adolf Hitler, who overran his European neighbors, those who favor homosexual marriage are determined to make it legal, regardless of the democratic processes that stand in their way.[37]

Here Dobson draws a direct analogy between the way Hitler operated and the tactics of same-sex marriage advocates. But there is more.

Opponents of same-sex marriage often complain that proponents use Nazi-like tactics against them. Writing in the *AFA Journal,* Donald Wildmon explains:

> Today, if you dare to oppose homosexuality—even with reason, humility and mercy—you can expect to be ridiculed or censored by the liberal media and the cultural elites. You would have thought Senator Lott was Adolph Hitler the way the media and gay advocacy groups jumped on him after he referred to homosexuality as sinful behavior.
>
> Another example: About two months ago AFA learned that our website had been blocked by CyberPatrol, the most popular Internet filtering software, on the grounds of "intolerance" for our opposition to the homosexual movement. The category was previously reserved for Nazis and Klansmen.[38]

Thus, opponents of same-sex marriage use the Nazi allusions in two distinct ways—as direct analogies to the gay marriage movement and as illustrations of how same-sex marriage proponents try to intimidate them through linkage to known hate groups.

And, in point of fact, sometimes the advocates of same-sex marriage do try to make such a linkage. In a twenty-two-page report titled "Anti-Gay Groups Active in Massachusetts: A Closer Look," the National Gay and Lesbian Task Force, writing about the Massachusetts Family Institute, notes that on the group's website are "links to an excerpt from the book *The Pink Swastika* suggesting that Nazism is intrinsically linked to homosexuality." While this is, literally, just a linking of same-sex opponents to Nazi ideas, advocates of gay marriage also draw direct analogies: "The strategy of blaming gays for the problems of marriage is an example of *scapegoating*—blaming or stigmatizing a relatively powerless minority for the problems of the majority. Hitler and his Nazi party were master at this game, and they convinced the German population that the Jews were to blame for every wrong, real or imaginary. Will the American people fall for the same trick . . . ?"[39]

Perhaps it should not be surprising that opponents, many of whom conceive themselves to be at war and ready, at least linguistically, to hurl nuclear weapons at their opponent in order to save humanity from the evil that they represent, should imagine that opponent in the most horrific terms—as Nazis led by Hitlers.

The metaphor of war, the images of death and destruction, and the analogies to the Nazis are linguistic indicators of extremism—and they are found on both sides of this debate. While both sides tell coherent stories that seem to resonate with those parts of the national audience that already agree with their values and presuppositions, neither side seems to be appealing to the vast majority of the American people who are not extremists and who do not perceive themselves to be at war. Indeed, a careful examination of the rhetoric of same-sex marriage advocates shows that it is targeted primarily to the courts and the legal system. The appeal to rights is an appeal to law, as are the appeals to equal protection against discrimination. The analogy to the black civil rights movement works well in this scenario because it was, in fact, primarily the federal courts that broke the back of racial segregation in America. Advocates of same-sex marriage are following a similar strategic path. Opponents of same-sex marriage are clearly speaking primarily to those with a religious worldview who already believe that nature and creation dictate against same-sex marriage. Their rhetoric seems intended more to arouse and motivate those who already believe in the cause than to persuade those who are ambivalent or opposed to the traditional view. And so, in a sense, we have a standoff, just as Fisher predicted twenty-five years ago, when he wrote: "When arguers appealing to justice and equality contend with adversaries who base their case on success, survival, and liberty, they talk past each other."[40]

Audiences, Civic Culture, and Public Morality

To even begin to deal with this debate we need to establish some working assumptions. First, we need to acknowledge that no one is inherently evil or beyond the pale of potential persuasion. Second, advocates on both sides need to start talking to one another and to the American public at large. Third, we need to be willing to admit differences not only between opposing camps but within each camp as well. We must recognize degrees of difference—latitudes of acceptance and rejection. And we must acknowledge the legitimate concerns of all parties, including those of the culture at large.

The rhetorical strategy of demonization is as old as humankind itself, but it is ultimately self-defeating, especially in a democratic polity. Neither those advocating same-sex marriage nor those opposing it are evil people. They are people who disagree and whose disagreements run deep, touching worldviews, religious commitments, and self-definitions. Nothing could be more fundamental. Yet even in the face of such disagreements, there must be more that binds people together than that separates them. For those opponents who are Christians, one central truth remains: Evan Wolfson, Andrew Sullivan, Mary Bonauto, Jonathan Rauch, Winnie Stachelberg, and all those advocating same-sex marriage are people created in the image of God and as such are precious human souls not only in the eyes of God, but in the eyes of all true Christians. As such, they are deserving of respect and love. For those advocates of same-sex marriage who are civil libertarians, one central truth remains:

James Dobson, Matt Daniels, Donald Wildmon, Tony Perkins, and yes, even George W. Bush are entitled, as citizens, to hold views grounded in any philosophical system, including biblical Christianity. Their views, too, must be respected. That's what the First Amendment is all about. Once respect is established on both sides, then and only then can opponents talk to one another rather than talk past one another.

What would it mean to talk to one another? First, it would require a change of strategy on the part of both proponents and opponents. For proponents it would mean giving up the ultimate weapon of a Supreme Court decision that legalizes same-sex marriage throughout the nation without any public input in the decision. For opponents, it would mean giving up the proposed constitutional amendment banning same-sex marriage. With such weapons of mass destruction being threatened, no real discussion can take place. Instead of talking to particular audiences, each side needs to talk to general audiences and to explain its concerns and fears rather than play upon them either to win sympathy or to create doomsday scenarios. A robust public debate about the strengths and weaknesses of same-sex marriage would go far toward breaking the narrative impasse and educating the public about why advocates believe as they do and what options the public has for responding to these needs.

Finally, each side needs to acknowledge the differences within its ranks, the latitudes of acceptance and rejection that exist, and the legitimate concerns of the other side. For example, proponents of same-sex marriage need to acknowledge that they do not speak for the entire gay rights movement, that some gays are, in fact, opposed to same-sex marriage laws, and that in any event a distinct minority of gay people ever avail themselves of same-sex marriage or civil unions, even in those countries where such marriages or unions have been legal for over a decade. In Vermont, where civil unions have been legal since July of 2000, less than 40 percent of gay couples have chosen to make that commitment. Opponents of same-sex marriage need to acknowledge that the institution of marriage was in trouble long before the advocates of same-sex marriage took their campaign public. To leave the impression that same-sex marriage is the lone or primary cause of the destruction of the American family and the death of cultural morality is to be willfully blind to many other forces. As David Frum notes:

The hard truth is that the demand for same-sex marriage is a *symptom* of the crisis in marriage much, much more than it is a *cause* of that crisis. To oppose same-sex marriage effectively, you have to believe that marriage is more than a contract between two consenting adults, more than a claim on employers and the government for economic benefits. You have to believe that children need mothers and fathers, *their own* mothers and fathers. You have to believe that unmarried cohabitation is wrong, even when heterosexuals do it. Lose those beliefs and the case for [traditional] marriage has been lost.[41]

In large measure it is heterosexuals who have debased the institution of marriage, and one might, as President Bush advised, remove the speck in one's own eye before worrying about the speck in the eye of one's neighbor. Opponents also tread on shaky ground when they purport to speak for all Christendom. Not all Christians think alike either.

There are latitudes of acceptance and rejection on both sides of this debate. On the same-sex marriage side there is a wide range, from those who just don't care whether it happens or not, to those who are satisfied with civil unions or domestic partnerships, to those who will be satisfied with nothing less that full rights to civil marriage, to an extreme fringe that seeks to undermine marriage as a tactic in a larger battle to disempower all forms of religious belief and morality. On the opposition side there is an equally wide range, from the fringe that claims to know (in their own despicable words) that "God hates fags,"[42] to those who don't care one way or the other about same-sex marriage, to those who favor some benefits and rights for homosexual couples, to those supporting full civil union or domestic partnership laws, to those even willing to have same-sex unions blessed in a religious ceremony. All, of course, stop short of endorsing same-sex marriage.[43]

Finally, each side needs to acknowledge that the other has at least some legitimate concerns. One can debate whether same-sex relationships are deserving of various economic benefits—and that debate should take place in the public arena. But other issues seem, to me, to be matters of common human decency, not law or social policy. Such basic issues as shelter, employment, personal dignity and respect, safety, and the full rights of citizenship should be matters beyond debate. So, too, should hospital visitation, survivorship benefits, and those economic benefits that have little or no direct relationship to traditional marriage, issues such as insurance rates and employee benefits of various kinds. These are legitimate concerns all of which, in my judgment, can—and should—be addressed, short of full marriage rights. Opponents have legitimate concerns, too. Worrying about the institution of marriage—even if some of that worry is misplaced—is not without merit. If traditional marriage is both a personal and a public good—and I believe that it is—then working to strengthen it and avoiding actions that would weaken it are legitimate activities. If people believe that homosexual activity is morally wrong, whether inside a same-sex marriage or outside of that arrangement, then it is not illegitimate for such people to ask what the result of a Supreme Court decision legalizing same-sex marriage might mean in such areas as public education (would textbooks be required to treat homosexual marriage equally with heterosexual marriage?), tax policy (would churches that teach that homosexuality is wrong lose their tax exemptions?), and social policy (would religious social service agencies that deal with adoption, spousal abuse, substance abuse, or medical care be prohibited from using their religious principles as guides for providing such services?). All such concerns need to be aired in public debate, but that won't happen as long as one side is addressing the courts and the other is addressing its base.

Ultimately, the issue of same-sex marriage will be determined by the American people. It would be better, in my judgment, if such a determination were to result from a prolonged and detailed discussion in every statehouse and every legislative body. For as Celeste Condit has rightly noted, "It is precisely the practice of public rhetoric that converts individual desires into something more—something carrying *moral* import, which can anchor the will of the community." Such a discussion would doubtless result in different bodies reaching somewhat different conclusions. But respect for differences is the essence of true civilization. Extremists on both sides of the same-sex marriage debate will probably not be satisfied with this path, for it is likely to result neither in universal same-sex marriage nor in universal traditional marriage. But whatever it ends up being, it will be the result, in Condit's words, "of slow, painful moral resolutions in the public realm." Condit is right:

To the extent that dominant elites control the means of communication and the public vocabulary, they can represent singular partisan interests as universal or moral ones. They can thereby evade the modifications, compromises, and larger goods wrought through agonistic competition between values and interests. Dominant elites thus hijack the moral potential for partisan ends.[44]

To date, both the advocates of same-sex marriage and their opponents have been hijacking the debate for partisan ends. It is time to insert into the dominant narratives the voices of the people and the people's representatives. In this ever-widening debate "the final judgment of what to believe or do," will, in the words of Fisher, be "made by inspection of 'facts,' values, self, and society." Such a judgment will be "inevitably an intersubjective and pragmatic decision," Fisher holds, but it will also be a "rational one," because it will represent the confluence of influences that make up community life in these United States of America.[45] And in a true democracy that's about the best for which one can hope.

ADDENDUM

As this book goes to press, public moral arguments over same-sex marriage continue unabated. In May 2008, the California Supreme Court, by a four-to-three vote, declared the state's voter-approved ban on same-sex marriage to be in violation of the state constitution. On June 16, 2008, same-sex marriages became legal in California, with no input from the general public. Unsurprisingly, in response to the ruling, opponents of same-sex marriage gathered enough signatures to place a citizens' initiative (Proposition 8) on the November 2008 ballot, a proposition designed to restore the status quo ante and once again ban same-sex marriage.[46]

At this writing, the outcome of the California ballot proposition is too close to call. But from the perspective of a public morality grounded in rhetorical participation, legislative deliberation, and citizen consent, whichever side might "win" the election battle in California, the common rhetorical culture will be the loser. Consensus cannot be achieved by four-to-three votes of a judicial body or by 51–49 percent "victories" at the polls. We must find a way to craft a compromise that meets the legitimate needs of all sides.

For my own part, I believe that John Kerry was on the right track in 2004 when he tried to distinguish marriage "rights" from marriage as a "status." Marriage is a status issue that has certain rights attached to it. If we could separate the rights from the status, we might be able to find a middle way that all but the most extreme fringes could accept. This is the approach that has been taken by states such as Vermont, New Jersey, New Hampshire, Oregon, Hawaii, Maine, Washington, and the District of Columbia.[47] Through civil unions, domestic partnerships, or reciprocal beneficiary statutes, certain enumerated rights have been granted to same-sex partners. If we really want to make progress in this difficult moral terrain, then we should set aside the debate over "marriage" and start a more robust debate over the "rights" that people should have, and why they should have them, without regard to sexual orientation.[48]

Setting aside the debate over marriage for a season may seem like a cop-out to some, but it is the only way that I can see, at this point in time, of avoiding another protracted culture war that rends society, polarizes politics, and poisons the rhetorical atmosphere. Repeating the errors associated with *Roe v. Wade*, whatever one's position on abortion, is not the way to form a more perfect Union. Likewise, carrying on a rhetorical war over marriage is a formula for social and cultural disaster. It is time to lay down our weapons and reach for the compromise that may please no one totally, but yet be acceptable to the vast majority of citizens.

NOTES

I want to express my thanks to the people who read and commented on various drafts of this chapter, including Karlyn Kohrs Campbell, James Darsey, Stephen John Hartnett, Robert L. Ivie, Charles E. Morris III, Lester C. Olson, Shawn J. Parry-Giles, and Trevor Parry-Giles. The viewpoints expressed in the chapter are, of course, my own.

1. I am well aware that some gay rights activists did not view the Massachusetts decision as a great victory. As I note toward the end of this essay, the gay community holds a variety of views on the subject of same-sex marriage. Even so, those activists quoted in the mainstream news media, the primary site of investigation for this

study, did view May 17, 2004, as a day of victory and celebration. It is the public, not the private, controversy with which this chapter is concerned. On the history of the gay liberation movement see David Carter, *Stonewall: The Riots That Sparked the Gay Revolution* (New York: St. Martin's Press, 2004); Jennifer Smith, *The Gay Rights Movement* (San Diego: Greenhaven Press, 2003); Walter L. Williams and Yolanda Retter, eds., *Gay and Lesbian Rights in the United States: A Documentary History* (Westport, CT.: Greenwood Press, 2003); Vern L. Bullough, ed., *Before Stonewall: Activists for Gay and Lesbian Rights in Historical Context* (San Francisco: Harrington Park Press, 2002); Eric Marcus, *Making Gay History: The Half Century Fight for Lesbian and Gay Rights* (New York: Perennial, 2002); Craig Rimmerman, *From Identity to Politics: The Lesbian and Gay Movements in the United States* (Philadelphia: Temple University Press, 2001); Vincent J. Samar and Andrew Sullivan, *The Gay Rights Movement* (New York: Fitzroy Dearborn Publishers, 2001); Suzanna Danuta Walters, *All the Rage: The Story of Gay Visibility in America* (Chicago: University of Chicago Press, 2001); John D'Emilio, William B. Turner, and Urvashi Vaid, *Creating Change: Sexuality, Public Policy, and Civil Rights* (New York: St. Martin's Press, 2000). For an insider's account of the battle for gay marriage in Massachusetts see David Moats, *Civil Wars: A Battle for Gay Marriage* (Orlando: Harcourt, 2004). Also see George Chauncey, *Why Marriage? The History Shaping Today's Debate over Gay Equality* (New York: Basic Books, 2004). For a history of the legal develops that preceded and accompanied same-sex marriage see William N. Eskridge, Jr., *Equality Practice: Civil Unions and the Future of Gay Rights* (New York: Routledge, 2002).

2. For a transcript of the Defense of Marriage Act (DOMA) and a legislative summary and analysis see "'Defense of Marriage Act' 5/96 H.R. 3396 Summary/Analysis" at http://www.lectlaw.com/files/leg23.htm. For the statement of President Bush endorsing a federal constitutional amendment see "Remarks by the President" at http://www.cnn.com/2004/ALLPOLITICS/02/24/elec04.prez.bush.transcript/index.html. On the polls during this period see the Pew Research Center for the People and the Press, "Republicans Unified, Democrats Split on Gay Marriage," online at http://www.people-press.org.

3. The first court test of same-sex marriage was in 1971 in *Baker v. Nelson* when the Minnesota Supreme Court "rejected the argument that denying a same-sex couple the right to marry was the equivalent of racial discrimination. The court found: 'In common sense and constitutional sense, there is a clear distinction between a marital restriction based merely upon race and one based upon the fundamental

difference in sex.'" Quoted in Timothy J. Dailey, "The Slippery-Slope of Same-Sex Marriage," at http://www.frc.org/get.cfm?I=BC04C02.

4. There was considerable publicity on the subject of gay rights throughout the 1990s, but most of that attention centered on topics other than same-sex marriage. For a brief overview of the issues and events of this decade see Martin J. Medhurst, "George W. Bush, Public Faith, and the Culture War over Same-Sex Marriage," in *The Prospect of Presidential Rhetoric*, ed. James Arnt Aune and Martin J. Medhurst (College Station: Texas A&M University Press, 2008), 212–14.

5. It is important to note that this study is limited to discourse circulated publicly in the mainstream news media. I do not examine the debate within the gay community, which often takes place in gay publications and is directed inward to a specialized audience rather than outward to the general public. This study examines only the dominant public narratives.

6. Walter R. Fisher, "Narration as Human Communication Paradigm: The Case of Public Moral Argument," *Communication Monographs* 51 (1984): 12.

7. These eight elements were derived inductively from an examination of fragments of discourse found from Internet searches of *gay rights*, *same-sex marriage*, and *gay marriage*.

8. I searched the entire websites of these groups. Rhetoric from other groups was picked up through the broader Internet search.

9. Sources for the paragraph on "rights," in descending order on the page, include Stachelberg quoted in "Defining Marriage: To Amend or Not to Amend," *CNN.com* at http://www.cnn.com/TRANSCRIPTS/0401/24/cst.01.html; Kucinich quoted in Carla Marinucci, "Kucinich Gives Spirited Defense of Gay Marriage: Democratic Hopeful Chides His Rivals for Equivocating," *SFGate* at http://www.sfgate.com/cgi-bin/article.cgi?file=/c/a/2003/12/17/MNGV03P1GH1.DTL&type=printable; Newsom quoted in Dominique Crawley, "Students Oppose Bush's Same-Sex Marriage Ban," *The Hilltop-Politik* at http://www.thehilltoponline.com/2.4817/1.470402; Kerry quoted in E. J. Dionne, "The Muddled Middle of the Gay-Marriage Debate," *Seattle Times*, at http://community.seattletimes.nwsource.com/archive/?date=2004 0303&slug=dionne03.

10. Sources for the paragraph on "discrimination," in descending order on the page, include *Lawrence* and *Goodridge*; Roth quoted in "U.S.: Same-Sex Marriage Ruling Upholds Equality under Law," *Human Rights Watch* at http://www.hrw.org/en/news/2004/02/04/us-same-sex-marriage-ruling-upholds-equality-under-law; Newsom quoted in Rachel Gordon, "S.F. Defies Law, Marries Gays: Legal Battle

Looms," *SFGate* at http://sfgate.com/cgi-bin/article.cgi?file=/c/a/2004/02/13/MN-GUQ50FoJ1.DTL&type=Printable; Erlich quoted in Gordon, "S.F. Defies Law"; Kevin Naff, "With Friends Like These," *Washington Blade* at http://www.washblade.com/print.cfm?content_id=2180; Schuman quoted in "To and Fro on Same-Sex Marriage," *CBS News* at http://www.cbsnews.com/stories/2004/07/12/politics/printable628760.shtml.

11. Sources for the paragraph on "freedom," in descending order on the page, include *Lawrence v. Texas* (02-102) 41 S.W. 3rd 349, June 26, 2003 (Majority Opinion by Justice Kennedy) at http://supct.law.cornell.edu/supct/html/02-102.ZO.html; Perry, "Why I Believe in Marriage Equality," *SignOnSanDiego* at http://www.signonsandiego.com/uniontrib/20040314/news_mz1e14perry.html; Mead quoted in "State of the Unions," *Commonweal*, September 27, 2002, 5; Cote-Whitacre quoted in Pam Belluck, "Governor Seeks to Invalidate Some Same-Sex Marriages," *New York Times* at http://query.nytimes.com/gst/fullpage.html?res=9807E6D8113FF932A15756C0A9629C8B63.

12. Perry, "Marriage Equality."

13. Sources for the paragraph on "equality," in descending order on the page, include Tseng quoted in Liza Porteus, "'Marriage Protection Week' Likely to Spark Debate," *FOX News* at http://www.foxnews.com/printer_friendly_story/0,3566,99747,00.html; Jacques quoted in "Federal Marriage Amendment Sees New Life in Congress," *Siecus*, March 2004, at http://www.siecus.org/index.cfm?fuseaction=Feature.show Feature&featureid=1235&pageid=483&parentid=478; Perry, "Marriage Equality"; Dean quoted in Steven Waldman, "White House Word Play," *Beliefnet* at http://www.beliefnet.com/story/130/story_13037_1.html; Rauch, *Gay Marriage: Why It Is Good for Gays, Good for Straights, and Good for America* (New York: Henry Holt, 2004), 46; Evan Wolfson, "For Richer, for Poorer: Same-Sex Couples and the Freedom to Marry as a Civil Right," *DMI E-Journal* at http://www.drummajorinstitute.org/plugin/template/dmi/55/1693.

14. Sources for the paragraph on "love," in descending order on the page, include Wolfson, "All Together Now (A Blueprint for the Movement)," *The Advocate*, September 11, 2001, reprinted at http://www.freedomtomarry.org/evan_wolfson/by/all_together_now.php; for photograph of this placard go to *DontAmend.com* at http://www.dontamend.com/; Stachelberg quoted in "CBS News Transcripts—Face the Nation, August 3, 2003," at http://www.cbsnews.com/stories/2003/08/04/ftn/main566528.shtml; Wolfson quoted in Maggie Gallagher, "What Marriage Is For," *Weekly Standard*, August 4–11, 2003, at http://www.weeklystandard.com/Content/

Public/Articles/000/000/0021939pxiga.asp; Wolfson, "All Together Now."

15. Sources for the paragraph on "nature," in descending order on the page, include James Dobson, *Marriage under Fire: Why We Must Win This Battle* (Sisters, Ore.: Multnomah Publishers, 2004), 10, 18; Wilton Gregory, "Letter to United States Senators," July 6, 2004, at http://usccb.org/comm/archives/2004/04-128.shtml; William P. Fay, "Statement of Monsignor William P. Fay, General Secretary of the United States Conference of Catholic Bishops, on the Federal Amendment before the Senate of the United States," July 12, 2004, at http://www.usccbpublishing. org/client_pdfs/5-626pdf.pdf; Gen. 1:27–28; Wilton Gregory, "Broadcast FAX to the Catholic Bishops of the United States," June 24, 2004, at http://www.archdpdx.org/occ/occcivil.pdf; Jerry Falwell quoted in "Push toward Gay Marriage Bans," *CBS News*, February 12, 2004, at http://www.cbsnews.com/stories/2004/02/12/national/printable599954.shtml.

16. Sources for the paragraph on "tradition," in descending order on the page, include George W. Bush, "Transcript of Bush Statement," *CNN*, February 24, 2004, at http://www.cnn.com/2004/ALLPOLITICS/02/24/elec04.prez.bush.transcript/index.html ; Peter Sprigg, "Questions and Answers: What's Wrong with Letting Same-Sex Couples 'Marry'?" *Family Research Council*, June 1, 2004, at http://www.frc.org/get.cfm?i=IFo3Ho1&v=PRINT; D. James Kennedy, "Dr. Kennedy Calls for Constitutional 'Firewall' to Protect Marriage," *Center for Reclaiming America*, November 19, 2003, at http://www.reclaimamerica.org/Pages/pressreleasepage.asp?story=1460.

17. Kenneth Burke, *The Philosophy of Literary Form*, 3rd ed. (Berkeley: University of California Press, 1973), 55.

18. Sources for the paragraph on "sacred," in descending order on the page, include George W. Bush quoted in Michael Foust, "Bush Uses Radio Address to Push for Marriage Amendment," *BP News*, July 9, 2004, at http://www.bpnews.net/printer-friendly.asp?ID=18662; Miriam Guardado quoted in Don Lattin et al., "Religious Groups on Common Ground: Many Faiths Oppose Same-Sex Marriage," *SFGate*, March 14, 2004, at http://www.sfgate.com/cgi-bin/article.cgi?file=/c/a/2004/03/14/MNGJB5KB9N1.DTL.

19. Sources for the paragraph on "morality," in descending order on the page, include Gallagher, "What Marriage Is For"; Tom Minnery, "Supreme Court Strikes Down Texas Sodomy Law," *Family*, June 26, 2003, reprinted at http://www.glaad.org/publications/archive_detail.php?id=3431&PHPSESSID=f; Gary Lavy quoted in "National Gay and Lesbian Task Force Hails Massachusetts Court Advisory Opinion," *National Gay and Lesbian Task Force*, February 4, 2004, at http://www.thetaskforce.

org/press/releases/pr624_020404; James Dobson quoted in Art Moore, "Queerly Beloved: Same-Sex Marriage Barriers Erected," *WorldNetDaily.com*, May 25, 2004, at http://www.worldnetdaily.com/news/printer-friendly.asp?ARTICLE_ID=38639 (accessed June 6, 2004)

20. Sources for the paragraph on "children," in descending order on the page, include Sam Brownback quoted in Jody Brown, Bill Fancher, and Fred Jackson, "Debate on FMA Continues on Eve of Vote," *Agape Press*, July 13, 2004, at http://headlines. agapepress.org/archive/7/afa/132004b.asp; Ron Crews quoted in "Door-to-Door for Same-Sex Marriage," *CBS News*, March 27, 2004, at http://www.cbsnews.com/ stories/2004/03/24/politics/printable608372.shtml; George W. Bush, "Proclamation 7697—Family Day, 2003," *Weekly Compilation of Presidential Documents*, August 28, 2003, at http://fdsys/gpo/gov/fdsys/pkg/WCPD-2003-09-01/pdf/WCPD-2003-09-01-Pg1123-2.pdf ; "A Necessary Amendment," *National Review*, August 11, 2003, 15.

21. Sources for the first paragraph on "family," in descending order on the page, include Matt Daniels, "Marriage, Society," *Washington Times*, April 15, 2004, at http://www. washingtontimes.com/news/2004/apr/14/20040414-090033-8998r/; Matt Daniels quoted in The Editors, "Marriage Amendment Stakes," *World Magazine*, March 6, 2004, at http://www.worldmag.com/world/issue/03-06-04/cover_4.asp (accessed June 6, 2004); Beth Robinson quoted in Zana Bugaighis, "Alumna Gay Rights Lawyer Recalls Groundbreaking Cases," *The DartmouthOnline*, April 21, 2004, at http:// www.thedartmouth.com/article.php?aid=2004042101030&action=print; David Tseng quoted in Randall Mikkelsen, "Bush Stops Short on Constitution Gay Marriage Ban," *Reuters*, January 20, 2004, reprinted at http://www.chatarea.com/bollyWHAT.quote1910607; Cheryl Jacques quoted in Tom Musbach, "Bush Repeats Anti-Gay Marriage Stand," *Gay.com/PlanetOut.com*, January 21, 2004, reprinted at http://gay_blog.blogspot.com/2004/01/hrc-denounces-remarks-by-president-as. html; Howard Kurtz, "Gay Marriage Gets Million Dollar Ad Campaign," *Washington Post*, November 10, 2003, A04.; Andrew Sullivan, "Why the 'M' Word Matters to Me," *Independent Gay Forum* (reprinted from *Time Magazine*), February 16, 2004, at http://www.indegayforum.org/authors/sullivan/sullivan15.html.

22. Sources for the second paragraph on "family," in descending order on the page, include Ed Vitagliano, "What Is a Family? New Video Introduces Kids to Same-Sex Couples," *AFA Journal*, March 2001, at http://www.afa.net/journal/march/homosexuala.asp; Charles Colson, "An Unstable Balance," *Breakpoint*, May 6, 2003, at http://www.dfamily.com/philosophy/teach/hswt/extras/breakpoint-an-unstable-balance-wanting-both-ways.pdf.

23. Sources for the third paragraph on "family," in descending order on the page, include Barry Drewitt quoted in Vitagliano, "What Is a Family?"; Sheila Kuehl quoted in Vitagliano, "What Is a Family?"; Lou Sheldon quoted in Edward Epstein, "Same-Sex Marriage Ban of 'National Importance,'" *SFGate*, February 25, 2004, at http://www.sfgate.com/cgi-bin/article.cgi?file=/c/a/2004/02/25/MNG4J57N1P1.DTL; Karen Oliveto quoted in Moore, "Queerly Beloved."

24. Sources for the first paragraph on "protection," in descending order on the page, include Colin Stewart quoted in "President Bush Promises to Preserve Traditional Marriage," *Good News*, July 30, 2003, at http://www.goodnewsetc.com/093FAM1.htm; Human Rights Campaign quoted in "Massachusetts Court Backs Gay Marriage," *Christianity Today*, December 10, 2003, at http://www.christianitytoday.com/ct/2004/january18.21.html; *Romer v. Evans* quoted in "The American Gay Rights Movement: A Timeline," at http://print.infoplease.com/ipa/0/7/6/1/9/0/A0761909.html; *Goodridge v. Department of Health* quoted in "Gay Marriage Enters the Race," *CBS News*, November 19, 2003, at http://www.cbsnews.com/stories/2003/11/11/politics/main583048.shtml; Evan Wolfson quoted in "9 States Seek Tougher Gay Marriage Bans," *ABC News*, January 23, 2004, at http://abcnews.go.com/wire/US/ap20040123_1414.html (accessed June 6, 2004); Cheryl Jacques quoted in Suzanne Herel, "Court Halts Gay Vows," *SFGate*, March 12, 2004, at http://www.sfgate.com/cgi-bin/article.cgi?file=/c/a/2004/03/12/MNGOJ5J9PL1.DTL&typ. . . .

25. Sources for the second paragraph on "protection," in descending order on the page, include Dobson, *Marriage under Fire*, 66; Bill Maier quoted in "Focus on the Family Applauds Sen. Bill Frist for His Support of the Federal Marriage Amendment," *Family.org*, June 30, 2003, at http://www.family.org/welcome/press/a0026694.cfm (accessed June 6, 2004); Bush quoted in Joseph Curl, "California Gay 'Marriages' Pushing Bush to Act," *Washington Times*, February 19, 2004, at http://www.washingtontimes.com/news/2004/feb/18/20040218-110717-5492r/; Dobson, *Marriage under Fire*, 9, 27.

26. Sources for the first paragraph on the "common good," in descending order on the page, include *Lawrence v. Texas* (Majority opinion by Justice Kennedy); Fay, "Statement"; Joseph Ratzinger and Angelo Amato, "Considerations Regarding Proposals to Give Legal Recognition to Unions between Homosexual Persons," Congregation for the Doctrine of the Faith, June 3, 2003, at http://www.vatican.va/roman_curia/congregations/cfaith/documents/rc_con_cfaith_doc_20030731_homosexual-unions-en.html.

27. Sources for the second paragraph on the "common good," in descending order on

the page, include Rauch, *Gay Marriage*, 5–6; Gregory, "Letter to United States Senators."

28. Buchanan quoted in Joan Vennochi, "A 'Culture War' on Gay Marriage Could Hurt GOP," *CommonDreams.org* (reprinted from the *Boston Globe*), November 20, 2003, at http://www.commondreams.org/cgi-bin/print.cgi?file=/views03/1120-02.htm.

29. Sources for the first paragraph on "war," in descending order on the page, include Kevin Cathcart quoted in "Bush: Gay Marriage Ban May Be Too Soon," *Las Vegas Sun*, July 3, 2003, reprinted at http://www.lsdnews.com/news/story.aspx?id=29265&comview=1; Richard Kim, "Queer Cheer," *The Nation*, July 21–28, 2003, 6; Matt Foreman quoted in Paul Johnson, "Bush Gay Marriage Remarks 'Act of War,'" *Equality.com*, December 17, 2003, reprinted at http://www.chicagopride.com/news/article.cfm/articleid/1163296; Arline Issacson quoted in Rick Klein, "Vote Ties Civil Unions to Gay-Marriage Ban," *Boston.com*, March 30, 2004, at http://www.boston.com/news/specials/gay_marriage/articles/2004/03/30/vote_ties_civil_unions_to_gay_marriage_ban/ ; Wolfson, "All Together Now."

30. Sources for the second paragraph on "war," in descending order on the page, include B. K. Eakman, "How We Lost the Culture Wars," *Washington Times*, May 18, 1999, reprinted at http://www.radioliberty.com/nlmar00.htm; Colson quoted in Moore, "Queerly Beloved"; Tony Perkins, "State of the Union 2004: Bush Should Support FMA," *FRC.org*, January 13, 2004, at http://www.frc.org/get.cfm?i=CM04A10 (accessed June 6, 2004); Chuck McIlhenny quoted in Don Lattin, "The Battle over Same-Sex Marriage: Newsom Faces Wrath of God, Fundamentalist Leaders Say," *SFGate*, April 15, 2004, at http://sfgate.com/cgi-bin/article.cgi?file=/c/a/2004/04/15/BAGGR65BU01.DTL&type=pri . . . ; Gary Bauer quoted in Alan Eisner, "Gay Marriage Issue Fails to Excite Voters," *Reuters*, July 14, 2004, at http://www.reuters.co.uk/printerFriendlyPopup.jhtml?type=worldNews&storyID=54742 (accessed June 6, 2004); Ray Flynn quoted in "Massachusetts Court Supports Equal Marriage," *Equal Marriage.org*, November 18, 2003, at http://www.samesexmarriage.ca/advocacy/massachusetts.htm; Tony Perkins quoted in Robert Marus, "Bush Touts Faith, Charity, Abstinence in Third State of the Union Address," Associated Baptist Press, January 21, 2004, at http://www.abpnews.com/index2.php?option=com_content&task=view&id=2519&pop=1&page=0&Itemid=117.

31. Sources for the third paragraph on "war," in descending order on the page, include John Aman, "Attack on Marriage Builds," *Center for Reclaiming America*, June 26, 2003, at http://www.reclaimamerica.org/PAGES/NEWS/newspage.asp?story=1247 (accessed June 6, 2004); Richard Land quoted in "Pro-Family Groups Announce

Marriage Alliance," *Maranatha Christian Journal*, October 2003, reprinted at http://headlines.agapepress.org/archive/11/afa/102003d.asp; John Aravosis quoted in "2004 Events, July-11 to 13: 'Protect Marriage Sunday,' and the Senate Debate," *Religious-Tolerance.org*, July 11, 2004, at http://www.religioustolerance.org/mar_amend8.htm.

32. Sources for the first paragraph on "destruction," in descending order on the page, include Dobson quoted in Allie Martin, Bill Fancher, and Jody Brown, "Advocates of Biblical Marriage Rally in Memphis," *Agape Press*, July 12, 2004, at http://headlines.agapepress.org/archive/7/afa/122004a.asp; Daniels quoted in Karen S. Peterson, "Man behind the Marriage Amendment," *USA Today* April 12, 2004, at http://usatoday.com/life/people/2004-04-12-matt-daniels_x.htm; Santorum quoted in B. A. Robinson, "2004 Events, July-11–13: 'Protect Marriage Sunday,' and the Senate Debate"; Santorum quoted in Brown, Fancher, and Jackson, "Debate on FMA Continues "; Kennedy quoted in Aman, "Attack on Marriage Builds"; Dobson quoted in Brown, Fancher, and Jackson, "Debate on FMA Continues."

33. Sources for the second paragraph on "destruction," in descending order on the page, include Nadler quoted in Thomas Ferraro, "US to Curb Same-Sex Marriage," *Swissinfo*, July 22, 2004, at http://www.swissinfo.org/sen/Swissinfo.html?siteSect=41&sid=5100926 (accessed August 6, 2004); Bakan quoted in Robert Raketty, "House Passes Direct Attack on Constitution and Gay Americans," *Seattle Gay News*, July 22, 2004, at http://www.sgn.org/2004/07/22/ (accessed August 6, 2004); ACLU of Southern California, "Say No to Discrimination in Our Constitution," n.d at http://gai.org/aclu_sc_action/notice-description.tcl?newsletter_id=857043 (accessed August 6, 2004); Brumberger, "Gay Marriage a Secular, Personal Matter," *Las Vegas Mercury*, June 24, 2004, at http://www.lasvegasmercury.com/2004/MERC-Jun-24-Thu-2004/24118433.html.

34. Sources for the first paragraph on the analogy to "civil rights," in descending order on the page, include Fine quoted in "Bush & Vatican Stance on Gay Marriage Outrages San Francisco Community," *gmax*, August 4, 2003, at http://www.gmax.co.za/look/08/04-usmarriage2.html; Lewis, "At a Crossroads on Gay Unions," *Boston.com*, October 25, 2003, at http://www.boston.com/news/globe/editorial_opinion/oped/articles/2003/10/25/at_a_crossroads_on_gay_unions/; Wolfson, "Why Are the Polls on 'Gay Marriage' So Inconsistent?" *Freedom to Marry*, April 16, 2004, at http://www.freedomtomarry.org/evan_wolfson/by/why_are_polls_inconsistent.php.

35. Victor B. Flatt, "'Separate But Equal' Now Part of Gay Marriage Debate," *Salt Lake Tribune*, May 9, 2004, reprinted at http://transdada.blogspot.com/2004/05/separate-but-equal-now-part-of-gay.html.

36. Sources for the second paragraph on the analogy to "civil rights," in descending order on the page, include "Declaration," *DontAmend.com*, July 19, 2004, at http://www.dontamend.com/ (accessed August 6, 2004); Ministers quoted in Adelle M. Banks, "Black Churches Quiet on Gay Marriage," *Chicago Tribune*, May 7, 2004, reprinted at http://www.baptistpress.com/bpnews.asp?io=17941; de Leon quoted in "Legal, Civil Rights Arguments Fuel Gay Marriage Debate," *USA Today*, March 3, 2004, at http://usatoday.com/news/Washington/2004-03-03-gay-marriage_xhtm.

37. The source for the first paragraph on the analogy to the Nazis is Dobson, *Marriage under Fire*, 30–31, 41.

38. The sources for the second paragraph on the analogy to Nazis is Wildmon, "Principles Which Guide AFA's Opposition to the Homosexual Agenda," *American-FamilyAssociationOnline*, June 2004, at http://www.afa.net/homosexual_agenda/principles.asp.

39. The source for the third paragraph on the analogy to Nazis is Matt Foreman, "Anti-Gay Groups Active in Massachusetts: A Closer Look," *NGLTF*, March–April 2004, at http://www.ngltf.org.

40. Fisher, "Narration as Human Communication Paradigm," 14.

41. David Frum, "The North Goes South," *National Review*, July 14, 2003, 56.

42. Quoted in Herel "Court Halts Gay Vows."

43. To get a sense of the various positions in this debate see Andrew Sullivan, ed., *Same-Sex Marriage: Pro and Con: A Reader* (New York: Vintage, 1997); Robert M. Baird and Stuart E. Rosenbaum, eds., *Same-Sex Marriage: The Moral and Legal Debate* (Amherst, N.Y.: Prometheus Books, 1997); Urvashi Vaid, *Virtual Equality: The Mainstreaming of Gay and Lesbian Liberation* (New York: Doubleday, 1995); Evan Gerstmann, *Same-Sex Marriage and the Constitution* (Cambridge: Cambridge University Press, 2004); Marvin M. Ellison, *Same-Sex Marriage? A Christian Ethical Analysis* (Cleveland: Pilgrim Press, 2004); Robert P. George, *The Clash of Orthodoxies* (Wilmington, Del.: ISI Books, 2001); Michael Warner, *The Trouble with Normal: Sex, Politics, and the Ethics of Queer Life* (New York: Free Press, 1999); Paul Robinson, *Queer Wars: The New Gay Right and Its Critics* (Chicago: University of Chicago Press, 2005).

44. Celeste Michelle Condit, "Crafting Virtue: The Rhetorical Construction of Public Morality," *Quarterly Journal of Speech* 73 (1987): 82–83.

45. Walter R. Fisher, "Toward a Logic of Good Reasons," *Quarterly Journal of Speech* 64 (1978): 382.

46. California's Proposition 8 was placed on the November 2008 ballot after opponents

of same-sex marriage turned in 1.1 million signatures to the secretary of state's office on April 24, 2008. The petitions as circulated used the phrase "Limit on Marriage" as the title of the proposed amendment to the California constitution. On July 3, 2008, California attorney general Jerry Brown changed the title of the ballot initiative to read: "Eliminates the Right of Same-Sex Couples to Marry." The campaign was expected to cost in excess of $30 million. The actual cost was $83 million. For more details see "California Proposition 8 (2008)" at http://www.ballotpedia.org/wiki/index.php?title+California_Proposition_8_.

47. The state of Connecticut was originally part of this list, but on October 10, 2008, by a vote of four to three, the Connecticut Supreme Court ruled that the state's own civil union law was in violation of the state constitution. Writing for the majority, Justice Richard N. Palmer held: "Interpreting our state constitutional provisions in accordance with firmly established equal protection principles leads inevitably to the conclusion that gay persons are entitled to marry the otherwise qualified same-sex partner of their choice." In so ruling, the state supreme court voided the remedy passed by the state legislature—civil unions—and substituted its own judgment for that of the people's elected representatives. In my judgment, this is the exact antithesis of what it means to be a rhetorical republic and to valorize the input and voices of the people. State legislatures must be free to pass whatever remedies a particular state deems necessary and proper, without the fear that some judicial body will overrule what is clearly a legislative prerogative. In the rare cases where courts choose to intervene in making social policy—and they should be very rare, in my view—care must be taken to demonstrate that the court's views are a consensus view, not a momentary majority of one. The Warren Court, it must be remembered, voted nine to nothing in *Brown v. Board of Education* (1954). In so doing, they underscored their unanimity and gave a broad imprimatur to the new social policy. Votes of four to three do no such thing, without regard to which view is on the "winning" side. I repeat: No one wins in these kinds of "victories." Indeed, the imposition of judicial fiat will inevitably result in a broader push for a federal constitutional amendment banning same-sex marriage. It appears that some people really do want a nuclear war on the issue of same-sex marriage. See Robert D. McFadden, "Gay Marriage Is Ruled Legal In Connecticut," *New York Times*, October 11, 2008, online at http://www.nytimes.com/2008/10/11/nyregion/11marriage.html?_r=1&pagewanted=print&oref=slogin.

48. For a similar call in the aftermath of California's Proposition 8 see Richard Mouw, "Less Shouting, More Talking," *Newsweek*, February 9, 2009, 26.

Time, Space, and Generic Reconstitution: Martin Luther King's "A Time to Break Silence" as Radical Jeremiad

James Jasinski and John M. Murphy

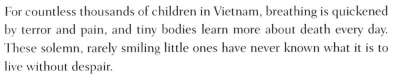

For countless thousands of children in Vietnam, breathing is quickened by terror and pain, and tiny bodies learn more about death every day. These solemn, rarely smiling little ones have never known what it is to live without despair.

They indeed know death, for it walks with them by day and accompanies their sleep at night. It is as omnipresent as the napalm that falls from the skies with the frequency and impartiality of the monsoon rain.

The horror of what we are doing to the children of Vietnam—"we," because napalm and white phosphorous are the weapons of America— is staggering. . . . There is no one to provide . . . care for most of the . . . horribly maimed children . . . and despite growing efforts by American and South Vietnamese authorities to conceal the fact, it's clear that there are hundreds of thousands of terribly injured children, with no hope for decent treatment on even a day-to-day basis, much less for the long months and years of restorative surgery needed to repair ten searing seconds of napalm.¹

This fragment from the opening of William Pepper's 1967 photo essay "The Children of Vietnam" is relevant to our essay because, as numerous scholars have noted, it was only after encountering Pepper's essay in *Ramparts* magazine sometime in early 1967 that Dr. Martin Luther King, Jr. decided to declare publicly his opposition to the war in Vietnam.² He included some antiwar remarks in a February 1967 speech in Los Angeles and a March speech in Chicago. But King delivered his most comprehensive indictment of the American war effort the following month. After initially planning to use the United Nations Building as the backdrop for his speech, King eventually concluded that it would be more advantageous to speak on familiar turf. So on April 4 he addressed an audience of over 3,000 at the Riverside Church in New York City at a meeting sponsored by the prominent antiwar group Clergy and Laymen Concerned About Vietnam. The speech he delivered that day is commonly known as either "A Time to Break Silence" or "Beyond Vietnam."

As he prepared the Riverside speech, King confronted a daunting rhetorical situation. Not only was he challenging a popular president who had provided crucial support during the legislative struggles on civil rights in 1964 and 1965 on an issue—foreign policy—thought to be beyond his area of expertise, he was also defying the position adopted at the time by virtually the entire civil rights establishment. Very few people thought it wise for Martin Luther King to oppose his nation's policies in Southeast Asia.³ But our focus is not on how King managed his considerable instrumental burden; rather, we turn our attention to the text's constitutive dimension as we seek to disclose its transformative action.

Previous critics have noted the text's "three thematic movements."⁴ After three introductory paragraphs in which he established "that the calling to speak is often a vocation of agony, but we must speak," King began the first section of the address. In this section King proleptically engaged those "many persons [who] have questioned me about the wisdom of my path. . . . Why are you speaking about the war, Dr. King? Why are you joining the voices of dissent? Peace and civil rights don't mix, they say. Aren't you hurting the cause of your people, they ask?" In response to these questions, King traced his "path from Dexter Avenue Baptist Church . . . to this sanctuary tonight."[5] That path led King to expand his "field of . . . moral vision," allowing him to identify seven ways to articulate the civil rights and the antiwar movements.[6]

The text's second section extended King's concluding observation in section 1 that because God "is deeply concerned especially for his suffering and helpless and outcast children, I come tonight to speak for them" (234). In this section King advanced a counternarrative of American involvement in Vietnam by adopting multiple perspectives (from the Viet Cong to American soldiers) and giving voice to their neglected needs and concerns. King concluded this second section by, first, "suggest[ing] five concrete things that our government should do immediately to begin the long and difficult process of extricating ourselves from this nightmarish conflict" (which included declaring a unilateral cease-fire and recognizing that the National Liberation Front must play a role in the negotiation process) and then urging Americans "to raise our voices if our nation persists in its perverse ways in Vietnam" (239).

King then acknowledged that "there is something seductively tempting about stopping . . . and sending us all off on what in some circles has become a popular crusade against the war in Vietnam" (240). King resisted the temptation, at least in part, because of the text's internal logic. By articulating his civil rights and antiwar commitments in the text's first section, King established that his mission extended beyond the problem of American race relations. In so doing he prepared his immediate audience and eventual readers for the text's second section, which moved beyond civil rights in order to examine the nation's policies in Southeast Asia. While focusing on Vietnam was tempting, King insisted that his audience continue moving, first beyond civil rights, and now beyond Vietnam. In the final section King challenged his audience to undertake "a radical revolution in values" that would undermine "the giant triplets of racism, materialism, and militarism" (240).

Throughout the three sections King deployed the three topoi—promise, decline, and redemption—common to the secularized, African American jeremiad.[7] King devoted considerable emphasis to the topos of decline. At the outset, he remarked: "Now, it should be incandescently clear that no one who has any concern for the integrity and life of America today can ignore the present war. If America's soul becomes totally poisoned, part of the autopsy must read Vietnam" (234). Toward the end of his counter-narrative in the address's middle section, he warned that "the image of America will never again be the image of revolution, freedom and democracy, but the image of violence and militarism" (238).

While the nation's decision to wage war in Vietnam threatened to poison its soul and destroy its image at home and abroad, that decision—and the specific political and military tactics through which it was implemented—was not King's exclusive concern in the speech. In what at first glance might have been considered an unusual move, as we have noted, he devoted the final section to three sub-topoi that were becoming more common in his discourse: "the giant triplets of racism, materialism, and militarism." While King acknowledged the temptation to focus solely on the war, he believed that the nation needed to confront a "more disturbing" truth. "The war in Vietnam," he declared, was merely "a symptom of a far deeper malady within the American spirit" (240).

Redemption was attainable, King believed, if the nation engaged in "a radical revolution in values" (240). Utilizing a loose anaphora pattern, he detailed the objectives of such a radical or "true revolution of values" in the speech's final section: "A true revolution of values will soon cause us to question the fairness and justice of our past and present policies. . . . A true revolution of values will soon look uneasily on the glaring contrast of poverty and wealth. . . . A true revolution in values will lay hands on the world order and say of war: 'This way of settling human differences is not just'" (240–41). Toward the end of this final section, King appropriated the voices of Kennedy and Lincoln to urge his audience: "Now let us begin. Now let us re-dedicate ourselves to the long and bitter—but beautiful—struggle for a new world" (243). Although there was no guarantee of success, redemption through rededication remained, he insisted, a real possibility.

King devoted the least amount of attention to the jeremiadic topic of promise, the community's original covenant with God or—once the form was secularized—with itself. He believed that the United States, like all Western nations, had once displayed "the revolutionary spirit" that played a crucial role in the "modern world['s]" emergence. While King did not explore the substance of this spirit in detail, it nevertheless anchored his jeremiadic appeal, since "our only hope today lies in our ability to recapture th[is] revolutionary spirit and go out into a sometimes hostile world declaring eternal hostility to poverty, racism, and militarism" (242). To redeem itself, King implied, the nation must be rededicated to its founding revolutionary spirit.

Given King's deployment of the jeremiad's conventional topoi, it might seem odd that George Dionisopoulos and his coauthors concluded their careful reading of the text by arguing: "In questioning the values of American society—rather than urging more stringent adherence to them—King rejected the jeremiad and, thus, the traditional form of American dissent."[8] We have not introduced this reading in order to engage in a narrow argument regarding generic classification. We suggest instead that the speech's disputed generic status raises important questions regarding rhetorical invention and rhetoric's capacity to engage in political and moral critique, particularly in time of war. As many scholars argue, presidential war rhetoric justifies military action, but it also constitutes the American people as a united community of virtuous warriors. This move is necessary, at least in part, because war demands brutality of a sort normally thought immoral. By refiguring the audience's identity, war rhetoric transforms such ferocity, defining it anew as the quality needed to defend the community from a savage Other.[9] As a result, war opponents must not only dispute the expediency of military action, but also take on the additional burden of reconstituting communal identity. They must address a question posed repeatedly over the years: what kind of people are we to be?

Identities, in turn, cannot be constructed ex nihilo. They must be constituted out of communal traditions and living genres.[10] We argue King's rhetorical art was constrained and enabled by those traditions of discourse in which he participated. Faced with the necessities imposed by the power of war rhetoric, this speech invoked alternative and subversive American idioms as well as forms. In doing so, he radicalized his available discursive resources. He collapsed the traditional distinction between individual and national moral agency and asserted that an ethical response to the war in Vietnam required an abandonment of American exceptionalism. By tracing this speech's temporal[11] and spatial dimensions, we hope to disclose the way King radicalized the American jeremiad as he transcended its parochial horizon, resulting in a truly innovative form of generic reconstitution that addressed his considerable burdens.

Jeremiadic Containment, Critical Memory, and the Tradition of Civic Republicanism

In his 1978 study *The American Jeremiad,* Sacvan Bercovitch introduced the idea of jeremiadic containment. He noted that for Americans in the late eighteenth and nineteenth centuries, "the symbol of America . . . [became] a vision designed to contain self-assertion." He then explained: "I mean *containment* in its double sense, as sustenance and restriction. The symbol set free titanic creative energies in our classic writers, and it confined their freedom to the terms of the American myth."[12] In Bercovitch's account, the symbol of America enabled social and political practice, but that practice was at the same time always constrained, contained, by the symbol. In short, social and political practices lack any generative or transformative capacity, no ability to go beyond the constraining and containing force of the American symbol.

Beginning in the late eighteenth century and continuing to the present day, the American Revolution has been one aspect of the broader American symbol frequently invoked in secular jeremiads. Within the jeremiadic imagination, the Revolution's norms and values established the terms of the political community's founding covenant, providing a frame of reference through which advocates could evaluate the community. According to Bercovitch: "In all cases, the ideal of the *American* revolution ruled out any basic challenge to the system. . . . In the United States, the summons to dissent, because it was grounded in a prescribed ritual form [the jeremiad], pre-empted the threat of radical alternatives." The jeremiad, he continued, ritualized political dissent, helping "to control the energies . . . unleashed" through the act of Revolution and "preclude . . . the possibility of fundamental social change."[13]

In a more recent essay, Bercovitch considered the purportedly radical rhetoric of Frederick Douglass, Henry David Thoreau, Elizabeth Cady

Stanton, Martin Luther King, Paul Goodman, and Gloria Steinem. "These dissenters," Bercovitch remarked, "miscalculated not just the power but the nature of rhetoric." He explained: "They had thought to appropriate America as a trope of the spirit, and so to turn the national symbol, now freed of its base historical content, into a vehicle of moral and political renovation. In the event, however, the symbol had refigured the moral and political terms of renovation—had rendered freedom, opportunity, democracy, and radicalism itself part of the American Way."[14] Bercovitch's reflections on American radicalism enabled him to recognize, if only implicitly, a perennial problem in rhetorical advocacy that J. Robert Cox has labeled the "scandal of *doxa*." Rhetorical advocates are, Cox maintains, caught in a bind because their inventional resources—common opinions, cultural values, or in short communal *doxa*—constrain their ability to generate new insights or perspectives. He writes: "In this context, public argument is suspect; it is the vessel of custom, blindness, and inaction. Drawn from *doxa,* from a continuity with all that is past, public moral argument can only rationalize what is. The effort to create the 'new' labors against this scandal of *doxa*."[15]

In his analysis of King's speech, Fred Antczak argues that it was essential to locate the text temporally "in the context of a larger moral tradition, our living tradition of revolution."[16] We agree with Antczak, but suggest that greater specificity may be in order. One way to grasp King's effort to radicalize the jeremiad and negotiate the scandal of *doxa* involves exploring its temporal dimension, which reveals the way his text incorporates important elements of the western European civic republican tradition. One of that tradition's foremost students, John Pocock, suggests that "the [civic republican] dread of corruption [was] the true heir of the [Puritan] jeremiad." Since the mid-eighteenth century, Americans have, Pocock maintains, "remained obsessively concerned by the threat of corruption."[17] Rereading King's critique of American society via the civic republican concept of corruption illustrates one way he radicalized the jeremiad.

As Gordon Wood and others document, since the revolutionary era Americans have deployed images of poison and disease to mark the presence of civic corruption, and we find King employing similar images in the speech. But even more important than the consistency of images over time is the way King harnessed an important civic republican distinction. Reflecting a strong individualistic ethos, the traditional Puritan jeremiad and its secularized kin imagined civic decline as a consequence of personal sin. As John Murphy notes: "The jeremiad deflects attention away from possible institutional or systemic flaws and toward considerations of individual sin. Redemption is achieved," he continues, "through the efforts of the American people, not through a change in the system itself."[18] But as Pocock has noted, the civic republican tradition eschews this individualistic fixation. In fact, he maintains that early modern civic republicans such as Machiavelli developed "a sociological as well as a merely moral analysis of corruption." According to Pocock, explicit "social analysis of the conditions propitious and unpropitious to republican government" constituted an important element of civic republican discourse. Given Pocock's observations regarding the civic republican concern with social analysis, we should not be surprised to find jeremiads manifesting forms of systemic critique as a counterbalance to individual moral decline.

Although King moralized the nation's Vietnam policy (a point developed in some detail by Dionisopoulos et al.), at one point demanding that the nation "atone" not just for policy "errors" but for "our sins . . . in Vietnam," he nevertheless resisted the tendency to collapse moral critique into a simple reaffirmation of individualism. The structures of American society generated the moral failures, the civic corruption, that King sought to uncover. By the middle of the twentieth century, a version of the sociological or systemic analysis of corruption that Pocock detected in Machiavelli had been resuscitated by intellectuals such as the maverick sociologist C. Wright Mills, by New Left advocates such as Tom Hayden, Carl Oglesby, and Paul Potter, and by black power activists such as Stokely Carmichael. By 1967 it had become common for King to claim that the civil rights movement was "forcing America to face all its interrelated flaws—racism, poverty, militarism, and materialism" and "exposing the evils that are deeply rooted in the whole structure of our society. It reveals systemic rather than superficial flaws and suggests that radical reconstruction of society itself is the real issue to be faced."[19] King's gradual embrace of systemic critique through the 1960s was, in all likelihood, due to a variety of influences, but his focus on materialism and militarism did not simply reflect unique mid-twentieth-century

American anxieties. By underscoring these forms of systemic corruption, King reanimated traditional civic republican concerns.[20]

Pocock, Wood, and other students of the civic republican tradition have recounted in some detail the civic republican antipathy for material self-interest, luxury, extravagance, dissipation, and venality, and King's condemnation of "a 'thing-oriented' society" where "machines and computers, profit motives and property rights are considered more important than people" echoed these themes. But by 1967 King had begun to perceive that America's materialistic spirit was not merely the "corrupt other" common in republican theory (as tyranny is the corrupt version of monarchy); it was an ineradicable feature of the nation's economic system. "A true revolution of values," he remarked at Riverside Church, "will soon look uneasily on the glaring contrast of poverty and wealth." "True compassion," he continued, "is more than flinging a coin to a beggar; it is not haphazard and superficial. It comes to see that an edifice which produces beggars needs restructuring" (240–41). King would continue his quest to restructure the economic edifice for the remainder of his life. For example, in his final Southern Christian Leadership Conference presidential address, he insisted that "the movement must address itself to the question of restructuring the whole of American society. There are forty million poor people here. And one day we must ask the question, 'Why are there forty million poor people in America?' And when you begin to ask that question, you are raising questions about the economic system, about a broader distribution of wealth. When you ask that question, you begin to question the capitalistic economy."[21] King's critique of materialism at Riverside Church should be located within his emerging rhetorical assault on American capitalism.[22]

The civic republican tradition's relationship to militarism and military conflict is, on the other hand, much more contested.[23] Emphasizing a distinction between professional armies (or a "standing army") and citizen militias, Pocock has argued that for Machiavelli and other early modern republicans "a man who should devote the whole of his energies to the *arte della Guerra* . . . is an infinitely greater danger" to the community's civic health than a man who devotes more energy to commerce than his civic responsibilities. Toward the end of *The Machiavellian Moment,* Pocock suggests that, given the tradition's emphasis on citizen-soldiers serving the nation through militia service, one part of the nation's "inherited rhetorical and conceptual structure" was a civic republican hostility toward "the growth of a military-industrial complex in government."[24] When in the early 1960s King challenged the "blind conformity" that "the military-industrial complex" helped inculcate, he echoed civic republican concerns that, for example, Anti-federalists had introduced during the ratification debate in the late eighteenth century.[25]

At Riverside Church, King at times defended his call for "wise restraint and calm reasonableness" in foreign affairs pragmatically, arguing that a reformed foreign/military policy would be a more effective weapon against communism since "our greatest defense against communism is to take offensive action on behalf of justice" (241). But his attack on American militarism frequently depicted it as a corrosive and corruptive force that undermined civic identity and civic morality. "A nation that continues year after year to spend more money on military defense than on programs of social uplift is," King insisted, "approaching spiritual death." He also stressed the war's impact on young American soldiers who were injected with "poisonous drugs of hate" and sent "home from dark and bloody battlefields physically handicapped and psychologically deranged" (241). If the nation did not reform its militaristic policies, King predicted, "we shall surely be dragged down the long dark and shameful corridors of time reserved for those who possess power without compassion, might without morality, and strength without sight" (243).

By reappropriating a systemic perspective on civic corruption and revoicing traditional civic republican themes,[26] King began the process of generic reconstitution. But the pervasive corruption of American values and ideals severely limited his ability to revitalize the nation's civic virtue. For this reason he could not enact the traditional jeremiadic strategy of, in Dionisopoulos and his coauthors' terms, "urging more stringent adherence to . . . the values of American society." As Fredrik Sunnemark recently remarked, by early 1967 "the Constitution and values of America [became] an accusation in [King's] rhetoric instead of a yet-to-be-fulfilled promise."[27] The corrupted communal *doxa* upon which King could draw only amplified his scandalous inventional dilemma: how to use existing rhetorical resources to craft a message that might move an audience beyond its existing conditions and its identity as a nation of warriors. Cox's speculations regarding critical memory's inventional potential provides, we maintain, some insight into the way King negotiated his dilemma.

Cox acknowledges that, as inventional strategies, history and public memory frequently engender either a simplistic civic nostalgia for the past or a reified present untroubled by historical contingency. Critical memory, Cox argues, rejects both nostalgia and reification. Instead, it seeks to disrupt the reified present and recover lost or forgotten possibilities. Echoing the civic republican antipathy to civic corruption, Cox describes the way nostalgia and reified history perpetuate communal "ideals" that have become "ideologically deformed." The practice of critical memory seeks to disturb or disavow deformed or corrupted traditions, enabling advocates to "re-collect" or recover a lost or forgotten "heritage." Transposed into the idiom of civic republicanism, critical memory seeks civic *rinnovazione* (renovation or *revitalization*) through a form of *ridurre ai principii* (a return to or recovery of first principles or fundamentals).[28]

Cox identifies a group of "transformative practices" that enable recovery of a lost heritage, "an appropriation of the seeds of a culture's past." One discursive practice to which Cox devotes considerable attention is the argument strategy of dissociation. Dissociation is powerful because it can "bring about a more or less profound change in the conceptual data that are used as the basis of argument." It is, in short, a discursive strategy for "remodeling our conceptions of reality."[29] According to Cox, in the context of communal memory practices "A dissociation holds 'deformed' parts of a tradition in tension with their historical alternatives. As arguers confront these possibilities critically, they disclose or liberate usable principles for contemporary practice."

Unlike, for example, Frederick Douglass's performance in Buffalo in 1852, King's speech occasion in April 1967 did not present an opportunity to explore the nation's revolutionary heritage in depth.[30] King did, however, deploy condensed dissociations throughout the speech, initially contrasting a superficial "smooth patriotism" with a more virtuous form of "firm dissent" (231), then in the middle portion of the address locating "the true meaning and value of compassion and nonviolence" in recovering "the enemy's point of view" (237). In the concluding section he continued his effort to recover "true compassion"—as we noted earlier—by distinguishing it from the merely "haphazard and superficial" (241). King reserved his most sustained use of the strategy for his effort to recover, or in his words, "recapture," the modern world's revolutionary spirit in order, as he put it, "to make democracy real" (242). King's invocation of the modern "revolutionary spirit," his desire to recapture that spirit, and his quest for a "genuine" or "a true revolution of values" all function as condensed dissociations; the adjective "true" and the rather transcendent noun "spirit" unleash a dissociative logic that seeks to disturb a domesticated revolutionary tradition (a tradition that has made the United States and the West, in King's judgment, "arch anti-revolutionaries") and recover a forgotten or repressed revolutionary heritage opposed to "exploitation and oppression" as well as "poverty, racism, and militarism" and committed to fostering "new systems of justice and equality . . . all over the globe" (242).

King's recurrent dissociations enacted a form of critical memory that sought a civic republican *ridurre,* a recovery of corrupted or deformed national values that would enable transformative political action (*rinnovazione*) by reconstituting our civic virtue. But as important as this temporal element is to the text's transformative action, we should follow King's advice and resist the temptation to stop here. By tracing the text's spatial dynamics, we come to see that a purely historical form of recovery is insufficient. In "A Time to Break Silence," King intimated that, for the nation to recover its (corrupted) virtue, its citizens must be willing to relinquish their parochial national identity.

Space, Movement, and Errand

To contend that a restoration of civic virtue requires movement in or through space should come as no surprise to students of American letters. Deeply embedded within U.S. public discourse is the faith that to move again is to be born again. If the world around us reeks of corruption, Huck Finn teaches, we can always "light out for the Territory." Space, however, assumes a particularly powerful role in the civic republican or Jeffersonian tradition of dissent that we have been tracing through King's text. In his germinal work on republican resistance to the Hamiltonian system in the early United States, Drew McCoy notes the widespread belief that corruption "could be forestalled in America as long as its citizens were able to expand across space rather than develop through time."[31]

His analysis suggests that, for the early republicans, time was the enemy. In their developmental view of human society, nations rose, flourished, and fell because of the ravages of time. The inevitable decline of "those who labour in the earth . . . the chosen people of God," in Jefferson's famous words, and the concomitant and equally inevitable growth of commerce introduces paper credit, stockjobbers, bankers, and lawyers. In short, the weeds of commerce kill the pastoral garden of republican virtue. Only movement to ever-new "empires of liberty" could save republican citizens. It was this opposition that leads Pocock to proclaim "that what was involved was a flight from modernity and a future no less than from antiquity and a past."[32] Such a perspective crafts this tradition's conception of space as a means to escape history, past and future. Thus, Pocock, as we have noted, links cries of corruption to Puritan outrage, arguing that the "jeremiad—that most American of all rhetorical modes— was merged with the language of classical republican theory to the point where one can almost speak of an apocalyptic Machiavellianism."[33]

His reservations about these flights notwithstanding, Pocock's productive link between the jeremiad and civic republicanism implies a means through which we can "re-collect," in Cox's terms, the transformative operations of movement through space as it works in this address. King's spatial dynamics reconfigured the traditions through which he spoke and engaged the audience in the task of national redemption. To begin, it is important to note, in the words of G. P. Mohrmann, "that when we talk of metaphorical space and place, we are not talking of passive constructs, but are talking instead of constructs alive with the potential for action, and their vigor often derives largely from that potential."[34] In the jeremiadic tradition, that incipient action flows powerfully from the Puritan interpretation of their "errand."

It is that concept which creates the most striking disagreement between those two great students of Puritan culture, Perry Miller and Sacvan Bercovitch. For Miller, an errand must either be for oneself *or* for someone else. That opposition leads to a series of debilitating dichotomies that result in a psychological reading of the jeremiad as a "self-defeating ritual of purgation."[35] It is a lament for an errand that was lost with the

restoration of monarchy in the Old England and the restoration of sinful-
ness in the New. For Bercovitch, an errand could be for oneself *and* for
someone else. He takes as his text Samuel Danforth's *Brief Recognition
of New England's Errand into the Wilderness*. Danforth takes as *his* text
Jesus' encomium for John the Baptist in Matthew 11:7–9. "What went ye
out into the wilderness to see?" is the question, and Danforth provides
the answer. Danforth, Bercovitch believes, "invests the errand with the
general import of *'pilgrimage.'*"[36] The wilderness is both in us, in our hard
hearts and recalcitrant wills, and outside of us, in the wilds of North
America. To encounter the latter is to change the former; such has been
the pilgrimage into the wilderness from Moses through the Baptist through
Christ and now to the people of the New Jerusalem. Pilgrimage through
space recovers the holy spirit of the original, yet progressive, revelation
of God. Paradoxically, to move outward through space is to recollect the
purity of the inner self. The errand is both/and; encountering the "other"
of an outer world transforms the inner self; both self and other change
and grow.

Yet the scandal of *doxa* intrudes again. For much of our history, Bercovitch implies, the locus of transformation rested not within the superior,
civilized self, but over and against the uncivilized other. He writes, "New
England was from the start an outpost of the modern world. It evolved from
its own origins, as it were, into a middle-class culture—a commercially
oriented society . . . a relatively homogenous society whose enterprise
was consecrated, according to its civic and clerical leadership, by a divine
plan of progress."[37] Sanctioned by divine capitalism, we would make the
other into our peaceful, civilized middle-class selves, from the Jacksonian
Trail of Tears to Remember the Alamo, from the Frontier Thesis to the
March of the Flag, from the jungles of Vietnam to the cities of Iraq. John
Pocock, too, recognizes the charge of this dominant spatial discourse,
identifying it with the dynamic force of Machiavellian *virtu* and paying
particular attention to its nineteenth-century exemplar: "When [Andrew]
Jackson is regularly praised as a general who won victories without attending to the formalities of international law, a president who made laws
and decisions without attending to constitutional niceties, it is clear that
we are dealing with a leader of *virtu* in a highly Machiavellian sense."[38]
The differing ways in which we view Jefferson and Jackson, the civilized

scholar and the uncouth general, trace nicely the transformation of virtue that occurred in U.S. political culture. Movement through space has often come to mean subjugation of place, a process we now sometimes term "pre-emptive war."

Moving uneasily in the shadows cast by the divine march of the flag is Huckleberry Finn. Recall that he determined to "light out" at novel's end, after his journey down the Mississippi with Jim, a trip that taught him the wonders of Jacksonian civilization and the fact that Jim "had a good heart in him and was a good man."[39] That journey made more movement inevitable: "But I reckon I got to light out for the Territory ahead of the rest, because Aunt Sally she's going to adopt me and sivilize me and I can't stand it. I been there before."[40] King, too, had been there before. The Aunt Sallies of white America sought to civilize him, by their own lights, and he, too, sought escape through movement. The restless energy of his texts flows, we suggest, from an invigoration of this subversive sense of movement in American public address, from a journey that changes the self as that self encounters the other in a place beyond ourselves. He reached for an aspect of the jeremiadic tradition, the full notion of an errand into the wilderness of the world and one's own soul and defined that moment, in a phrase borrowed from Buber, as a creative confrontation that changes an "I-It" relationship to an "I-Thou" relationship.

King's figuration of the transformative power of movement through space came not only from his reading of Buber and the like, but also from his biblical heritage. Malinda Snow, in her analysis of "Letter from Birmingham Jail," notes that the word *walk*, not a likely candidate for religious allusion, often comes to mean in the English Bible "the righteous person's safe passage through life . . . one who walks is both righteous and protected." After citing numerous examples from the Scriptures, she writes, "For King, to walk was as morally significant an action as to go to jail."[41] To put it another way, for King, every journey was alive with the possibility of Saul's trip to Damascus. We might all become Paul in our encounters with the faces of God. Such energy has not gone unnoticed in the previous fine readings of this address; Antczak, for example, reveals the "ever-widening contexts of duty" that King used to justify his right to speak.[42] Dionisopoulos and his colleagues do not engage the spatial axes that infuse the text, but their writing reflects the flux of King's images;

he offers not ideas, but "trajectories," his "trajectories" do not fit, they "collide," and he presents not a history from above, but "from below."[43] It remains to specify the textual movements that have sparked such critical agitation.

Those movements began at the beginning. King announced, "I come to this magnificent house of worship tonight because my conscience leaves me no other choice" (231). Not only does King "come" to the church, he was compelled to do so by an inner force, by his conscience. The insistent dialectic between movement and stasis, inner and outer, continued through the introduction. He acknowledged the "difficult" mission of opposition: "Even when pressed by the demands of *inner truth*, men do not easily assume the task of opposing their government's policy, especially in time of war. Nor does the human spirit *move* without great difficulty against all the apathy of conformist thought *within one's bosom and in the surrounding world*" (231, emphasis ours). "Apathy," the dictionary tells us, derives from the Greek: *a* meaning "without" and the rhetorically familiar *pathos* meaning "feeling" or "suffering." To be apathetic is to be without pathos. Conformist thought on Vietnam, much like racism, extended into "one's bosom," an analysis of our lives that echoes Samuel Danforth's both/ and errand and Herbert Marcuse's *One-Dimensional Man*.[44] To "move," in the face of these "outposts in our heads," to borrow Sally Kempton's feminist phrase, was terribly difficult, a problem King emphasized with another spatial image: "We are always on the verge of being *mesmerized* by uncertainty; but we must *move on*" (231, emphasis ours).

King used the introduction to present, in effect, his rhetorical obstacle. It was daunting. Conformist thought had left us without feeling, and thus, "The calling to speak is often a vocation of agony," similar to the pain that results from movement after a prolonged confinement. Our body, our conscience, was not used to the exercise because we had been "mesmerized." Yet King offered hope; the dissociation between a "smooth patriotism" and a "firm dissent" that we spoke of earlier was reinforced by spatial imagery—we should move to the "*high grounds* of a firm dissent. . . . Perhaps a new spirit is *rising* among us. If it is, let us *trace its movement* well and pray that our own *inner being* may be sensitive to its guidance for we are *deeply* in need of a *new way* beyond the darkness that seems *so close* around us" (231, emphasis ours). It may be possible to pack more spatial imagery into a sentence, but we are not sure how to do so. Consistent with archetypal metaphors, the new spirit rose, and, King implied, we must follow it to the good high ground.[45] Our "inner being," he suggested, could change as we "trace" the "movement." Movement upward and outward resulted in inner change, a "path," King then indicated, that he himself had followed.

The introduction proper ended as King turned to the issue of his dissent. As he "moved to break the betrayal of my own silences and to speak from the burnings of my own heart," many "have questioned me about the wisdom of my path" (232). As we noted at the outset, King asked their questions: Why you? Why dissent? Why mix civil rights and the war? This section resembled nothing so much as "Letter from Birmingham Jail," and, by linking these texts, King cast his nameless interlocutors as the white ministers in Birmingham, surely an uncomfortable position for many of his allies. Like the ministers, they wondered why he came here. As in his response to those earlier ministers, King was "greatly saddened" by the inquiries because such questions suggested that they "have not really known me, my commitment or my calling. Indeed, their questions suggest that they do not know the world in which they live" (232). Note the juxtaposition and the implied reversal. If they did not know King, they did not know the world; if they did not know the world, they did not know King. Like the apostle Paul once more wearily traveling out into the world to spread the good news, King must, again, explain why "the path from Dexter Avenue Baptist Church . . . leads clearly to this sanctuary tonight," just as it led clearly to Birmingham's jail (232). The condensed allusion to the "Letter" foreshadowed the powerful, explicit links King would draw between the civil rights movement and Vietnam. It also set in place the spatial dynamics that move through the succeeding three sections of the address—to know King is to know the world, and to know the world is to move as King moved.

Fred Antczak has discerned both the widening contexts of duty that form King's justification for dissent and the implicit model he offers his audience in the first section.[46] It is important to note, however, the two additional spatial axes that characterize this portion of the address. First, as King widened those contexts of duty, from his role as civil rights leader to his "calling to be a son of the living God" (234), as he moved out into

the world, he also moved inward into his own soul. His leadership of
civil rights was a political role; his calling was personal indeed. To move
outward through contexts of duty was to move inward to the burning of
one's own heart. He implicitly asked a similar move of the audience; a
"son of the living God" could not help but question the current path of
the United States in Vietnam. Second, King's use of space, the subversive
historical alternative, as Cox might put it, was held in tension with the
nation's past movement outward, the hegemonic tradition. In contrast to
King's movement, as the nation moved outward, "adventures like Vietnam
continued to draw men and skills and money [from the war on poverty]
like some demonic destructive suction tube." As the nation moved outward, it sent black men "to die in extraordinarily high proportions relative
to the rest of the population." As the nation moved outward, young men
in the ghetto asked King, was it not "using massive doses of violence to
solve its problems, to bring about the changes it wanted?" Why should
they not do so? (223). Even in what appeared to be a simple, defensive,
and enumerated justification of dissent, King's spatial movement foreshadowed the revolution in values for which he would call. The nation's
movement led to violence at home and abroad; his movement promised
redemption and learning, just as he had learned from those young people
in the ghetto.

Yet the question remained for King: How might he move the audience
as he himself had been moved by the spirit? Recall that King saw apathy
as a major rhetorical problem. As a result, pathos becomes a key strategy,
and Thomas Farrell's analysis of it helps us to understand King's text.
Pathos, Farrell notes, has created problems because it seems to traffic
in "excitations of emotion." If we regard the audience as an "agency of
logos and judgment," as King surely did, what can we say of emotion?
Farrell argues that the import of pathos rests in its ability to remove "us
from the immediacy of familiar appearance, thereby allowing us to for-
mulate conditions for appreciating the needs of others." As pathos acts
in rhetoric, "There is a doubly reflexive move, from awareness of our own
emotion (fear) to a recognition of what may be involved when it is others
who are suffering." From this view, emotions allow "the sense of recognition we require whenever we are taken outside of our own immediacy:
from the neighborhood to the moral community. . . . Without rhetoric's

intervention, we would have only the partiality of immediate interest, the familiar locale. We would end where we started."[47] Needless to say, we find Farrell's use of spatial metaphors suggestive. King moved us from our immediate locality to Vietnam, from apathy to a sense of recognition.

Throughout this section, the process was inductive as King moved us along. We were more likely to care about the peasants, those for whom we were supposedly acting, and so King began there. From there, he turned to the National Liberation Front (the Viet Cong) and then to the leaders in Hanoi. At each stage, he took us out of our immediacy and confronted us with our actions and their effects on others. For instance, speaking of the peasants, he said, "Now they languish under our bombs and consider us—not their fellow Vietnamese—the real enemy. They move sadly and apathetically as we herd them off the land of their fathers into concentration camps where minimal social needs are rarely met. They know they must move or be destroyed by our bombs" (236). The nation's movement in space inevitably led to the tragic movement of the people in Vietnam; King wished us to experience that movement, to understand it, perhaps, as an ironic revelation. They had become as apathetic as our national conscience. The bombing brutalized both Americans and Vietnamese. In using emotion in this way, to borrow again from Farrell, King constituted his audience as "an agency capable of character, of 'social emotions.'"[48] By moving us successively further away from ourselves, even unto the thoughts of Ho Chi Minh (238), King constituted us as an agency capable of judgment. We were no longer apathetic; we were moved. We had feeling again and could assume moral responsibility for our choices.

That responsibility was a heavy burden on our journey. It required not only dissent on the issue of Vietnam, but also that "true revolution of values" of which we have spoken. To this point, we have traced the movements of King's spirit in time as he reached back to recollect and revitalize our lost and forgotten revolutionary heritage. That move gained energy from an equally palpable pilgrimage through space as King's spirit lifted us out of our immediate locale to embrace a moral community that included the peoples of Vietnam. Much as the recovery of a civic republican discourse of dissent radicalized that journey through time by invoking a systemic critique, so, too, did the recollection of the full import of a pilgrimage through space radicalize our identity as an audience. The journey changed us. As King turned to the revolution, he revealingly said, "There is something seductively tempting about stopping there and sending us all off on what in some circles has become a popular crusade against the war in Vietnam" (240). Note that "stopping" had a dual meaning. You may stop an action in time or you may stop a trip and settle into place. A true revolution of values allowed neither. Awakened to the responsibility of moral choice, we were driven to move forward and outward. It was, to invoke the speech's two common titles, both a time to break silence and a move beyond Vietnam.

Two passages illustrate King's final theme. First, in a remarkably inventive use of the parable of the Good Samaritan, King said, "We are called to play the Good Samaritan on life's roadside; but that will be only an initial act. One day we must come to see that the whole Jericho road must be transformed so that men and women will not be constantly beaten and robbed as they make their journey on life's highway" (241). Recall the question that sparked this parable. A lawyer sought to test Jesus by asking, "Teacher, what must I do to inherit eternal life?" Jesus, as he often did, answered a question with a question, "What is written in the law?" Then, the famous answer: "You shall love the Lord your God with all your heart and with all your soul and with all your strength, and with all your mind; and your neighbor as yourself." Love, in other words, was the answer to the question, and King's invocation of this parable foreshadowed his belief, articulated later, that the power of love can transform this highway. In addition, the power of this parable resulted partly from the social status of those on the road—the priest, the Levite, and the disdained Samaritan. Samaritans were despised because they thought themselves superior, pure adherents of the faith who treated only the Pentateuch as holy and disdained the rest of the Scriptures as tainted.[49] An intriguing possibility existed here; as the Samaritan made his journey, encountered the man, and was "moved with pity" (New Revised Standard Version), the Samaritan, too, was changed. That was why he stopped. Yet for us to stop, as the individualistic ethos of the jeremiad suggests, was not enough, King insisted. To act truly in the Samaritan's spirit, to change as he changed, we must make the entire road safe for all.

To do that meant to lift ourselves out of our parochial identities, to make priest, Levite, and Samaritan one. As King prepared for that crucial move, he reiterated the themes we have identified. He then used them to refigure his famous Dream: "Our only hope today lies in our ability to recapture that revolutionary spirit and go out into a sometimes hostile world declaring eternal hostility to poverty, racism, and militarism. With this powerful commitment we shall boldly challenge the status quo and unjust mores and thereby speed the day when 'every valley shall be exalted, and every mountain and hill shall be made low, and the crooked shall be made straight and the rough places plain'" (242). The spirit of the American Revolution, in King's view, would inspire movement against that triplet. The jeremiad's call for reform was deepened and strengthened here by a systemic critique rooted in the civic republican tradition; that tradition, in turn, was then redeemed by the eschatological promise of the jeremiad.

Perhaps more revealing in this context, however, was King's effort to reinterpret his own advocacy. As Cox notes, King's August 28, 1963, dream found "its denouement in the words of comfort Isaiah spoke to those whose exile in Babylon in the sixth century B.C.E. would soon end."[50] It is but a small exaggeration to claim that the civil rights movement came to be culturally defined through that speech, that the speech came to be defined through King's dream, and that his dream located its promise in the authority of Isaiah. By so using Isaiah at Riverside, King made of civil rights, racism, poverty, militarism, and war a whole cloth; one must address all to address any. Whatever the case in 1963, the promise of "I Have a Dream" in 1967 could only be redeemed through a comprehensive re-vision of American society. That required a new identity. King then said: "A genuine revolution of values means in the final analysis that our loyalties must become ecumenical rather than sectional. Every nation must now develop an overriding loyalty to mankind as a whole in order to preserve the best in individual societies. This call for a world-wide fellowship that lifts neighborly concern beyond one's tribe, race, class and nation is in reality a call for an all-embracing and unconditional love for all men" (242).

King's call, indeed the speech, asked us to discard our belief in American exceptionalism.[51] We were not special. We were not different. As a result, we had to join with others, much as the Samaritan joined the man with no name, no religion, and no identity along the road. All people were citizens in a worldwide fellowship. Taylor Branch describes King's errand in this way: "To curtail unspeakable cruelty and waste, Americans must refine their cherished ideal of freedom by accepting that they could support but not impose it in Vietnam. To honor sacrifice with understanding, Americans must grant the Vietnamese people the elementary respect of citizens in disagreement. The lesson was at once wrenching and obvious, in the way modern people might be chastened by the centuries it took to establish that the Inquisition's bloody enforcement profaned rather than championed Christian belief."[52] It was this call that incited critics to read the speech as ineradicably radical. In a sense, King did not so much reject the values of American society and the jeremiad as extend them to all people. But to see the enemy as citizens was to obliterate the difference that had constituted American identity in war. If they were no longer the savage Other, then who were we? In King's eyes, we were citizens and neighbors. All people, not only Americans, but all people were chosen and beloved of God.

Speculative Conclusion

This assessment of King's call helps to account for the negative response that greeted him; to dispense with exceptionalism was no easy task. Generally, the nation's opinion leaders attacked King for speaking on Vietnam and urged him to keep to civil rights. Branch bitingly summarizes the reaction: "The call for segregated silence on Vietnam dashed any expectation that King's freedom movement had validated the citizenship credentials of blacks by historic mediation between the powerful and dispossessed. It relegated him again to the back of the bus, conspicuous yet invisible."[53] It is also important to note, however, that those same pundits were wrong about the outcome of the Vietnam War, wrong about the inevitability of Lyndon Johnson's reelection, wrong about the political potential of Eugene McCarthy, and, in general, wrong about the political developments in that long and terrible year following this speech. In short, assessment of the instrumental power of this speech is forever held in suspension by the assassination of its author and of the strongest antiwar presidential candidate, Senator Robert F. Kennedy.

Our analysis, instead, has sought to locate King's rhetoric through two traditions of American dissent, civic republicanism and the jeremiad. We argue that he reconstitutes these languages by interanimating them, shining the light of one through the other. In a statement that possesses the virtues and vices of oversimplification, we might say: the resources of the civic republican tradition, particularly the invigoration of *ridurre,* allow for a systemic critique; the resources of the Puritan tradition, particularly the invigoration of "errand," allow for the transformative possibilities of movement. These two axes of time and space constitute American political culture in such a way as to unite the critique of the individual and systemic. That is the genius of this address. Each of us must stop along the road to Jericho. Yet we must also rebuild that road together.

King's words at Riverside Church make of this charge a living possibility. James Boyd White writes of such rhetoric, "Whenever you speak, you define a character for yourself and for at least one other—your audience—and make a community at least between the two of you; and you do this in a language that is of necessity provided to you by others and modified in your use of it."[54] To craft an effective ethical response to the powerful imperatives of presidential war rhetoric asks such character work of dissidents. An end to war means an end to the communal identity that sustained the slaughter and a refiguration of the community in light of such experiences. Much as Lincoln sought to conclude his war with "malice towards none; with charity for all," so, too, did King call for a new fellowship among all in the multiple idioms of American life. As a result of this inventional action, the possibilities for dissent, particularly in time of war, are widened, strengthened, and deepened. Our languages are modified in the wake of this speech.

Equally important, King's speech did not stand alone. It participated in a swirl of "respectable" rhetoric that questioned American exceptionalism and refused to equate American identity with some sort of special status. Compare King's denial with these words: "For, in the final analysis, our most basic common link is that we all inhabit this small planet. We all breathe the same air. We all cherish children's future. And we are all mortal." President Kennedy rejected the notion that exceptionalism would save us from the effects of nuclear war. A month before the Riverside Church address, Senator Robert Kennedy asked us to take moral responsibility for

the carnage: "Let us reflect for a moment not on the wisdom and necessity of our cause . . . , but on the horror. . . . [War] is the vacant moment
of amazed fear as a mother and child watch death by fire fall from the
improbable machine sent by a country they barely comprehend. . . . All
we say and all we do must be informed by our awareness that this horror
is partly our responsibility; not just a nation's responsibility but yours and
mine. It is we who live in abundance and send our young men out to
die. It is our chemicals that scorch the children and our bombs that level
the villages."⁵⁵ So, we conclude as we began—with the chemicals that
scorch the children. As one of us has argued elsewhere, Kennedy did not
quite reach the high moral ground of systemic critique we see in Riverside
Church. But the Reverend King did not stand alone, nor did this address
fail to shape interpretations of our "errand into the wilderness."

In his April 30, 1970, address to the nation on the situation in Southeast Asia, Richard Nixon insisted: "It is not our power but our will and
character that is being tested tonight. The question all Americans must
ask and answer tonight is this: Does the richest and strongest nation
in the history of the world have the character to meet a challenge by a
group which rejects every effort to win a just peace, ignores our warn-
ing, tramples on solemn agreements, violates the neutrality of unarmed
people, and uses our prisoners as hostages?"⁵⁶ Like most skilled political
advocates, Nixon framed his rhetorical question in a way that he believed
precluded all answers but one. However ironic it might seem, had Martin
Luther King, Jr. been able to evade the assassin's bullet, he would have
endorsed the initial shape of Nixon's question. King believed in 1967 that
the war in Vietnam *was* testing the nation's character in the way all wars
test a nation's character. Nixon tried to use his April 1970 speech to affirm
the community's identity as virtuous warriors. At Riverside Church three
years earlier, King drew on multiple discursive resources in an effort to
reconstitute the possibilities of communal identity in a time of war. King
challenged Americans to recover and realize their radical potential, their
true identity as revolutionaries, but he insisted that to do so they would
paradoxically have to stop being Americans. He challenged the nation to
think and exist in multiple registers and idioms. More than forty years
later, with the nation engaged in another war, the question recurs: what
kind of people, what kind of nation, do we wish to be?

NOTES

1. William Pepper, "The Children of Vietnam" *Ramparts*, January 1967, 53.
2. For example, see Adam Fairclough, "Martin Luther King, Jr. and the War in Vietnam," *Phylon* 45 (March 1984), esp. 28–29; David Garrow, *Bearing the Cross: Martin Luther King, Jr. and the Southern Christian Leadership Conference* (New York: William Morrow, 1986), esp. 543–544; Stephen B. Oates, *Let the Trumpet Sound: The Life of Martin Luther King, Jr.* (New York: Harper and Row, 1982), esp. 427.
3. For a discussion of the debate between King and his associates regarding this speech, see Taylor Branch, *At Canaan's Edge: America in the King Years, 1965–68* (New York: Simon and Schuster, 2006), 584–586.
4. See George N. Dionisopoulos, Victoria J. Gallagher, Steven R. Goldzwig, and David Zarefsky, "Martin Luther King, the American Dream, and Vietnam: A Collision of Rhetorical Trajectories," *Western Journal of Communication* 56 (1992): 99.
5. "A Time to Break Silence" in *A Testament of Hope: The Essential Writings and Speeches of Martin Luther King, Jr.*, ed. James M. Washington (New York: Harper Collins, 1986), 231. Subsequent references will be made parenthetically in the text.
6. Dionisopoulos et al. summarize the seven reasons for linking the two movements: "1) it [the war] distracted the nation from civil rights and poverty, 2) blacks were dying in disproportionate numbers, 3) it made a mockery of calls for nonviolence, 4) it destroyed the [nation's] soul, 5) his dissent was required by the mission he assumed in accepting the Nobel Peace Prize, 6) it [his public opposition] was also required by his status as a man of God, and 7) he would prefer to focus on the needs of the poor" ("Martin Luther King," 100). We are not sure how Dionisopoulos and his coauthors reconstructed their seventh reason. King's final point in this opening section was that he "must be true to my conviction that I share with all men the calling to be a son of the living God. Beyond the calling of race or nation or creed is this vocation of sonship and brotherhood." This final comment appears consistent with their sixth reason. Dionisopoulos et al. fail to note King's effort to use the SCLC's motto "To save the soul of America" as an articulatory resource (see 233).
7. See David Howard-Pitney, *The Afro-American Jeremiad: Appeals for Justice in America* (Philadelphia: Temple University Press, 1990).
8. See Dionisopoulos et al., "Martin Luther King," 98.
9. For discussions of war rhetoric, see Karlyn Kohrs Campbell and Kathleen Hall

Jamieson, *Deeds Done in Words: Presidential Rhetoric and the Genres of Governance* (Chicago: University of Chicago Press, 1990), 101–126; Robert L. Ivie, "Images of Savagery in American Justifications for War," *Communication Monographs* 47 (1980): 279–294; John M. Murphy, "'Our Mission and Our Moment': George W. Bush and September 11," *Rhetoric and Public Affairs* 6 (2003): 607–632.

10. For a discussion of war dissent and its burdens, see John M. Murphy, "Epideictic and Deliberative Strategies in Opposition to War: The Paradox of Honor and Expediency," *Communication Studies* 43 (1992): 65–78.

11. While it is possible to follow Michael Leff's lead and examine a text's internal temporal rhythm, our approach to the temporality of King's speech concentrates instead on its external dynamics, specifically the way the speech reanimates the tradition of civic republicanism and exhibits a form of critical memory that recovers forgotten or deformed possibilities. Leff exemplifies the way a critic might engage a text's internal temporality in "Rhetorical Timing in Lincoln's 'House Divided' Speech," The Van Zelst Lecture in Communication, Northwestern University School of Speech, May 1983.

12. Sacvan Bercovitch, *The American Jeremiad* (Madison: University of Wisconsin Press, 1978), 180.

13. Ibid., 160, 174, 179.

14. Sacvan Bercovitch, *The Rites of Assent: Transformations in the Symbolic Construction of America* (New York: Routledge, 1993), 19. Bercovitch inserted this passage at the outset of a discussion of radicalism in America. During the course of his analysis, he acknowledged the problem of simple binary oppositions (such as radicalism and reform; co-optation and dissent) and admitted that "in all these cases, dissent was demonstrably an appeal to, and through, the rhetoric and values of the dominant culture; and in every case, it issued in a fundamental challenge to the system" (20). Nevertheless, he concluded that critical or political dissensus remains unable to "transcend" its ideological context. Attempts to create critical "distinctions" function "to exclude alternatives to the dominant culture by limiting opposition to terms which are intrinsic to the patterns of dominance" (22).

15. J. Robert Cox, "Cultural Memory and Public Moral Argument," The Van Zelst Lecture in Communication, Northwestern University, May 1987, 7.

16. Frederick J. Antczak, "When 'Silence Is Betrayal': An Ethical Criticism of the Revolution of Values in the Speech at Riverside Church," in *Martin Luther King, Jr. and the Sermonic Power of Public Discourse*, ed. Carolyn Calloway-Thomas and John L. Lucaites (Tuscaloosa: University of Alabama Press, 1993), 140–141.

17. J. G. A. Pocock, *The Machiavellian Moment: Florentine Political Thought and the Atlantic Republican Tradition* (Princeton, N.J.: Princeton University Press, 1975), 545, 548.

18. John M. Murphy, "'A Time of Shame and Sorrow': Robert F. Kennedy and the American Jeremiad," *Quarterly Journal of Speech* 76 (1990): 402.

19. Quoted in Vincent Harding, *Martin Luther King: The Inconvenient Hero* (Maryknoll, N.Y.: Orbis, 1996), 76.

20. Of King's "giant triplets," only racism—rooted in a liberal natural rights vision of equality—does not have deep roots in the civic republican tradition. Civic republicanism typically accentuated an economic or material sense of equality, as opposed to the more contemporary natural rights position that, thanks in part to Locke and Jefferson, has dominated American public discourse.

21. Martin Luther King, Jr., "Where Do We Go From Here?" in *Testament of Hope*, 250. On King's radicalism, see Harding, *Martin Luther King*, esp. 69–81, and Fredrik Sunnemark, *Ring Out Freedom! The Voice of Martin Luther King, Jr. and the Making of the Civil Rights Movement* (Bloomington: Indiana University Press, 2004), esp. 195–232.

22. See Michael Eric Dyson, *I May Not Get There with You: The True Martin Luther King, Jr.* (New York: Touchstone, 2000), 78–100.

23. For example, Paul Rahe represents a strand of scholarship that emphasizes the militaristic nature of the tradition. See *Republics Ancient and Modern*, 3 vols. (1992; rpt. Chapel Hill: University of North Carolina Press, 1994).

24. Pocock, *Machiavellian Moment*, 200, 548.

25. See King, *Strength to Love* (New York: Harper and Row, 1963), 10. On antifederal criticism of a "standing army" as inimical to civic character, see James Jasinski, "Rhetorical Practice and Its Visions of the Public in the Ratification Debate of 1787–1788," Ph.D. diss., Northwestern University, 1986.

26. It is also worth noting that King's critique of "our proneness to adjust to injustice" introduced another element of the civic republican tradition—the tension between accommodation and audacity—that has helped shape American public discourse. On this tension see James Jasinski, "Idioms of Prudence in Three Antebellum Controversies: Revolution, Constitution, and Slavery," in *Prudence: Classical Virtue, Postmodern Practice*, ed. Robert Hariman (University Park: Penn State University Press, 2003), 145–188.

27. Sunnemark, *Ring Out Freedom!* 198.

28. In addition to "Cultural Memory and Public Moral Argument," this paragraph and

the one to follow draws upon Cox, "Argument and Usable Traditions," in *Argument across the Lines of Disciplines*, ed. Frans H. van Eemeren et al. (Dordrecht: Foris Publishing, 1987), 93–99, and Cox, "Memory, Critical Theory, and the Argument from History," *Argumentation and Advocacy* 27 (1990): 1–13.

29. Chaim Perelman and Lucie Olbrechts-Tyteca, *The New Rhetoric: A Treatise on Argumentation*, trans. John Wilkinson and Purcell Weaver (Notre Dame, Ind.: University of Notre Dame Press, 1969), 412–413.

30. References to the Revolution assume greater prominence in King's 1967 discourse. For example, King concluded his first Massey lecture for the Canadian Broadcasting Corporation "Impasse in Race Relations" by noting "a shattering historical irony that the American Revolution of 1776 was the consequence of many of the same conditions that prevail today." He then likens the "American Negro of 1967" to Crispus Attucks, remarking that former, like the latter, "may be the vanguard in a prolonged struggle that may change the shape of the world." In King, *The Trumpet of Conscience* (New York: Harper and Row, 1968), 16–17.

31. Drew McCoy, *The Elusive Republic* (Chapel Hill: University of North Carolina Press, 1980), 62.

32. Pocock, *Machiavellian Moment*, 462.

33. Ibid., 512.

34. G. P. Mohrmann (ed. and rev. by Michael Leff), "Place and Space: Calhoun's Fatal Security," *Western Journal of Speech Communication* 51 (1987): 147.

35. Bercovitch, *American Jeremiad*, 10.

36. Ibid., 12.

37. Ibid., 20.

38. Pocock, *Machiavellian Moment*, 536.

39. Mark Twain, *The Adventures of Huckleberry Finn* (New York: Barnes and Noble Classics, 2003), 286.

40. Ibid., 293.

41. Malinda Snow, "Martin Luther King's 'Letter from Birmingham Jail' as Pauline Epistle," *Quarterly Journal of Speech* 71 (1985): 326–327.

42. Antczak, "Silence," 142.

43. Dionisopoulos et al., "Martin Luther King.""

44. Herbert Marcuse, *One-Dimensional Man: Studies in the Ideology of Advanced Industrial Society* (Boston: Beacon, 1966).

45. For a fine analysis of King's use of space, archetypes, and "rhetorical distance" in "Letter from Birmingham Jail," see Michael Osborn, "Rhetorical Distance in

"Letter from Birmingham Jail,'" *Rhetoric and Public Affairs* 7 (2004): 23–36.

46. Antczak, "Silence," 142.

47. Thomas Farrell, *Norms of Rhetorical Culture* (New Haven: Yale University Press, 1993), 71.

48. Ibid.

49. Richard Coggins, "Samaritans," in *The Oxford Companion to the Bible*, ed. Bruce M. Metzger and Michael D. Coogan (New York: Oxford University Press, 1993), 671–673.

50. J. Robert Cox, "The Fulfillment of Time: King's 'I Have a Dream' Speech," in *Texts in Context: Critical Dialogues on Significant Episodes in American Political Rhetoric*, ed. Michael C. Leff and Fred Kauffeld (Davis, Calif.: Hermagoras Press, 1989), 200.

51. According to Albert J. Raboteau "African American Christianity has continuously confronted the nation with troubling questions about American exceptionalism. Perhaps the most troubling was this: 'If Christ came as the Suffering Servant, who resembled Him more, the master or the slave?' Suffering-slave Christianity stood as a prophetic condemnation of America's obsession with power, status, and possessions. African-American Christians perceived in American exceptionalism a dangerous tendency to turn the nation into an idol and Christianity into a clan religion. Divine election brings not preeminence, elevation, and glory, but—as black Christians know all too well—humiliation, suffering, and rejection." King's Riverside speech reaffirms Raboteau's observations regarding African-American Christianity, especially the way that tradition nurtures "a critique of national ambition and hubris." See Raboteau, "American Salvation: The Place of Christianity in Public Life," *Boston Review* 30 (2005), http://bostonreview.net/BR30.2/raboteau.html (accessed September 20, 2006).

52. Branch, *At Canaan's Edge*, 597.

53. Ibid.

54. James Boyd White, *When Words Lose Their Meaning: Constitutions and Reconstitutions of Language, Character, and Community* (Chicago: University of Chicago Press, 1984), xi.

55. Robert F. Kennedy, *RFK: Collected Speeches*, ed. Edwin O. Guthman and C. Richard Allen (New York: Viking, 1993), 293.

56. Richard Nixon, "Address to the Nation on the Situation in Southeast Asia," April 30, 1970, in *Public Papers of the President of the United States, 1970* (Washington, D.C.: Government Printing Office, 1971), 409.

From Civilians to Soldiers and Back Again: Domestic Propaganda and the Discourse of Public Reconstitution in the U.S. Treasury's World War II Bond Campaign

James J. Kimble

> In America we are apparently confronting the need to change from a commercial-liberal-monetary nexus of motives to a collective-sacrificial-military nexus of motives as the principle shaping the logic of the nation's efforts.
>
> —Kenneth Burke, November 1942

The chaos and destruction of World War II largely spared the U.S. mainland. Although at times millions of Americans worried about a Japanese invasion or German submarine attacks in domestic harbors, these fears were generally unfounded. Separated from the war fronts by two oceans, most of the public had the luxury of exhibiting a profound "ignorance of war's reality."[1] The vast majority of citizens experienced the devastating events of the conflict as they were filtered through several levels of public discourse, leaving returning soldiers to point out that "the real war will never get in the books."[2]

America's isolation from the war fronts was a significant concern for the Roosevelt administration. Officials constantly worried that the secure population would lose its war focus. Such concerns plagued the administration as early as 1940, when it witnessed the stunning defeat of France by Nazi forces. The utter defeat, believed many of the president's advisors, was due less to German military strength than to a lack of unity among the French.[3] Compounding the problem on the domestic front was the emerging debate between the Committee to Defend America and its rival, the America First Committee. The groups—each founded in 1940—served to organize the isolationist and the interventionist camps, giving voice to partisans on both sides who were powerful, articulate, and passionately committed to their polar positions.[4] Realizing that the unification of such a divided public would be a tremendous challenge if the United States were to end up fighting in the war, the administration began to consider ways to unite the country despite its seclusion from the ongoing conflict.

The government's challenges in uniting the fractious nation, however, were quite significant. In addition to the bitter divide between interventionists and isolationists, the lingering excesses of the previous war ensured that Americans were quite aware that their government was not above using domestic propaganda to attempt to shape public opinion in wartime.[5] These suspicions were so great that Roosevelt's official propaganda agencies—the successive Office of Civilian Defense, the Office of Facts and Figures, and the Office of War Information—failed to gain public trust. By 1943, there was no officially recognized propaganda agency operating on the home front.

Despite these challenges, there is evidence to suggest that public unity during the war became very strong. Geoffrey Perrett argues that the war "was the supreme collective social experience in modern American history," an experience in which "a disparate people was fused into a community."[6] Charles C. Alexander suggests that during the war Americans "felt the greatest sense of national unity and collective purpose in their history."[7] And Allan Nevins points out that "it is universally agreed" that the nation's "unity of sentiment" during World War II was much greater than in previous wars.[8]

The transformation of fractious prewar America into a unified society capable of producing thousands of planes and tanks, millions of rifles and artillery shells, and billions in war funds is startling, to say the least. Such a juxtaposition resembles what anthropologist Victor Turner describes as the transition of societies from structured to antistructural, or from socially divided to socially united. Usually occurring during periods of liminality, or crisis, this transformation signifies the emergence of *communitas*, a strong sense of solidarity that "produces in men their highest pitch of self-consciousness." Here a society's previous structures become flexible, easing or even erasing traditional social distinctions as a group coalesces "within the integuments of myth, symbol, and ritual."[9]

The *communitas* that emerged during the liminal crisis of World War II America had a distinct militaristic flavor. Poster artists began to depict factory workers in military garb, their rivets as rifles. Children found themselves learning under the guidance of the "schools at war" program.[10] And, soon after Pearl Harbor, citizens were told that they, too, needed to "Attack Now!"[11] Although these Americans did not experience a real battlefield, they did experience a *rhetorical* battlefield, complete with a vast national army fighting out the war in factories, fields, offices, and schools. Here was the *home front*, a virtual struggle in which politics, religion, class, and race became secondary to the solidarity of the domestic fighting force.

The pervasiveness of the militarized *communitas* during the war years invites further scrutiny, particularly in light of the fractured community that preceded it. Although Turner believed that *communitas* was usually transitory, organic, and spontaneous, the home front's militarized solidarity lasted for the duration, visible even through its waxing and waning phases.[12] The sheer scale of this virtual mobilization and its maintenance throughout the war years suggests that the government found at least some answers in its prewar quest to find ways to unite the country. George H. Roeder, Jr., agrees with this assessment, arguing that "the preponderance of evidence indicates that the Roosevelt administration was largely successful" in its efforts "to encourage widespread and enthusiastic participation in the war effort."[13]

Unable to rely on its official propaganda agencies to build and maintain this militarized *communitas*, the Roosevelt administration at times found support in a variety of less objectionable propaganda sources. Frank Fox, for example, has shown that the work of the War Advertising Council—a private operation run from Madison Avenue—was frequently done at the behest of government advisors. Gerd Horten has pointed to the importance of radio propaganda on the home front, much of which was produced locally. There were, in fact, many other campaigns, such as those for victory gardens, civilian defense activities, and scrap metal drives. Most of these efforts minimized their connections with the administration's recognized propaganda channels, understanding that citizens were suspicious of such official efforts.[14]

Despite the visibility of these unofficial propaganda campaigns on the home front, however, the Roosevelt administration ultimately found itself relying on a publicity effort centered just blocks from the White House. This effort was the U.S. Treasury and its war bond sales program—a vast and continuous operation that grew to be as much as ten times larger than any other wartime government campaign.[15] The war bond machine emerged in early 1941 from the creative mind of Treasury secretary Henry Morgenthau, Jr. The secretary, a close personal friend of President Roosevelt, recognized that the Nazis' defeat of the French implied a need for greater American unity in case of war. He also recognized that Roosevelt's efforts to create a propaganda agency for that very task were likely to fail.[16] Morgenthau's response was to create the Defense Savings Staff, an arm of the Treasury whose publicly declared aims were to sell bonds to citizens "for defense against present-day methods of aggression" and to "help prevent price inflation."[17] Privately, Morgenthau and Roosevelt both recognized that the program's primary task would be to use its bond publicity to shape public morale.[18] This morale task, however, was rarely discussed explicitly in public, giving the Treasury's propagandists a much better chance of reaching the wary home front than the publicly acknowledged information agencies. Not surprisingly, then, members of the Defense Savings Staff came to feel even before Pearl Harbor that the bond program was "carrying the load of morale work or propaganda . . . in preparing a considerably divided America for war."[19]

This chapter contends that the Treasury's widespread domestic propaganda campaign helped construct the home front's militarized *communitas* by constituting and reconstituting the public at several points during the war years. In so arguing, the chapter offers an important case study in the mechanics of top-down constitutive rhetoric. While the Treasury's campaign was an unusual historical case in some ways, its size, scope, and longevity present an intriguing opportunity to elaborate on two specific ways that such constitutive rhetoric can work to call its subjects into being.

First, an analysis of the war bond campaign's appeals suggests the importance of metaphoric processes to theories of constitutive rhetoric. To this point, the primary machinery of constitutionality has appeared to be *narrative* processes. Such "narrative discourse," argues Jasinski, "helps constitute the ways we speak and act with others."[20] Charland similarly contends that audience identification normally "occurs through a series of ideological effects arising from the narrative structure of constitutive rhetoric."[21] Yet while narratives did play a role in the Treasury's construction of home front *communitas*, this chapter shows that the primary tool of American reconstitution during the war was a systematic cognitive metaphor.

Second, scrutiny of the Treasury's home front campaign highlights how central visual imagery can be in constitutive metaphors. We are beginning to appreciate how important visual texts are to the construction of a public. More precisely, as Robert Hariman and John Louis Lucaites point out, we know that constitutive rhetors can rely on both verbal and visual appeals.[22] The war bond propaganda, however, specifically shows how visual appeals work hand in hand with metaphoric processes. The Treasury's constitutive *communitas*, in other words, emerged from a series of complex metaphors that appeared in both verbal and visual formats— and often both at once. Such iconotexts, to use Peter Wagner's term, offer a glimpse of the resources available to constitutive rhetors, particularly those well versed in propaganda technique and with access to mediated channels of communication.[23]

From a broader perspective, the mechanisms of constitutive rhetoric implicate important ethical considerations. When rhetors constitute audiences, their moral values are on display. As Ronald Walter Greene argues, for example, a text is ultimately "morally responsible for the audiences it affirms and negates."[24] Yet when the text in question emerges from a government agency—and when it takes on the form of widespread domestic propaganda in a context of war—such ethical assessments are all the more vital. The analysis that follows, then, concludes that while the Treasury's war bond appeals served a cause that history generally acknowledges as worthy, both the means toward that end and the constitutive norms modeled in the campaign call the essential ethics of the effort into question.

In reaching these conclusions this chapter draws on public and private archival documents to plot the Treasury's attempts to constitute and reconstitute the American public throughout the war. It shows that the centerpiece of the Treasury's propaganda was a series of metaphoric messages that conflated the missions of at-home civilians and battlefield GIs. This conflation, I argue, was the primary facilitating mechanism underlying the psychological transformation of civilians into home front soldiers during the war, and of their metaphoric return to civilian status near the war's end. The chapter tracks this dynamic conflation through three primary wartime phases: (1) metaphoric congruence; (2) metaphoric irony; and (3) metaphoric reversion. It concludes by returning to the moral implications of the Treasury's constitutive discourse.

Metaphoric Congruence: 1941–1943

Secretary Morgenthau began to construct the war bond machine nearly a year before Pearl Harbor. One of his first acts was to recruit Peter H. Odegard, an Amherst political scientist, to advise the Treasury on its new propaganda role.[25] Odegard quickly focused on ways to unite the fractured public. "In a democratic society," he wrote, "national unity is achieved not by force but by persuasion, not by the liquidation of minority interest groups but by their incorporation into the framework of the nation."[26] The contexts of "modern warfare and modern defense require national mobilization in the literal sense," he argued, concluding that "every man and woman in the nation must contribute in some manner to the common defense."[27]

The problem was how to achieve this unified mobilization. Here Odegard proposed dramatizing the part that home front Americans might play in the war. His thinking is worth quoting at length, since it shaped many of the Treasury's appeals throughout the war:

At a time when national energies . . . are directed toward military and naval objectives it is of the utmost importance that these individuals and groups be related to those ends. We might say: "These are heroes in the factory and on the farm as well as on the drill ground and the battlefield. Soldiers of freedom are to be found in overalls as well as in khaki. Workers operating drills, engines, bending over drawing boards, farmers tilling the soil, women at typewriters, teachers in classrooms, scientists in the laboratory, and mothers in the home, are as truly enlisted in the defense of democracy as the men who carry rifles or the admirals who command the fleet."[28]

Clearly, Odegard was proposing the development of what Roeder calls "the home front analogy," the comparison of domestic people and activities with those on the battlefront.[29] As Odegard concluded in his brainstorming notes, the war bond program needed to "take the people into the camps, air fields and on the ships at sea—either actually or by proxy."[30]

Following this logic, the Treasury's new program quickly became a tremendous publicity effort that militarized the public even as it sold bonds. The campaign's attempts to portray the civilian world in militarized terms initially developed on two main fronts. First, the campaign developed a sense of *metaphoric congruence* through the pervasive use of a primary cognitive metaphor: CIVILIANS are SOLDIERS. Because this device relates "one rich image with one other rich image," it belongs in the category that George Lakoff and Mark Turner have dubbed "image-metaphors."[31] Here, one domain—the source—shapes the way one comes to view the second domain—the target. For example, in the metaphor PEOPLE are PLANTS, what we know about the source domain, PLANTS, structures what we come to see in the target domain, PEOPLE. Through the lens of this metaphor one could describe a human life in terms of plant growth; flowering would correspond with maturation, seeds with offspring, and harvesting (or being cut down) with death. This metaphor allows humans to comprehend descriptions of an individual as "a young sprout," as "in full bloom," or as "withering away."[32] In a similar way, the Treasury's propaganda early in the war attempted to shape an understanding of its target domain, CIVILIANS, in terms of the logic of its source domain, SOLDIERS.

Consider, for example, an editorial cartoon disseminated by the Treasury not long after Pearl Harbor. The cartoon (see figure 1) featured an inset of the bond program's logo—a silhouette of Daniel Chester French's *Minute Man* sculpture, positioned to feature his musket and minimize his plow.[33] The cartoon's central figure, however, was an ordinary civilian, with eyeglasses, a moustache, and even a cigar. This figure was standing in an obvious echo of the *Minute Man*. However, the figure was holding an oversized, rolled-up defense bond in place of a musket. Appropriately, the cartoon's caption suggested that the way to "be an "Up-to-the-Minute-Man" was to purchase bonds, thereby becoming a soldier and crushing the Axis. Or, consider an early Treasury illustration that was used in various versions of war bond publicity. This image portrayed a woman striding determinedly toward the viewer, her shadow cast as a silhouette of the Minute Man, its musket emphasized. "We're Ready, Too," intoned the image—"Buy War Bonds."[34] Such images worked to establish metaphoric congruence between the worlds of the civilian and the soldier. Each depiction offered a new understanding of the domain CIVILIANS by mapping onto it characteristics of the domain SOLDIERS. Thus, viewers could identify themselves as citizens who could, metaphorically at least, join up with a military service, march with the troops, serve with distinction, and earn the respect of other soldiers. And, as the second image implied, this role was available to both home front men and women.

Many of the Treasury's visual appeals worked in symbiotic fashion with accompanying verbal texts, offering additional ways that CIVILIANS were indeed SOLDIERS. To offer just one example, in a December 1942 ad viewers could see Uncle Sam striding forward, flanked by a sailor, a soldier, a nurse, and a worker. Behind them, the image showed a crowd of perhaps one hundred civilians, each marching in Uncle Sam's footsteps, many waving American flags. The image's caption underlined the message: "130,000,000 Americans . . . With *One Thought—One Purpose—* VICTORY!" The explanatory text below offered more reinforcement of this unified martial image, proclaiming, "They asked for it at Pearl Harbor. And today, just twelve months later, we're dishing it out!" "Yes," continued the text, "this 'soft, luxury-loving nation' of ours . . . [has] turned with one thought and one purpose to the grim designs of war."[35] Here the text offered a deeper perspective on the visual mapping between CIVILIANS and SOLDIERS. Not only does the description unite the missions of home front soldiers and battlefield soldiers, it also characterizes the home front's actions as "dishing it out," an implied reference to the violence that soldiers—apparently even home front soldiers—must employ to achieve victory.

These appeals reveal a second metaphoric front in the Treasury's discourse. To make sense of the concept that civilians can enact violence, just as soldiers do, the submetaphor BONDS are WEAPONS is necessary. As the initial image discussed above implied, a bond could serve as a rifle. After all, the bespectacled civilian was carrying an enlarged, rolled-up war bond *in the same position* as the *Minute Man* was holding his musket. The Treasury reinforced this metaphoric congruence between bonds and weapons in as many ways as it could, often equating a number of war bonds with the exact amount of munitions or supplies that it could purchase for the military. For instance, in the first newsreel released for the Second War Loan in early 1943, President Roosevelt asked General George C. Marshall and Admiral Ernest J. King what the $13 billion goal for the drive would mean for the military. Marshall replied that it "would produce more than eighty five thousand" tanks, while King said the navy would probably focus on "aircraft carriers, escort ships, submarines, [and] landing barges." Fittingly, the newsreel's opening title emphasized the direct part that the home front would play in these purchases. It displayed the first half of the drive's slogan—"They Give Their Lives"—with shots of the military in action, then displayed the second half of the slogan— "You Lend Your Money!"—with images of civilian workers producing, presumably, the materiel to be used by the nation's soldiers.[36] In such ways, BONDS became metaphoric WEAPONS, reinforcing the overall suggestion that CIVILIANS were indeed SOLDIERS.

The Treasury's attempts to create metaphoric congruence between the domains of CIVILIANS and SOLDIERS and the domains of BONDS and WEAPONS signified a constitutive element in the war bond program's discourse. To paraphrase Greene, the Treasury's rhetoric *spoke a world* through two distinct constitutive stages.[37] First, the construction CIVILIANS are SOLDIERS performs a rhetorical sleight-of-hand. Its most obvious emphasis is on the transference of properties from source to target. But in the act of referencing the target domain—CIVILIANS—the metaphor instantly treats the existence of that domain as a given. Put another way, in the metaphoric mapping of a people as something else, the people are assumed to be a stable domain to begin with even as they are transformed. If one were to protest the transformation (e.g., "We are *not* soldiers!"), the protest itself would be assuming a stable initial identity (there is no protest of the "we"), meaning that much of the initial constitutive impact is paradoxically within the target domain. This effect is similar to what Charland describes as interpellation, the tendency of ideological discourse to call a particular audience into being even as it implies that that audience existed prior to its recent discursive constitution. In this case, the unity of the home front is assumed to be beyond question, treated as "always already" present.[38] Since the undisclosed "psychological purpose of the Defense Savings Program was national unity,"[39] this initial metaphoric stage was thus offering a powerful vision of home front *communitas*.

Yet in addition to positioning CIVILIANS as a stable subject, the Treasury's early war propaganda presented civilians with *metaphoric possibility*.[40] Here citizens, once accepting the premise of a united people, were offered a vision of what *kind* of people they could be, and what *action* was required for that sort of people. The kind of people they could be was structured by the primary source domain, SOLDIERS. The resulting entailments provided a character blueprint for the newly constituted public. Odegard's initial plans for the war bond program included a list of forty-two "personality traits" that the Treasury was interested in suggesting to its home front citizens. They included such characteristics as "alert," "determined," "vigilant," "unflagging," "unflinching," "dauntless," and "undivided."[41] If Americans accepted the Treasury's metaphoric possibilities, these characteristics circumscribed the sort of people they would become—a fighting force strongly identified with the contemporary depictions of that nation's heroic battlefield soldiers.

The Treasury's metaphoric possibilities thus offered subjects the opportunity to both *become* soldiers and to *enact* that becoming in a concrete way. John Poulakos argues that "the rhetoric of possibility assumes an incomplete universe," one that audiences "must bring closer to completion."[42] Through the metaphor CIVILIANS are SOLDIERS, subjects could perceive that they would hasten their own completion by becoming more soldier-like. Then, through the logic of BONDS as WEAPONS, they would face an immediate telos—to purchase bonds and thereby participate in the collective unity of the home front.[43] In this way, the Treasury constituted the home front both as a fighting unit and, more specifically, as a united group.

Metaphoric Irony: 1944

By late 1943, the Allies were indisputably winning on most battlefronts. While this was good news, the Roosevelt administration recognized that the public's growing assurance of ultimate victory in the war would likely encourage home front apathy or even frustration as the war gradually finished its course.[44] An April 1944 survey appeared to confirm this worry, as 66 percent of those polled agreed that "most people in this country do not take the war seriously enough."[45] Declaring "It's not over yet," the Treasury warned staffers that they would need "to combat this spirit of overconfidence." *"The enemy,"* it suggested with a touch of hyperbole, *"is more powerful today than at the beginning of the war."*[46]

Thus, in early 1944, the Treasury shifted the tenor of its publicity for the continuing war bond program, adopting appeals aimed directly at home front complacency. Hoping to shock the public out of its growing malaise regarding the war, the war bond staff adopted material for the campaign that had previously been censored as unsuitable for public consumption. While such depictions had been, according to Richard W. Steele, "withheld for fear they might unnerve the public," now the Treasury seemed determined to do exactly that.[47] 1944's war bond publicity greeted the home front with grisly and often realistic images and descriptions of combat, injured soldiers, and mangled bodies.

These starker appeals heralded a challenging shift in the central metaphor underlying the Treasury's war bond campaign. By embracing a new approach that one could describe as *metaphoric irony*, the war bond machine was signaling to its home front subjects that they were no longer serving in a valiant manner. True, they were still enlisted in the cause, remaining caught up in the CIVILIANS are SOLDIERS metaphor. Now, however, the war bond propagandists were suggesting that the home front soldiers were failing in their mission; compared to the soldiers on the battlefronts they were, in fact, mediocre soldiers at best.

This unexpected turn in the Treasury's war bond discourse is reminiscent of Kenneth Burke's "over-all ironic formula" that "what goes forth as A returns as non-A."[48] Indeed, the sudden contrast between CIVILIANS and SOLDIERS—even as they continued to be forced into their metaphoric relationship—embodied the classic version of irony: "incongruity between what is expected and what occurs."[49] After some two-and-a-half years of enacting their soldierly roles and being praised for it, now, shockingly, home front soldiers found that their success in fulfilling the mission was wavering badly. From the Treasury's perspective, such a "strategic moment of reversal" seemingly facilitated every civilian's reconsideration of his or her individual contribution to the war effort, and—ideally—a renewed and more intense commitment to the cause.[50] In terms of metaphoric possibility, American citizens could now choose to identify themselves as *poor* soldiers, or to elevate their former status into that of soldiers who were willing to offer truly dramatic sacrifices in the name of the war effort.

The Treasury's 1944 appeals established this tension-filled metaphoric irony with two juxtaposed perspectives. The first perspective implied or even directly stated that the home front was failing in its duties as compared with those on the battlefield. Whether it was boredom, excuses, or just a desire to do something besides help with the war effort, this perspective suggested, civilians on the home front were just not doing their part. One national ad, for instance, featured a GI confronting a dancing couple. "Like to swap night clubs, pal?" he asked with biting sarcasm. For entertainment on the battlefront, he continued, "You got a nice little 4-piece orchestra of Jap mortars, Zeros, machine guns, and your best friend screaming in the next foxhole." He then repeated his invitation: "Come any time, pal. The show goes on all night . . . There's never a cover charge. Not even for the flag they put over you when they carry you out."[51] This ironic and even scornful contrast between the battlefront and the lax home front was visually reinforced by the ad's main image, in which the couple—dressed in formal attire—gazed in open-mouthed shock at the GI, in his helmet and combat fatigues. Whereas previous war bond images had shown a visual equivalence between soldiers and civilians, here there was little but guilty contrast. The ad's message was clear: the home front was in danger of losing its focus, even as America's soldiers continued to do their jobs on behalf of the unfaithful civilians. That the home front might be out enjoying itself *instead of buying bonds*, as the ad suggested, was all the more dramatic given the Treasury's earlier equation of bonds and weapons.

A mid-1944 newspaper advertisement offered a similar contrast between the battlefront and the home front. This one (see figure 2) offered a realistic visual of a GI—injured, dirty, and bloody, lying on a battlefield with barbed wire, tanks, and explosions filling the background. He is lifting his head up to the viewer, one hand outstretched, asking, "Why am I dying?" "I didn't ask to come out here—to live in mud and filth . . . to shoot at and *be* shot!" the text continued in his voice. "I did know that you folks back home were depending upon me to do a job for you—to rid the earth of those hateful forces trying to destroy our way of life. I believed in that. I believed in you. That's why I'm dying." Here the pathetic image of a GI near death was dramatic enough on its own. But even more dramatic was the Treasury's implied message—this soldier was dying *because the home front let him down*. Indeed, the visual showed him without a helmet or rifle, and with tattered clothing, suggesting that more bond purchases might have equipped him properly and saved his life.[52] Again, the contrast between battlefront and home front was glaring, a perspective that must have been quite difficult for those domestic Americans who were used to thinking of themselves as effective soldiers.

This damning perspective on the home front, though, was juxtaposed in the Treasury's 1944 publicity with a second, more redeeming perspective. Symbolized, in part, by the dying soldier's pleading, outstretched hand, the war bond propagandists offered those on the home front a chance to rededicate themselves to the mission by buying more bonds. In this way, the Treasury implied, civilians could turn their backs on complacency and devote themselves more than ever to their soldierly duties. But the cost of this recommitment would be steep. For instance, to be able to receive a Treasury banner proclaiming that a household had sacrificed to purchase extra bonds in the Fourth War Loan drive, the program insisted that civilians would need "to earn it by self-denial, [and] by digging to the quick in order to buy more [bonds]."[53]

The potential for heightened rededication by the home front's slacking soldiers was prevalent in many of the Treasury's 1944 appeals. One national ad portrayed a soldier in the midst of battle, offering an urgent face-to-face message directly to home front viewers. Acknowledging the challenges faced by the civilian-soldiers, he was reassuring, suggesting that "if we all get together and do *all* we can, we'll be over this hurdle and well on our way to complete and crushing victory." The caption for the ad, meanwhile, took a more scolding tone: "Come On America! *It's 1944!*"⁵⁴ Another ad showed a photograph of charging marines in a battle scene on Tarawa, one of the bloodiest battles of the war. Initially contrasting the Marines with the home front, the ad urged, "THINK OF THESE BOYS—AND ASK YOURSELF THIS QUESTION—Which of you—these boys or yourself—could more truthfully have said: 'I'm sorry—I've done all I can?'" After this initial unflattering contrast, however, the ad offered readers a chance to recommit to the cause: "THINK IT OVER—and help get this war over sooner by doing your share." The ad's caption, meanwhile, seemed to speak for both battlefield soldiers and rededicated home front soldiers: "The Command is 'Forward.'"⁵⁵

The ironic contrast of SOLDIERS and CIVILIANS in the Treasury's 1944 discourse constructed what Burke would call "perspective by incongruity."⁵⁶ As Martha Solomon points out, over time humans develop strong orientations that resist differing perspectives. She argues that "new views seem 'impious' to us because they violate our 'sense of what properly goes with what.'" Once forced to examine a contradictory viewpoint, however, the resulting "perspective by incongruity stimulates the receiver to resolve the contradiction, ideally by developing a new set of meanings."⁵⁷ In the Treasury's 1944 propaganda, home front civilians were forced to confront the value of their own exertions as soldiers, and to question whether they were really doing enough for the war effort. Their choices in resolving the contradiction were to reject the CIVILIANS are SOLDIERS metaphor altogether, or, goaded by the Treasury's increasingly demanding tone, to rededicate themselves to the war effort as never before. Having failed once in the government's view, they were offered a chance to push even harder in their war-buying efforts; only in this way could they transcend the contradiction in the Treasury's rhetoric.

From a constitutive perspective, the war bond program's use of metaphoric irony in its 1944 efforts marked a period of revised subjectivity. Charland comments that "tensions in the realm of the symbolic render possible the rhetorical repositioning . . . of subjects."[58] Bonnie J. Dow agrees that some constitutive rhetorics can play a "role in the rhetorical de-construction and re-construction of identity."[59] Here, the Treasury revised its creation of the American home front in a second level of reconstitution. Having been constituted once as a unified group, then reconstituted as home front soldiers, now the public was being reconstituted again, this time as conflicted soldiers who faced a choice of accepting their new characterization as poor soldiers, or of rededicating themselves as *renewed* soldiers who would fight even harder for the cause.

Thus, in 1944's war bond propaganda the Treasury repositioned its subjects in reaction to perceived public apathy and complacence about the war. The war bond program was no longer allowing civilians to purchase a few bonds and thereby feel that they were a vital part of the war effort. Instead, bond propaganda began to portray home front soldiers as *presumptively* contemptible, and made the price for demonstrating otherwise a steep one in terms of money, effort, and sacrifice. As before, the Treasury's reconstitutive rhetoric offered the public metaphoric possibility. But considering the program's ironic contrast between CIVILIANS and SOLDIERS, the home front's choice of which possibility it should take was clear. Perhaps, then, it is not surprising to find that by April 1944 no less than 80 percent of respondents in a national poll agreed that they expected "to have to make more sacrifices" before the war would come to a close.[60] The home front's *communitas*, it seems, had lived through the Treasury's metaphoric irony, emerging as a civilian army even more determined to do its part in the war.

Metaphoric Reversion: 1945

The German army's last desperate attack through the Ardennes Forest—the "Battle of the Bulge"—was halted by Allied forces in mid-January 1945. After this point it was clear that the Nazis would soon be forced to surrender. Although progress in the Pacific theater was not going quite so quickly, most observers agreed that the war was in its final stages. As Nevins wrote a few years later, "Early in 1945 . . . it became clear that the end of the war was in sight."⁶¹ Back home, the Treasury was concerned about the effect of this public perception on the war bond program's agenda. As Ted R. Gamble, the program's national director, wrote, "The problems we face change with the progress of the war. As the war in Europe approaches an end and as it is stepped up in the Asiatic theatre people will come to view their bond-buying in a somewhat different light."⁶²

In truth, the Treasury faced two related challenges in the closing year of the war, each understandable from the perspective of military commanders as the final victory appears to approach. The initial challenge is to motivate soldiers for one more dramatic effort to secure the enemy's defeat. Thus, commanders must cajole the troops in a climactic fashion, asking them for their final and most complete effort so that they can return home as victors. Unfortunately, this difficulty leads to a related challenge, the cognitive transformation of soldiers back into civilians. Logistically, it is relatively easy to take soldiers home from the war zone. But to remove the war zone from the soldiers' minds is another task altogether.

The war bond program faced similar problems regarding its civilian soldiers on the home front. With the war reaching an apparent climax, the Treasury had an overwhelming interest in spurring the public into one last urgent push. Not only was it important to maintain the national *communitas* at the most urgent point of the war, it was also imperative that the purchase of war bonds reach a crescendo to help pay for the dramatic cost of the fight in the Pacific. The idea of a climactic push, however, simultaneously brings with it the idea of a postclimactic resolution. Thus, even as the Treasury portrayed its home front soldiers as nearing a point of ultimate effort, it was at the same time inevitably preparing them for a return to civilian-hood.

This two-part challenge faced by the Treasury's staffers emerged in 1945's war bond propaganda as a kind of *metaphoric reversion*. In this final stage of its central metaphoric mapping, the bond program continued to equate the domains of CIVILIANS and SOLDIERS. Once again, however, it altered the source domain to transform the image of the home front. No longer were CIVILIANS active or engaged soldiers; neither were they painted as mediocre soldiers. In 1945's depictions, home front civilians became *cathartic* soldiers. The word *cathartic* is useful here because it captures the new metaphoric equation's almost entelechial potential for transformation. It is akin to metaphorically describing adolescents as caterpillars—an image that dramatically restructures one's understanding; instead of gawky, uncomfortable individuals, here are people poised on the precipice of transformation, awaiting just the right moment for a miraculous change.

The Treasury's subjects, of course, were not growing into teenhood, but returning to their original civilian status—once they negotiated the final climactic home front push. William H. Rueckert explains such cathartic effects through the analogy of "a work of art," which "can be considered as something which induces tensions in the audience and then resolves them." When a person is exposed to such work, he continues, "the resolution of the work effects a resolution of his own tensions, so that he leaves the work a 'changed man,' having somehow been purged and restored to 'normal' by the cathartic exaltation produced in him." The Treasury's 1945 domestic propaganda, I suggest, used metaphor to encompass both aspects of such a "purgative journey."[63]

The Treasury's initial appeals in the last year of the war focused on constructing its home front soldiers as engaged in one final home front push. In appeal after appeal, the war bond publicity blared its climactic theme. For instance, a sample speech—written by Treasury staff but intended for use by local speakers—declared, "You've gone a long way! Those war loans have nearly completed your job. But . . . ANYTHING SHORT OF SUCCESS IS FAILURE! There is no 'nearly' nor 'almost.'" "Put your money in cheerfully or put your money in grimly," the speech continued, "BUT KEEP BUYING THOSE WAR BONDS UNTIL THE DIVIDEND IS IN!"[64] Similarly, many of the Treasury's advertisements agitated for one final, tremendous effort. "*This is no time for half-way measures!*" boomed one ad. "At this crucial time in the war Uncle Sam is calling on *all* of us to go whole hog—to produce more food, to build more equipment, to do *all* we can to hit the enemy—HARD—without a let-up."[65] "All right, America, let's go!" said another. "We've got our enemies on the run—now we've got to put everything into *one great effort!*"[66] As these examples indicate, the war bond campaign's verbal appeals reached a climactic fever pitch as the war came to a close.

The Treasury's images reinforced these verbal appeals. The ubiquitous illustration of the recent Iwo Jima flag-raising—on posters, in advertisements, on billboards, and nearly everywhere else—was a primary Treasury symbol, with its depiction of an ascendant American flag almost (but not quite) raised in victory. As one ad (see figure 3) using the image declared, "Every American is determined to win the final victory, no matter what the cost!" "Here at home," it continued, "we're engaged in the *greatest*, the most *urgent* War Bond drive of the war. It will take more bond purchases than ever before to put it over the top."[67] Paired with the already-famous Iwo Jima image, the phrase "put it over the top" was an unmistakable suggestion that home front soldiers, too, were helping to raise the flag and, indeed, were nearly done with the task. Another ad featured a middle-aged male civilian's face, grimly looking into the viewer's eyes. Three soldiers, bayonets at the ready, were running toward the viewer in the distance. The civilian's proximity to the evident combat—and the serious determination in his eyes—indicated his direct involvement in the final battle, even as the text proclaimed, "We can, We Must, WE WILL."[68] Such images combined with the Treasury's verbal depictions in much of the 1945 war bond publicity, together portraying a public that was intimately involved in one final, dramatic, climactic effort to win the war as home front soldiers.

At the same time, however, the Treasury's climactic rhetoric in the final year of the war was also sowing the seeds of the domestic soldier's return to being a civilian. Rueckert argues that this kind of "mysterious process" can "function as a rhetoric of rebirth,"[69] and, indeed, in the Treasury's 1945 discourse the rhetorical transformation of home front soldiers back into civilians was ever present, if not always overt. In many cases, this shift appeared in the changed qualities and uses of the bonds themselves. For instance, while in previous years the Treasury's publicity had occasionally visited the idea of war bonds as investments, in 1945 staffers privately decided that the "personal advantages of [war bond] ownership will become increasingly effective as other appeals decline."[70] Bonds were still weapons in some appeals, but more and more often in 1945 they were becoming the bond buyer's ticket to a postwar future. War bonds, proclaimed an editorial written by *Vogue* and disseminated nationally by the Treasury, "will make possible increased purchasing power after the war . . . with the money you save in War Bonds, after the war, you will build and rebuild houses, buy helicopters, cars, radios, [and] ice boxes."[71] "The possibility of an early victory in Europe," added a sample speech, "has aroused in the minds of many people the question as to what is to be done with these savings when the war is over." The speech went on to discuss several objectives clearly targeted at postwar civilians, including the "education of children," the "purchase of a home or a farm," a "plan for self-retirement or increased income in [the] post-war period," and the "establishment of a small business."[72] In such descriptions, war bonds were beginning to show the signs of transformation from their earlier construction as weapons. Meanwhile, those who purchased the war bonds were—even as they engaged in the final push at war's end—portrayed as increasingly involved in the postwar world and their role as civilians in the months and years to come.

The theme of transformation became more poignant after the Japanese surrender in August 1945. At this point the war bond program shifted its primary sales product from *war* bonds to *victory* bonds. The mighty push to end the war was over, and home front soldiers could finally embrace their transition back to civilians. While images of soldiers returning home dominated many of the Treasury's postwar messages, the bond propagandists were also careful to feature civilians adjusting to their new lives after the grueling years of war. "It's up to you and me," intoned a civilian in one advertisement, "to make certain *their* America is strong and prosperous."[73] This voice belonged to a young man, cap tilted back at a jaunty angle, leaning with his arm against the bottom of the image's frame in a friendly, personal way, emphasizing his connection with the viewer. He was referring to two children and a pet dog, all playing under a tree in the near background. Whereas ads featuring these characters during the war might have shown the man with worried or fearful or determined eyes, and the children as endangered or grieving at the loss of a relative to the war, here the three exuded a sense of serenity and of peace. Another advertisement showed a handsome couple greeting a bond sales representative at their front door. During the war years, the images of bond sellers making house calls typically featured an *external* view of the house, thus denying readers a glimpse of the area within. Such external wartime perspectives emphasized the outside world and the struggle it embodied. In this postwar image, however, viewers were comfortably situated *inside* the couple's home, while the only reminder of the war—the bond seller—stood outside in the darkness. Here was another sign of the climactic transformation of those on the home front from soldiers to civilians. As veterans, so to speak, this civilian couple still had responsibilities to the postwar recovery efforts. But their primary focus was now on their home, their life together, and on their postwar future. As the ad's text confirmed, this was the bond program's "last call."[74]

The Treasury's 1945 rhetoric, then, provided a final and climactic series of moments for its metaphoric logic. By reconstructing the relationship between CIVILIANS and SOLDIERS as a cathartic exchange in which the home front army could achieve an entelechial transcendence, the war bond propagandists allowed for a rhetorical space wherein the directionality of its central metaphor actually reversed. Whereas once the domain SOLDIERS served as a source, shaping the target domain CIVILIANS, now—at the ultimate moment of transformation—the domain CIVILIANS became the source, shaping a new target domain: SOLDIERS. To put it another way, the bond program spent much of the war metaphorically depicting civilians in the guise of soldiers. Here, at war's end, those civilians finally reached the apex of their soldier-ness, only to find that the very moment they fully personified the domain SOLDIERS was the same cathartic moment they completed their "purgative journey"[75] and returned to the domain CIVILIANS. Thus, in the postwar world it was now appropriate to say that the final metaphoric reversion had occurred, creating a *new* metaphor: the home front SOLDIERS were now CIVILIANS.

This metaphoric reversion had implications for the constitutive elements of the war bond propaganda. Once again the Treasury had revised the subjectivity of its constituents, continuing its pattern of reconstructing the nature of the home front's *communitas*. In this reconstitution the Treasury's metaphoric irony faded and was replaced with a vision of transcendent home front soldiers. These soldiers were depicted as working toward a final burst of *communitas* to reach what Turner describes as "reaggregation"—the last stage of the liminal process in which "the passage is consummated" and its group of participants "reenters the social structure."[76] Therefore, the war bond propaganda at war's end constituted a public both united by its final militarized mission and readied for a metaphoric demobilization. In both aspects of this ultimate

transformation, the Treasury's reconstitutive propaganda was demonstrating yet again that "the character or identity of the 'peuple' [is] open
to rhetorical revision."[77]

Metaphoric Myopia and the Morality
of Domestic Propaganda

My primary aim in this chapter has been to sketch the important role that
metaphoric processes can play in large-scale constitutive campaigns. The
Treasury's massive war bond operation offers an excellent case in point
because its propaganda worked tirelessly to convince Americans that they
were home front soldiers fighting with war bonds, just as their GIs were
fighting with munitions. The consistent conflation of SOLDIERS and CIVIL-
IANS functioned at the level of role identification, constructing *communitas* because it placed Americans in a common character position. This
sort of identification is, at heart, a matter of metaphoric transformation,
moving identity from one conceptual domain to another.

The war bond metaphors that promoted this identification emerged
in visual as well as in verbal forms. Citizens on the home front could read
about, listen to, and visualize their metaphoric roles in the war. Sometimes,
as in a newsreel, they could do all three at once. These various ways of
constructing *communitas* gave the Roosevelt administration—using the
largest government-sponsored campaign of the conflict—an ever-present
means of influencing the average citizen. The Treasury's effort was, in
other words, a comprehensive campaign that aimed to saturate the home
front with motivational appeals of all sorts, a significant percentage of
them metaphorically reconstituting CIVILIANS in terms of SOLDIERS.

Yet while metaphoric discourse, both verbal and visual, appears to
have been the primary process driving the Treasury's wartime appeals,
there is no doubt that narratives ultimately played a part as well. Once
constituted as home front soldiers, civilians inevitably became part of a
larger story. Early in the war, for instance, the Treasury's implied story line
featured civilians' dauntless participation in the war effort as courageous
soldiers. This ongoing mentality, because it developed a trajectory and
even a plot, was—in at least some respects—a narrative effect.

Still, the Treasury's narratives appear to have emerged from its metaphors in a sort of cause-and-effect relationship. Once the propaganda constructed civilians as a particular kind of soldier, the role itself suggested what kind of narrative trajectory was appropriate for the newly constituted character. To put it another way, the case of the Treasury's war bond propaganda suggests that while constitutive discourse can rely on both metaphors and on narratives, it is the initial metaphoric process that ushers in a narrative trajectory; the rhetoric of possibility puts us into a character's role *before* we are motivated to live that character's story. Richard D. Johnson Sheehan agrees with this perspective, contending that "metaphors serve as a basis for inventing narratives," and even that "the majority, maybe all, of our thoughts and language . . . [is] constituted—or at least shaped—by cultural metanarratives invented through metaphors."[78]

As I have suggested, the Treasury's metaphoric characterizations changed dramatically during the war. These metaphoric shifts required narrative changes as well; when the character changes, so must the story line. Thus, civilians on the home front were initially depicted as dauntless GIs enthusiastically purchasing war bonds to crush the enemy. In 1944 that story line was abandoned as they became mediocre soldiers, moved to participate in the war through guilt and sarcasm, yet still struggling determinedly to keep fighting. At war's end, the mediocre narrative disappeared as civilians suddenly became cathartic soldiers, primed for a tremendous final push in order to transform back into civilians. With each metaphoric change, the associated narrative trajectories had to change, too.

Such metaphoric shifting provided little in the way of continuity for the Treasury's constituted and reconstituted audience. It is evident that each of the Treasury's metaphoric stages offered home front citizens a clear telos: purchase bonds and in the process enact or prove or achieve one's rightful status as a home front soldier. Yet because each stage shifted unpredictably, the associated narratives were necessarily truncated. As a result, civilians on the home front—much like soldiers at the lowest level of a military operation—had a confusing overall picture or rationale for their constructed military persona. The Treasury's constitutive metaphors placed these civilians into a character slot, but provided little ongoing logic for that slot's motivation.

The Treasury's constitutive discourse, then, might have helped produce a sense of what one could call *metaphoric myopia*. The home front soldiers seemingly knew that they had to fight, but the narrow confines of their contextual interpellation militated against careful, responsive thought in the face of the Treasury's ubiquitous propaganda. This reading is consistent with contemporary accounts of the home front's mentality. Nevins, for instance, pointed out that "the mood of the United States in this war differed perceptibly from that in previous conflicts. There was less of parades, brass bands, and fireworks; there was more of grim, determined, businesslike attention to the job."[79] Archibald MacLeish, director of the defunct Office of Facts and Figures, offered a similar perspective, describing many Americans "who are willing, if need be, to die to help their people win it; but who are nevertheless unable to understand clearly, or to imagine precisely, what our victory in this war will be." "American morale during the Second World War," concludes Alexander, "was clearly of the 'practical' type."[80] Evidently, Americans experienced a dogged sense of *communitas* on the home front, but they were often unable to articulate the reasons for their solidarity and why they were struggling to keep it intact. I contend, then, that their metaphoric *communitas* presented an immediate telos but allowed little space for consideration, deliberation, or opportunity for resistance.

This argument prompts a return to the essential question of the morality of the Treasury's home front propaganda. Jacques Ellul believed that "propaganda seeks to induce action, adherence, and participation—with as little thought as possible."[81] This perspective seems to be consistent with the Treasury's reconstitutive efforts. Consider, too, that the war bond program failed to acknowledge publicly its mission to shape home front morale. As I have suggested, this omission allowed the Treasury's messages to reach the public, while the administration's *official* information or propaganda agencies could not. Odegard himself, in fact, admitted early in the war that "one of the principles of propaganda is that you must be unobtrusive as to motive in order to be effective."[82]

In many ways, then, one must offer a negative moral judgment of the Treasury's wartime propaganda activities. After all, here was discourse that seemingly inhibited public deliberation, that reduced the potential for resistance, and that failed to disclose its underlying agenda. As such, the war bond program's attempts to constitute and reconstitute its home front subjects could be seen as essentially immoral, or at least as damaging to the values of public debate and self-determination.

Yet James Boyd White suggests that in making moral judgments about the constitution of communities, one might take into account the interaction between means and ends. Following White, it makes sense to consider whether an action that initially seems morally questionable can become worthy if directed against acknowledged evils.[83] In the context of World War II's domestic propaganda this question becomes rather intriguing. What if the home front had *not* been united, potentially causing morale to crumble, production to plummet, and public resistance to the war to crescendo? Fictional alternative histories often speculate on how an Axis victory in World War II might have shaped the world differently. Not surprisingly, almost all of them paint a very negative vision.[84] More tellingly, after interviewing scores of the war's veterans—including those who served on the home front—Studs Terkel wrote that the conflict "had been a different kind of war." "It was," he concluded, "a 'just war' if there is any such animal."[85] From one important viewpoint, it would seem, the Allied victory was a *moral* one. What happens, then, if one assumes that the Treasury's essentially immoral propaganda operation served a higher, longer-term moral cause?

Such a perspective certainly mitigates some moral criticism of the Treasury's efforts. Yet taking rhetorical ends into account cannot absolve critics from considering rhetorical means. It also cannot absolve rhetors for the possible normative implications of their discourse over the long term. To be specific, when the Treasury's campaign methods resurfaced in other government-sponsored efforts during the Cold War, it was clear that a later generation of propagandists had noted the Treasury's wartime approach, and had elected to use it in another context.[86] Thus, even if the war bond operation's original context provided some moral justification for its methods, the campaign's attempted replication in a later context shows how thinly veiled such a justification can become. It might be true that the war bond campaign ultimately served a higher good, playing an integral role in what Odegard argued was "a people's war."[87] Given the inherent moral questionability of its approach, however, one is led to wonder if there might have been another, more ethical way for the government to direct the war on the home front.

How to Be an Up-to-the-Minute Man

FIGURE 1. The U.S. civilian as a soldier. From the Treasury's *Field Organization Newsletter*, 27 December 1941.

FIGURE 2. In 1944, war bond appeals became starker. From *Ammunition! 5th War Loan Official Daily Newspaper Ads*, [1944]. Courtesy Franklin D. Roosevelt Library.

FIGURE 3. With the end of the war approaching, many Treasury ads relied on urgent appeals. From *America's Greatest Challenge*, [1945]. Courtesy National Archives.

NOTES

1. Michael C. C. Adams, *The Best War Ever: America and World War II* (Baltimore: Johns Hopkins University Press, 1994), 73.

2. Paul Fussell, *Wartime: Understanding and Behavior in the Second World War* (New York: Oxford University Press, 1989), 267.

3. Richard W. Steele, "Preparing the Public for War: Efforts to Establish a National Propaganda Agency," *American Historical Review* 75 (1970): 1641.

4. Lise Namikas, "The Committee to Defend America and the Debate between Internationalists and Interventionists, 1939–1941," *Historian* 61 (1999): 843–863.

5. J. Michael Sproule, "Propaganda Studies in American Social Science: The Rise and Fall of the Critical Paradigm," *Quarterly Journal of Speech* 73 (1987): 63–64.

6. Geoffrey Perrett, *Days of Sadness, Years of Triumph: The American People, 1939–1945* (New York: Coward, McCann and Geoghegan, 1973), 433.

7. Charles C. Alexander, *Nationalism in American Thought: 1930–1945* (Chicago: Rand McNally, 1969), 190.

8. Allan Nevins, "How We Felt about the War," in *While You Were Gone: A Report on Wartime Life in the United States*, ed. Jack Goodman (New York: De Capo Press, 1946), 11.

9. Victor Turner, *Dramas, Fields, and Metaphors: Symbolic Action in Human Society* (Ithaca, N.Y.: Cornell University Press, 1974), 255, 259.

10. Robert W. Kirk, *Earning Their Stripes: The Mobilization of American Children in the Second World War* (New York: Peter Lang, 1994), 87–88.

11. Perrett, *Days of Sadness,* 209.

12. Turner, *Dramas, Fields, and Metaphors,* 274.

13. George H. Roeder, Jr., *The Censored War: American Visual Experience during World War Two* (New Haven: Yale University Press, 1993), 64.

14. Amy Bentley, *Eating for Victory: Food Rationing and the Politics of Domesticity* (Urbana: University of Illinois Press, 1998); Frank Fox, *Madison Avenue Goes to War: The Strange Military Career of American Advertising, 1941–1945* (Provo, Utah: Brigham Young University Press, 1975); Gerd Horten, *Radio Goes to War: The Cultural Politics of Propaganda during World War II* (Berkeley and Los Angeles: University of California Press, 2002); James J. Kimble, "The Militarization of the Prairie: Scrap Drives, Metaphors, and the *Omaha World-Herald*'s 1942 "Nebraska Plan,'" *Great Plains Quarterly* 27 (2007): 83–99; and Elwyn A. Mauck, "A History of Civilian Defense in the United States, 1941–1945," *Bulletin of Atomic Scientists,* August–September 1950, 265–270.

15. Assessments of size are necessarily subjective; however, one of the Treasury's internal studies concluded that the war bond program's posters were displayed in store fronts in numbers greater than the combined total of all other governmental campaigns combined. See Dorwin P. Cartwright to Peter H. Odegard, August 2, 1945, 5, Box 13, Folder 2, Peter H. Odegard Papers, Franklin D. Roosevelt Presidential Library, Hyde Park, N.Y. (Hereafter referred to as "Odegard Papers.")

16. Beginning in the summer of 1940, several members of the administration had encouraged FDR to construct a domestic propaganda agency. The advisors were split over the best way to organize such a program, however, and the president delayed his decision indefinitely (although he eventually created the Office of Civilian Defense the following May). Morgenthau was aware of these discussions, but soon lost patience, planning the defense bond program to both raise funds for a war effort and to raise public morale. In doing so he agreed, in principle, with Secretary of the Interior Harold Ickes, who complained that the administration was doing little or nothing to help bolster domestic morale. See discussion in James J. Kimble, *Mobilizing the Home Front: War Bonds and Domestic Propaganda* (College Station: Texas A&M University Press, 2006), 20–21.

17. Treasury Department, *Defense Savings Bonds and Stamps . . . What They Are and the Part They Play in the Defense Program* (Washington, D.C.: Government Printing Office, 1941), 2, 14. Over the war years, the Defense Savings Staff changed incarnations, becoming first the War Savings Staff, then the War Finance Division. The war bonds were created to help discourage Americans from spending cash (earned in increasing amounts in the wartime economy) on scarce goods needed for the war. Citizens could purchase a $25 bond for $18.75. The Treasury promised to pay purchasers the full face value of the bond after ten years. From 1941 to 1945, the war bond operation raised some $185 billion for the war effort in this way. For more details, see Kimble, *Mobilizing the Home Front*.

18. John Morton Blum, *From the Morgenthau Diaries: Years of War, 1941–1945* (Boston: Houghton Mifflin, 1967), 17.

19. Julian Street, Jr., "High Lights of My Work with Writers and Artists for the Treasury Department," [1946], 2, Box 35, Odegard Papers. This chapter adopts Shawn J. Parry-Giles's definition of propaganda: "strategically-devised messages that are disseminated to masses of people by an institution for the purpose of generating action benefiting its source." See Parry-Giles, "'Camouflaged' Propaganda: The Truman and Eisenhower Administrations' Covert Manipulation of News," *Western Journal of Communication* 60 (1996): 162.

20. James Jasinski, "(Re)Constituting Community through Narrative Argument: *Eros*

and *Philia* in *The Big Chill*," *Quarterly Journal of Speech* 79 (1993): 480.

21. Maurice Charland, "Constitutive Rhetoric: The Case of the *Peuple Québécois*," *Quarterly Journal of Speech* 73 (1987): 134.

22. Robert Hariman and John Louis Lucaites, *No Caption Needed: Iconic Photographs, Public Culture, and Liberal Democracy* (Chicago: University of Chicago Press, 2007), 25. For evidence that constitutive rhetoric can use both verbal and visual texts, Nathaniel I. Córdova, "The Constitutive Force of the *Catecismo del Pueblo* in Puerto Rico's Popular Democratic Party Campaign of 1938–1940," *Quarterly Journal of Speech* 90 (2004): 212–233; and Bernadette Marie Calafell and Fernando Delgado, "Reading Latina/o Images: Interrogating *Americanos*," *Critical Studies in Media Communication* 21 (2004): 1–22. For a detailed explanation of the concept of visual metaphors, see Paul Messaris, *Visual Persuasion: The Role of Images in Advertising* (Thousand Oaks, Calif.: Sage, 1997), 10–17.

23. Peter Wagner, *Reading Iconotexts: From Swift to the French Revolution* (London: Reaktion, 1995).

24. Ronald Walter Greene, "The Aesthetic Turn and the Rhetorical Perspective on Argumentation," *Argumentation and Advocacy* 35 (1998): 25. See also Edwin Black, "The Second Persona," *Quarterly Journal of Speech* 56 (1970): 109–119.

25. Laurence M. Olney, *The War Bond Story* (Washington, D.C.: U.S. Savings Bonds Division, 1971), vii. Odegard was coauthor of a prominent book on national politics, including material describing "the fine art of propaganda." See Peter H. Odegard and E. Allen Helms, *American Politics: A Study in Political Dynamics* (New York: Harper and Brothers, 1938), 545.

26. Peter Odegard to Harold Graves, April 12, 1941, 3, Box 4, Folder 2, Odegard Papers.

27. [Peter H. Odegard], "Every Time of National Crisis," [1941], 4, Box 3, Folder 2, Odegard Papers.

28. Ibid.

29. Roeder, *The Censored War*, 59.

30. [Peter H. Odegard], "Literature" [1941], 1, Box 8, Folder 3, Odegard Papers.

31. George Lakoff and Mark Turner, *More Than Cool Reason: A Field Guide to Poetic Metaphor* (Chicago: University of Chicago Press, 1989), 99.

32. Ibid., 12–14, 6.

33. *Field Organization Newsletter*, December 27, 1941, 2. The Treasury's newsletter reprinted the cartoon from the *Chicago Sun*. On the Treasury's use of the *Minute Man*, see Kimble, *Mobilizing the Home Front*, 26–28, 127–28.

34. "We're Ready, Too," illustration, [1941?] in RG 56, Records of the Savings Bond Division (Including Records of its Predecessor, the War Finance Division), Women's Section, Historical and Promotional Records, 1941–1960, Photographs, Kits, and Posters, Box 9, Folder 7, National Archives, College Park, Md. (Hereafter "National Archives.")

35. "130,000,000 Americans," advertisement, *Des Moines Register*, December 3, 1942, 4.

36. "Continuity for First Newsreel Release for Second War Loan," April 7, 1943, 2–3, 1. Roosevelt Official File 4408, Box 2, Folder 2, Franklin D. Roosevelt Presidential Library, Hyde Park, N.Y.

37. Greene, "The Aesthetic Turn," 24.

38. Charland, "Constitutive Rhetoric," 134.

39. Peter H. Odegard and Jarvis M. Morse, "History of War Finance" (unpublished book manuscript), chap. 2, p. 1, Box 32, Folder 4, Odegard Papers.

40. Kirkwood stresses that "the need to evoke possibilities of the human condition is central to the rhetorical enterprise." Poulakos suggests that the rhetoric of possibility "is necessarily metaphorical." William G. Kirkwood, "Narrative and the Rhetoric of Possibility," *Communication Monographs* 59 (1992): 32; John Poulakos, "Rhetoric, the Sophists, and the Possible," *Communication Monographs* 51 (1984): 224.

41. [Peter H. Odegard], "Selected List of Personality Trait Names," [1941], 4, Box 8, Folder 3, Odegard Papers.

42. Poulakos, "Rhetoric," 223.

43. Here I am using *telos* in the Aristotelian sense, to mean an end, or inherent purpose.

44. Richard W. Steele, "News of the 'Good War': World War II News Management," *Journalism Quarterly* 62 (1985): 712.

45. Hadley Cantril, *Public Opinion: 1935–1946* (Princeton, N.J.: Princeton University Press, 1951), 484.

46. "It's Not Over Yet," *The Minute Man*, 15 Jan. 1944, 12.

47. Steele, "News of the 'Good War,'" 712.

48. Kenneth Burke, *A Grammar of Motives* (Berkeley and Los Angeles: University of California Press, 1969), 517.

49. Karen A. Foss and Stephen W. Littlejohn, "*The Day After*: Rhetorical Vision in an Ironic Frame," *Critical Studies in Mass Communication* 3 (1986): 328.

50. Burke, *A Grammar of Motives*, 517. See a deeper development of this point in Kimble, *Mobilizing the Home Front*, 75–84.

51. "Like to Swap Night Clubs, Pal?" advertisement, [1944], in RG 56, Records of the

Savings Bond Division (Including Records of its Predecessor, the War Finance Division), Records of the Field Directors, 1941–47, vol. 42, National Archives.

52. "Why Am I Dying?" advertisement, in Treasury Department, War Finance Division, *Ammunition! 5th War Loan Official Daily Newspaper Ads* (Washington, D.C.: Government Printing Office, [1944]), 12, Box 11, Folder 5, Odegard Papers.

53. "Your Copy Theme Is . . . 'Sacrifice—To Buy Extra War Bonds,'" in Treasury Department, War Finance Division, *4th War Loan Campaign Book* (Washington, D.C.: Government Printing Office, [1944]), 3, Box 11, Folder 5, Odegard Papers.

54. "Come On America! *It's 1944!*" advertisement, *Washington Evening Star*, January 31, 1944, A3.

55. "The Command is 'Forward,'" advertisement, *Tucson Daily Citizen*, January 17, 1944, 7.

56. Kenneth Burke, *Permanence and Change: An Anatomy of Purpose*, 3rd ed. (Berkeley and Los Angeles: University of California Press, 1984), 90.

57. Martha Solomon, "Ideology as Rhetorical Constraint: The Anarchist Agitation of 'Red Emma' Goldman," *Quarterly Journal of Speech* 74 (1988): 187. Solomon is quoting Burke, *Permanence and Change*, 74–75.

58. Charland, "Constitutive Rhetoric," 147.

59. Bonnie J. Dow, "AIDS, Perspective by Incongruity, and Gay Identity in Larry Kramer's '1,112 and Counting,'" *Communication Studies* 45 (1994): 227.

60. Cantril, *Public Opinion*, 1179. The Treasury's difficult rhetorical posturing might have had a negligible impact on war bond sales; during 1944 sales of bonds leveled off compared to earlier points in the war. See Kimble, *Mobilizing the Home Front*, 68–71.

61. Nevins, "How We Felt," 24.

62. Ted R. Gamble, foreword, in Treasury Department, War Finance Division, *Forward to the Seventh War Loan* (Washington, D.C.: United States Treasury, [March 1945]), 3.

63. William H. Rueckert, *Kenneth Burke and the Drama of Human Relations*, 2nd ed. (Berkeley and Los Angeles: University of California Press, 1982), 25–26.

64. "Victory is Your Business," speech text, in Treasury Department, War Finance Division, *For Speakers Only—7th War Loan* (Washington, D.C.: Government Printing Office, [1945]), 19.

65. "This is No Time for Half-way Measures!" advertisement, in Treasury Department, War Finance Division, *America's Greatest Challenge: The Big 7th War Loan Advertising Portfolio for Daily Newspapers* (Washington, D.C.: Government Printing Office,

[1945]), 9, in RG 56, Records of the Savings Bond Division (Including Records of its Predecessor, the War Finance Division), Publicity and Promotion Division—War Loan Drives—Promotional Material, Box 1, Folder 6, National Archives.

66. "Give 'em the Gun in the MIGHTY SEVENTH," advertisement, in Treasury Department, War Finance Division, *America's Greatest Challenge*, 10.

67. "Americans! *Victory Can't Wait!*" advertisement, in Treasury Department, War Finance Division, *America's Greatest Challenge*, 7.

68. "We Can, We Must, WE WILL," advertisement, *Bismarck Tribune*, May 16, 1945, 2.

69. Rueckert, *Kenneth Burke*, 27.

70. Treasury Department, War Finance Division, *Forward to the Seventh War Loan*, 11.

71. "An Editorial," in Treasury Department, War Finance Division, *For Speakers Only*, 4.

72. "What Your War Bonds Mean to Uncle Sam," speech text, in Treasury Department, War Finance Division, *For Speakers Only*, 9.

73. "It's Up to You and Me," advertisement, *Bismarck Tribune*, November 16, 1945, 2.

74. "Last Call, Neighbor!" advertisement, *Bismarck Tribune*, November 14, 1945, 8. For an example of an exterior sales call, "Welcome Him When He Knocks at Your Door," advertisement, [1944], in RG 56, Records of the Savings Bond Division (Including Records of its Predecessor, the War Finance Division), Records of the Field Directors, 1941–1947, vol. 42, National Archives.

75. Rueckert, *Kenneth Burke*, 26.

76. Turner, *Dramas, Fields, and Metaphors*, 232.

77. Charland, "Constitutive Rhetoric," 136.

78. Richard D. Johnson Sheehan, "Metaphor as Hermeneutic," *Rhetoric Society Quarterly* 29 (1999): 48, 61.

79. Nevins, "How We Felt," 8.

80. Quoted in Alexander, *Nationalism in American Thought*, 192. Alexander is paraphrasing Herbert Blumer here, but he provides no citation.

81. Jacques Ellul, *Propaganda: The Formation of Men's Attitudes* (New York: Vintage, 1965), 180. Note that Ellul views propaganda as almost any widespread communication, including, for instance, "public and human relations" (xiii).

82. Peter H. Odegard, "Strategies of Political and Moral Warfare" (panel discussion, University of Virginia, Charlottesville, July 9, 1942), 15–16, Box 20, Folder 4, Odegard Papers.

83. James Boyd White, *Heracles' Bow: Essays on the Rhetoric and Poetics of the Law* (Madison: University of Wisconsin Press, 1985), 4–5.

84. One recent example of this common genre is Philip Roth's *The Plot against America* (New York: Houghton Mifflin, 2004), which constructs a very clear picture of the moral nature of the actual historical victory over the Axis.

85. Studs Terkel, *"The Good War": An Oral History of World War Two* (New York: Ballantine, 1984), 13.

86. See Kimble, *Mobilizing the Home Front*, 135.

87. Peter H. Odegard, untitled message, in Treasury Department, War Finance Division, *For Speakers Only*, 11.

6

Constituting Benevolent War and Imperial Peace: U.S. Nationalism and Idyllic Notions of Peace and War

Shawn J. Parry-Giles

During a commencement address at American University on June 10, 1963, President John F. Kennedy voiced a commonplace of U.S. foreign policy: "The United States, as the world knows, will never start a war."[1] President Ronald Reagan issued a similar edict during a March 23, 1983, speech on national security in an intensifying Cold War context—"The defense policy of the United States is based on a simple premise: The United States does not start fights. We will never be the aggressor."[2]

Of course, many can identify situations where the U.S. government did initiate acts of aggression—the CIA ousting of President Jacobo Arbenz Guzman from Guatemala in 1954;[3] the charge that U.S. soldiers fired the first shots in the Gulf of Tonkin;[4] and the 1986 "preemptive action against [Libyan] terrorist installations."[5] Most recently, though, a movement toward a more emboldened doctrine of preemption is visible in the public discourse and military actions of the George W. Bush administration. Bush argued in his 2003 State of the Union speech that "some have said we must not act until the threat is imminent. Since when have terrorists and tyrants announced their intentions. . . . If this threat is permitted to fully and suddenly emerge, all actions, all words, and all recriminations would come too late."[6] In response to charges that he acted without the support of the United Nations and allies like France and Canada in the Iraq war, Bush promised in his 2004 State of the Union address that "America will never seek a permission slip to defend the security of our country."[7]

Although President Bush and his supporters believed that the terrorist attacks on September 11, 2001, warranted such preemptive measures, Bush's Democratic rivals in the 2004 presidential primary challenged the president's preemptive actions in the Iraq conflict. Senator John F. Kerry (Mass.) noted in a speech before the Council on Foreign Relations, "We have a President who has developed and exalted a strategy of war—unilateral; pre-emptive; and in my view, profoundly threatening to America's place in the world and the safety and prosperity of our own society."[8] During an October 23, 2003, address to the Center for American Progress, General Wesley Clark responded to the Bush administration's policies: "We are not a nation that disdains our allies or starts wars without just cause. That is not who we are. America was born to end all that."[9]

Such arguments that our presidents or our presidential candidates offer about peace and war are significant. As Mary E. Stuckey asserts, the president acts as the nation's "interpreter-in-chief. He tells us stories about ourselves, and in so doing he tells us what sort of people we are, how we are constituted as a community."[10] By examining the chronological constructions of peace and war by presidents in the context of U.S. nationalism, this essay reveals how their historical, ideological, and discursive legacies created an institutional logic that prepared the way for a preemptive doctrine at the turn of the twenty-first century. Such a logic was predicated on the shared beliefs that exalted a sense of American exceptionalism because of the nation's commitment to democratic principles. As John Collins and Ross Glover assert, "Processes of meaning-making don't happen overnight; rather, they happen historically, through repeated . . . and generally selective usage."[11]

Progressing from George Washington through George W. Bush, this chapter assesses the influence of a nineteenth-century construction and commitment to benevolence in addressing matters of the nation's "others"—African Americans, Native Americans, and immigrants—a rhetorical legacy that reappears in twentieth-century *war* discourse. As the rhetoric of the Cold War takes shape, *benevolent war* constructions exist alongside rhetorics of an *imperial peace*. So as to combat images of an aggressor nation, a discourse of benevolence integral to the idealism of American exceptionalism functions to temper American commitments to militarism. Yet, because of the perceived equation of peace with weakness and war with strength, linguistic usages of peace assume a more imperial focus, where commanders-in-chief accentuate U.S. supremacy and power, another key discursive image of American exceptionalism.

Such connections of peace with weakness and war with power also exhibit a gendering of U.S. war rhetoric, as peace is often discursively feminized or demasculinized and war is masculinized. The chapter further demonstrates how references to peace in certain instances during the Cold War reflect a language of morality, honor, truth, cooperation, idealism, submissiveness, and piety, traits often associated with women's "essence" and their contributions to U.S. political culture.[12] In contrast, war images assume characteristics of power, strength, and decisiveness, attributes that have defined the so-called nature of men throughout U.S. history. These depictions reflect an anxiety over peace because of its linguistic feminizations and demasculinizations in international relations, encouraging an emboldened rhetoric of power that prompts doctrines of preemption. Ultimately, such language use is constitutive, particularly of public morality. As Robin Tolmach Lakoff explains, "Language is just air after all—it is not a gun. . . . Yet it changes reality."[13]

In the end, this chapter demonstrates the symbiotic and contested relationship between war and peace, a historical and contemporary commitment to the masculinization of the presidency, and the use of peace and benevolence to justify U.S. exceptionalism, preemptive commitments, and acts of aggression against nations of color in particular. Such a discourse helps form the foundation of moral responsibility integral to the social contract as the government acts to secure its people with an all-empowered military force; the role of the American people in turn is to unify around such military efforts. As J. Ann Tickner explains, out of this militarized nationalist context, the "valorization of war" occurs.[14]

U.S. Benevolence and Commitments to Peace and War

Precedents were established early in U.S. history that vested decisions over foreign policy in the office of the presidency.[15] As presidents committed themselves to neutrality in international relations, they simultaneously evidenced imperialist acts and arguments, especially in relation to African Americans, Native Americans, and immigrants. A discourse of benevolence worked to justify such imperial actions—arguments that began to infiltrate U.S. foreign policy rhetoric by the twentieth century. In the end, benevolent war arguments coexisted with notions of an imperial peace during the Cold War, demonstrating the contestation over matters of peace and war in U.S. foreign policy rhetoric.

Presidents found themselves embroiled in many external conflicts early on, and this external focus helped fashion U.S. nationalism. Publicly, several presidents committed themselves to neutrality on matters of foreign policy unless such affairs affected the United States directly. President George Washington, of course, called for "holding a neutral conduct" on European matters because of the dangers associated with "a passionate attachment of one nation for another [that] produces a variety of evils."[16] In addition to large-scale wars such as the War of 1812, where President James Madison declared that Great Britain "Abandon[ed] . . . respect for the neutral rights of the United States . . . on the high seas,"[17] there were smaller military excursions that often involved battles at sea over trading and piracy.[18] Such conflicts, while designed to protect U.S. economic interests, can be viewed as the initial stages of U.S. imperialism. The Monroe Doctrine, issued by President James Monroe on December 2, 1823, ostensibly was designed to declare America's neutrality in European skirmishes and to dissuade against future colonialist actions in the Western Hemisphere. It likewise exhibited the country's "imperialist tendency" in "anti-imperialist" terms, Michael Hardt and Antonio Negri contend;[19] Monroe announced, for example, that "any attempt" to "extend their [Europe's] system to any portion of this hemisphere [was] dangerous to our peace and safety" and would be viewed as an invasion of *American* "rights."[20]

Even before and certainly after the United States declared its protectionist interests in the Americas, presidents exhibited expansionist tendencies. By the beginning of the Civil War, the United States had acquired new territory from the Louisiana Purchase (1803), and the Mississippi (1804), Orleans (1804), Michigan (1805), Illinois (1809), and Indiana (1809) territories. The Texas Annexation occurred in the same year as the acquisition of the Oregon territories (1845), and the Mexican cession followed three years later (1848). Albert K. Weinberg links America's expansionist activities to "the evolution of American nationalism," in which the "moral doctrines that have been advanced in justification of this extension of the national domain [are espoused] at the expense of other and—usually weaker—peoples."[21]

Within this expansionist context, the ideology of "Manifest Destiny" was popularized at a time when a discourse of nationalism and benevolence flourished in the pre–Civil War era. Manifest destiny is a concept attributed to John O'Sullivan,[22] who as the editor of the *Democratic Review* declared in 1839, "The far-reaching, the boundless future will be the era of American greatness. . . . Its floor shall be a hemisphere—its roof the firmament of the star-studded heavens, and its congregation an Union of many Republics . . . governed by God's natural and moral law of equality."[23] Manifest destiny principles were associated most commonly with those of "Anglo-Saxon, Protestant roots," which were granted "the divine right 'of united white people' to govern the entire continent."[24] Vanessa B. Beasley explains that "because the American people have never been characterized by the level of ethnic or religious homogeneity that has historically marked . . . most other nations, Americans have always had to imagine their national political community in alternative . . . ways."[25] Manifest destiny and a commitment to benevolence were key ideologies in that national identity project.

Such a sense of moral and religious superiority helped propel America's missionary spirit. The commitment to benevolence became a major part of U.S. nationalism as Americans embarked on "religious work, medical work, relief work, and political activism . . . throughout the world."[26] Benevolent topoi, Gordon S. Wood proclaims, were grounded in the Enlightenment and the American Revolution, which encouraged "educated and enlightened people . . . to secularize Christian love and find in human nature itself a scientific imperative for loving one's neighbor as oneself."[27] Yet Joseph Conforti refers to such actions of spreading a white Anglo-Saxon version of Christianity as "disinterested benevolence," where the greater emphasis was placed on testing one's own holiness rather than on successfully aiding "others," who were often viewed as incapable of achieving salvation or civilization.[28]

Benevolent commitments were soon used to justify the colonization of free blacks. The American Colonization Society (ACS) was formed in 1816 to colonize blacks in Africa[29]—a plan that attracted the support of such presidents as Thomas Jefferson, James Madison, John Quincy Adams, and Abraham Lincoln.[30] For some, acts of slavery were viewed benevolently as a means to "Christianize" the genetically "inferior" Africans.[31] Colonization efforts were likewise understood in benevolent terms; John H. B. Latrobe of the ACS argued that "Africa will be civilized, and civilized by the descendants of those torn from the land," spreading "over this vast continent . . . civilization and gospel."[32] Segregation, of course, represented the eventual alternative to colonization, acting as the means, Kirt H. Wilson argues, "to keep blacks in carefully controlled spaces."[33]

Benevolent moralities and "ethnocultural" commitments also reified the treatment of Native Americans. Early political leaders often expressed guilt over Native American removal, Rogan Kersh suggests, yet by 1820, "an era of removal" emerged that "featured little of the discomfort expressed by . . . constitutional framers."[34] While George Washington viewed American Indians as foreigners who necessitated the creation of treaties, Thomas Jefferson instituted the notion of civilizing the Native Americans, transforming them from savages to productive inhabitants of the nation.[35] President Andrew Jackson, however, grew impatient with the civilization experiments and instead inculcated a rhetoric of benevolence, championing the 1830 Indian Removal Act in such terms. He argued during his "Second Annual Message" to Congress: "It gives me pleasure to announce to Congress that the benevolent policy of the Government . . . in relation to the removal of the Indians beyond the white settlements is approaching to a happy consummation."[36]

While the republic attended to matters of relocation and Reconstruction after the Civil War, immigration increased and the nation's boundaries expanded. Kersh asserts that these forces magnified the "notions of national union limited to a divinely chosen, homogeneous white American 'race.'"[37] While still committed to benevolence, Lucy Hayes's post–First Lady speech to the Woman's Home Missionary Society evidences the fears over increased immigration in the latter half of the nineteenth century: "The cornerstone to practical religion is the Golden Rule. . . . We would reflect on no other benevolent enterprise. . . . [Yet] the stream of unchristian tendencies from abroad and the flood of indifference and vice of our own country, shall overwhelm the institutions of our fathers, the missions of every Christian Church, both home and foreign, will suffer alike by the common calamity."[38] Sharing such concerns, Theodore Roosevelt called for "Americanizing . . . the new-comers to our shores. . . . We must Americanize them in every way, in speech, in political ideas and principles, and in their way of looking at the relations between Church and State."[39] Gary Gerstle suggests that Roosevelt "subscribed to the racial notion that America, despite its civic creed, ought to maximize the opportunities for its 'racial superiors' and limit those of its 'racial detractors.'"[40]

AN ERA OF INTERNATIONAL EXPANSION
IN BENEVOLENT TERMS

As the country prepared to enter the twentieth century, notions of expansionism began to transcend the contiguous lands of North America—the nation's manifest destiny, predicated on an American exceptionalism, inspired the progression into new parts of the world. A rhetoric of benevolence, formerly aligned with missionary acts abroad and marginalized peoples within the nation's borders, became visible in U.S. foreign policy discourse. Such a discourse of war, however, was likewise predicated on a rhetoric of power. The twin commitments of imperialism and benevolence were featured components in U.S. war discourse in the early twentieth century.

Part of the ideological power of manifest destiny and expansionism as key components of U.S. nationalism is linked to what Frederick J. Turner defined as the "frontier thesis." When the Superintendent for the Census declared in 1890 that the frontier regions would no longer be noted in the census reports, Turner identified this policy shift as "the closing of a great historic movement" that acted as a "meeting point between savagery and civilization" and "the line of most rapid and effective Americanization." Linking the frontier to militarization and nationalism, Turner concluded that "the frontier" functioned "as a military training school, keeping alive the power of resistance to aggression."[41] As the nineteenth century came to a close, Amy Kaplan suggests, the "United States shifted from continental expansion to overseas empire, from absorbing new territories into the domestic space of the nation, to acquiring foreign colonies and protectorates abroad."[42]

By the time of the Spanish-American War, when the United States battled a colonial power for control over developing nations of color, presidential discourse reflected the ideologies of imperialism, benevolence, and militarism. Governor Theodore Roosevelt (N.Y.), the eventual vice president for President William McKinley, wrote and spoke about "the strenuous life" in his essay under that title, where he called for the United States to "undertake the task of governing the Philippines," because "their population includes half-caste and native Christians, warlike Moslems, and wild pagans . . . people . . . utterly unfit for self-government." To illustrate his argument, Roosevelt compared the U.S.-Filipino relationship to "England's rule in India and Egypt"; he also argued that if the United States were to "shrink" from the task of governing the Philippines, the country should "leave the Apaches of Arizona to work out their own salvation," to show the absurdity of self-governance in the Southeast Asian country.[43]

McKinley did embark on a four-year-long war to govern the Philippines in the aftermath of the Spanish-American War—what many view as the nation's first battle on international soil outside of the Americas. McKinley also expanded presidential war powers by sending troops to defend against the Boxers in China without congressional approval. McKinley faced formidable opposition from political leaders like William Jennings Bryan.[44] Nonetheless, after McKinley's assassination in 1901, Roosevelt expanded the parameters of the Monroe Doctrine during a speech in Chautauqua, New York, on August 11, 1905, in which he emphasized the nation's benevolent morality: "In the interest of justice, it is as necessary to exercise the police power as to show charity and helpful generosity."[45] Cuba acted as the key example of U.S. military success and was invoked to warrant similar actions in other areas of Latin America. As John Higham claims, Roosevelt's "The Strenuous Life" "sounded the tocsin of a new era."[46]

For Roosevelt, battle readiness was the key component of U.S. nationalism, as he expressed in his 1903 book *American Ideals*: "A peaceful and commercial civilization is always in danger of suffering the loss of the virile fighting qualities without which no nation, however cultured . . . and prosperous, can ever amount to anything. Every citizen should be taught . . . that while he must avoid brawling and quarrelling, it is his duty to stand up for his rights." Roosevelt also conflated the skills of the warrior and politician, declaring, "A politician who really serves his country well and deserves his country's gratitude, must usually possess some of the hardy virtues which we admire in the soldier who serves his country well in the field."[47] Roosevelt's discourse of nationalism was dependent on visions of U.S. moral superiority as ordained by God, justifying American imperialism—often against developing countries populated by persons of color. Kersh maintains that "for the first time apart from actual armed hostilities, patriotic spirit in the late nineteenth century was strongly associated with martial virtue among Americans, especially young men and even boys."[48]

During Woodrow Wilson's presidency, conceptions of American internationalism were conjoined with a benevolent spirit in U.S. foreign policy as the United States joined the battle of the colonial powers. In his war address, Wilson opined that "armed neutrality . . . is impracticable" in relation to the "German Imperial Government" because of the attack on what the British identified as a passenger ship (*Lusitania*) that carried Americans as well as the interception of the German-authored Zimmerman Letter that sought to incite a Mexican insurgence against its northern neighbor. As he called for America's entrance into the Great War, Wilson assured that "we have no selfish ends to serve. We desire no conquest, no domination. . . . We are but one of the champions of the rights of mankind."[49] Similar benevolent undercurrents were visible in Wilson's "14 Points Address" of January 8, 1918, where he asserted, "What we demand in this war . . . is nothing peculiar to ourselves. It is that the world be made fit and safe to live in; and particularly that it be made safe for every peace-loving nation."[50] Alexander DeConde refers to such arguments as the "caregiving aspect . . . of [U.S.] exceptionalism."[51]

World War II furthered the ongoing contest among the colonial powers. Although securing America's safety represented the primary call to war, the legacy of benevolence was still visible. In his Lend-Lease plan of 1940, which was designed to arm the Allies, President Franklin Roosevelt urged, "We must be the great arsenal of democracy. . . . We have no excuse for defeatism. We have every good reason for hope—hope for peace, hope for the defense of our civilization and for the building of a better civilization in the future." For Roosevelt, the Monroe Doctrine's call for neutrality in European matters represented a nineteenth-century relic, because "the width of those oceans is not what it was in the days of the clipper ships . . . today we have planes that could fly from the British Isles to New England and back again without refueling."[52] In his 1942 State of the Union address, FDR's discourse reflected the ideologies of benevolent manifest destiny in wartime: "We are fighting today for security, for progress, and for peace, not only for ourselves but for all men. . . . We on our side are striving to be true to that divine heritage. We are fighting, as our fathers have fought, to uphold the doctrine that all men are equal in the sight of God." U.S. imperialism was further evidenced in FDR's call "to see that the Stars and Stripes will fly again over Wake and Guam."[53]

The persistent militarism of U.S. nationalism helped expand the power of the executive branch during the twentieth century and reify the relationships among war, nationalism, and the presidency. Forrest McDonald identifies Wilson's and Franklin Roosevelt's "war powers" actions during World War I and II as reaching "near" or, in the case of FDR, actually achieving "truly dictatorial powers."[54] Of Roosevelt, Erwin C. Hargrove writes that his views of "international relations were a blend of the realism of Theodore Roosevelt, who recognized the importance of national power in a lawless world, and the idealism of Woodrow Wilson, who envisioned the United States as the apostle of peace and law among nations." FDR likewise evinced an ability to "misuse the powers of the presidency if institutions did not restrain him," as in the case of the Lend-Lease program of World War II,[55] which he implemented secretly before achieving congressional approval. Such presidential prerogatives had considerable consequences for foreign policy matters, where the president is given extensive authority. The increased power of the presidency occurred at a period when the "nation-state tide reached full flood," Benedict Anderson contends, where the European and American models of nationalism exhibited "the legacy of imperialist official nationalism."[56] Such a vision of an all-empowered nation was most explicit in the Cold War discourse of the United States.

Cold War Realism, Benevolent War, and Imperial Peace

In part, the presidential rhetoric of the Cold War reflected a commitment to an all-empowered nation, reflective of the realist notions of U.S. foreign policy. Such realist tendencies, however, were tempered by the rhetoric of benevolence—discursive legacies traceable to the nineteenth-century missionary spirit. In explicating the tenets of realism, Francis A. Beer and Robert Hariman refer to the "narrative of world politics," which is rooted in classical and medieval governments and appears as a "natural outgrowth of the . . . formation of the nation-state," expressing the "permanent essence of politics between nations."[57] Benjamin Frankel details the "theories in the realist family" that share the common assumption that "international politics" represents a "constant struggle for, and conflict over, power and security," as nations attempt to "protect and preserve themselves in an anarchic environment in which dangers to security and welfare are always present."[58] As Tickner argues, "Realists believe that, in an anarchical world of sovereign, self-interested states, war is always a possibility; therefore, states must rely on their own power and capabilities rather than international agreements to enhance their national security."[59]

The presidential rhetoric of the Cold War helped reify the nation's superpower status, which required a perpetual renewal of U.S. military prowess to help protect domestic and international peace. In a June 1963 speech in Frankfurt, Germany, Kennedy called for a "united strength" to work toward "real peace between us and the Communists." He warned, though, that "We will not be second in that effort."[60] President Lyndon B. Johnson spoke of America as the "most powerful of all nations,"[61] a national creed that required "the strong [to] help the weak defend their freedom."[62] For President Richard M. Nixon, such "strong military defenses" represented "not the enemy of peace" but "the guardians of peace";[63] they helped "prevent a third world war for more than a generation," President Gerald R. Ford concluded.[64] President Jimmy Carter's words in his 1978 State of the Union address reflected the underlying assumptions at work in U.S. foreign policy during the Cold War period: "Because we are strong, our Nation is at peace with the world."[65]

So as to temper charges of imperialism during the Cold War, benevolent images of war dominated presidential justificatory discourse, reflective of arguments posited by Wilson and Roosevelt decades earlier. As Jean Pickering and Suzanne Kehde assert, "In times of change or crisis, nations look to the past and infer a narrative that erases all confusion and contradiction."[66] In his March 12, 1947, address that enunciated what later came to be called the Truman Doctrine, President Harry Truman remarked, "The free peoples of the world look to us for support in maintaining their freedom. If we falter in our leadership, we may endanger the peace of the world."[67] Extending such expressions during his inaugural address of January 20, 1949, Truman assured the nation: "We have sought no territory. We have imposed our will on none. We have asked for no privileges we would not extend to others. . . . Our efforts have brought new hope to all mankind."[68] Johnson made similar arguments in relation to the Vietnam conflict: "We covet no territory, we seek no domination, we fear no nation, we despise no people. With our arms we seek to shelter the peace of mankind."[69] Nixon went so far as to suggest that "never in history have men fought for less selfish motives—not for conquest, not for glory, but only for the right of a people far away to choose the kind of government they want." Nixon, like Ford, accentuated the benevolent acts of the United States in Vietnam and elsewhere in the world, which involved "building schools, roads, hospitals, clinics,"[70] evidencing "a compassionate America, its heart reaching out to orphans, to refugees, and to our fellow human beings afflicted by war, by tyranny, and hunger."[71]

A rhetoric of imperialism framed in benevolent terms also carries into the post–Cold War period as U.S. presidents justify new U.S. foreign policy actions in similarly munificent terms. In portraying the U.S. mission in the Persian Gulf War, President George H. W. Bush argued: "We went halfway around the world to do what is moral and just and right. . . . We lifted the yoke of aggression and tyranny from a small country that many Americans never even heard of, and we ask nothing in return."[72] President Bill Clinton hailed the country's heroic actions that "saved the world from tyranny in two World Wars and a long Cold War, and time and again reached out across the globe to millions who, like us, longed for the blessings of liberty."[73] Finally, President George W. Bush also offered benevolent depictions of contemporary U.S. foreign policy goals: "We have no desire to dominate, no ambitions of empire. Our aim is a democratic peace."[74] The discursive legacy of the Cold War, Robert L. Ivie contends, "is a tragic framework of interpretation that constitutes the perils of hubris in the image of a heroic nation struggling globally to redeem itself by contesting the relentless forces of chaos and establishing a New World Order."[75] Such actions evidenced, Michael Rogin contends, "the imperialist tendencies of the United States, where foreign policy is conducted by theatrical events—Grenada invasion, Libyan bombing, Persian Gulf flagging . . . [where] their significance lies less in stopping the local spread of 'Communism' than in convincing elite and mass publics that America has the power to have its way."[76]

THE FORCE OF AN AMERICAN PEACE

To justify U.S. interventions in these developing nations, the United States also pledged a commitment to peace, which seemingly distinguished the nation from its Cold War opponent to further miligate against claims of imperialism. Yet, because of the perceptions of weakness associated with peace, an American peace was portrayed in more empowering terms. As Kennedy asserted, "Even the Soviets could not objectively regard our resumption of [nuclear] tests . . . as provocative" because "our reasons for testing and our peaceful intentions are clear."[77] Such an assumption is premised on the "democratic peace theory," where peace is understood "as a function of a more robustly democratic internationalism," Ivie explains.[78] Yet as the Cold War progressed, anxieties about "peace" became visible in presidential discourse; after all, the absence of war did not ensure U.S. safety in the battle between democracy and communism. In this context of heightened tension, peace assumed qualities of weakness and was marginalized at times, reflective of common realist assumptions.[79] President Dwight D. Eisenhower's Psychological Strategy Board noted in July 1953, for example, that "no good policy was ever made with either peace or compromise as its main ingredient."[80] In his memoirs, *The Vantage Point*, President Lyndon Johnson relayed a comment from Clark Clifford, advisor to Presidents Truman, Kennedy, and Johnson: "Any objective citizen knows the government's position. Talk of peace is interpreted as a sign of weakness."[81] Nixon talked also of the "peace of humiliation" and a "flimsy peace" in his Vietnam discourse.[82] In his 1985 book, *No More Vietnams*, Nixon argued that "any nation [that] decides the way to achieve peace is to use only peaceful means is a nation that will soon be a piece of another nation."[83] Such a position of "national weakness," Carter argued, "can tempt aggression and thus cause war";[84] similarly, Reagan suggested that a weakened state "only invites aggression."[85] Explaining the presidential logic, Tickner asserts that "the valorization of war . . . depends on a . . . devalued notion of peace as seen as unattainable and unrealistic."[86]

The alternative when speaking of the ultimate goal during the Cold War was to portray peace with metaphors of power and strength. In a speech to the United Nations in 1963, Kennedy spoke of peace as a "weapon" and of the "peacekeeping machinery" required during the Cold War.[87] Presidents often equated peace with a "competition";[88] others sought to "win the peace"[89] while still others like Reagan popularized the phrase "peace through strength."[90] Clinton noted that "We will stand mighty for peace and freedom";[91] George W. Bush called for a "durable peace."[92] Speculating about the future of peace constructions, Francis A. Beer argues that "peace may be the name of the overarching framework of great-power relations within which smaller creatures may still fight and the elephants may occasionally trample the ants and the grass."[93]

In furthering America's authority, idyllic images of an imperial peace were common in presidential discourse, ensuring that the nation would not only lead the world during wartime but also maintain such power in times of greater tranquility. Johnson speaks of an "American covenant" that "called on us to help show the way for the liberation of man."[94] In his State of the Union message of 1970, Nixon invoked the ideals of manifest destiny in prayer-like fashion, proclaiming, "May God give us the wisdom . . . so that America can fulfill its destiny of being the world's best hope for liberty, for opportunity, for progress and peace for all people."[95] Reagan similarly hails the ideology of manifest destiny, which ordained the United States with the leadership role for all time: "We raise our voices to the God who is the Author of this most tender music . . . as we fill the world with our sound . . . one people under God, dedicated to the dream of freedom that He has placed in the human heart, called upon now to pass that dream on to a waiting and hopeful world."[96] In justifying the bombing of Iraqi military installations, Clinton argued, "we'll have a remarkable opportunity to shape a future more peaceful than the past."[97] Such a rhetorical legacy conjoining manifest destiny, imperialism, and U.S. exceptionalism reified the idyllic beliefs of American nationalism— beliefs that are likewise reflected in George W. Bush's conceptualization of the Iraq war: "The goal of a free and peaceful Iraq unites our coalition. And this goal comes from the deepest convictions of America. The freedom you defend is the right of every person and the future of every nation. This liberty we prize is not America's gift to the world; it is God's gift to humanity."[98] Such reliance on an ideology of manifest destiny that hails a "theological image," Lyon Rathbun asserts, is "reassuring to anxious Americans"[99] in times of international conflict and nervous tranquility.

When presidents work to reify an ideology of "manifest destiny," they locate the source of their power in a higher, extra-constitutional authority. Such age-old discursive strategies function to justify U.S. acts of aggression, even preemptive ones. Focusing exclusively on arguments made about the Middle East, Carter threatened in his 1980 State of the Union address that "An attempt by any outside force to gain control of the Persian Gulf region will be regarded as an assault on the vital interests of the United States . . . and such an assault will be repelled by any means necessary, including military force."[100] U.S. imperial control over the enriched oil region far from the nation's borders is thus normalized by Carter, warranting a militaristic response. In justifying what he called a "preemptive action against terrorist installations" in Libya, Reagan also threatened that "It must be the core of Western policy that there be no sanctuary for terror."[101] Like his predecessors in Middle East matters, George W. Bush warns in his 2003 State of the Union address: "We will consult. But let there be no misunderstanding. If Saddam Hussein does not fully disarm, for the safety of our people and for the peace of the world, we will lead a coalition to disarm him."[102] Thus, the linguistic and political responses to Middle East conflicts and to terrorism in particular were well established before the Bush presidency and the September 11th tragedy. As Bush concluded in his 2002 State of the Union speech, which furthered his rhetoric of preemption in relation to the "axis of evil" (North Korea, Iran and Iraq), "I will not wait on events, while dangers gather. I will not stand by, as peril draws closer and closer."[103]

Combining benevolent war images with notions of imperial peace work to justify preeminent actions in the developing world and reify imperialist notions of U.S. nationalism. French philosopher Etienne Balibar suggests that oppressive nationalisms are generally invisible and "present themselves, rather, as political and cultural universalisms in which religious and economic components may exist."[104] The end result of such "telling of history," Otto Bauer contends, is that "the nation is linked with the idea of its destiny, with the memory of heroic struggles . . . with triumphs and defeats. The whole rapport that someone today may feel with the struggling people in the past is then transformed into love for the bearers of this motley fate, the nation."[105] Such nationalism exercises, though, as Pickering and Kehde suggest, "is the field over which gender differences are played out,"[106] offering further explanations for the historical and contemporary conceptions of peace and war in presidential oratory and decision making.

The Feminization/Demasculinization of Peace; The Masculinization of War

Conceptions of peace are frequently equated with weakness while war is associated with power—a process that genders militarism *and* pacifism. Today, Tickner argues, "nationalist identities are more ambiguously gendered,"[107] helped in part by the emergence of the "New Man" image in the 1970s, which impacted presidential constructions of peace and war. Yet, the masculinization of the presidency makes such allegiances to power difficult to disrupt. As George P. Fletcher argues, "To sit back and suffer attack, without responding in kind, is to accept a form of national humiliation."[108]

The gendering of U.S. nationalism is historically rooted. Grounding patriarchal principles in "classical republicanism," Carroll Smith-Rosenberg contends that the "eighteenth-century Anglo-American republican political body was always emphatically male."[109] During this period, R. W. Connell maintains, "women were certainly regarded as different from men, but different in the sense of being incomplete or inferior examples of the same character."[110] Schools also participated in the national project, John Beynon suggests, instituting a curriculum that trained elite white males in first world cultures to exhibit "grit, self-reliance, determination, leadership and initiative." These nineteenth-century qualities were "acquired in male company from exposure to the 'great outdoors' far removed from the domestic and the feminine." Athletics also represented an important means for socializing male children for participation in the public world; Beynon maintains that "a direct link [was] made between all-male games and sport . . . and patriotism and Empire-building,"[111] which helped inspirit feelings of "national superiority."[112] "Classical republicanism had . . . banished women from the political arena," Smith-Rosenberg asserts, because they were seemingly void of the necessary "physical strength and martial skills [needed] to defend their nation's . . . honour" as well as the "economic independence that made manly civic virtue possible."[113]

Women's national roles, though, were important in their own right as exemplified by the ideology of "Republican Motherhood"; the practice of benevolence in fact represented a feminine sphere of authority. Mothers of the revolutionary era and beyond were expected to commit themselves to the promulgation of "civic virtue." The republican mother was imbued with the power to prepare her sons in particular for citizenship. As Linda K. Kerber asserts, "she educated her sons for it, she condemned and corrected her husband's lapses" from such moral expectations.[114] Although women's political acts were centered in the private-domestic sphere, the republican mother's purview of activity ultimately expanded to include volunteer spaces. The "Benevolence Empire," in fact, represented a late eighteenth-century Christian force that elite and middle-class women "extend their maternal and domestic expertise to those of the community less able to care for themselves."[115] As Kersh explains, "the roots of union talk run deep in Protestant Christianity,"[116] as do the lingering values of true womanhood, which constructs the ideal woman as naturally more religious, more moral and pious, and submissive to their husbands—a power dynamic rooted in the Bible.[117]

Theodore Roosevelt was one president that reinforced traditional gender roles in a U.S. nationalist context. In "The Strenuous Life," he asserted that "the man must be glad to do a man's work, to dare and endure and to labor . . . The woman must be the housewife . . . the wise and fearless mother of many healthy children." Such roles carried national consequences for Roosevelt: "When men fear work or fear of righteous war, when women fear motherhood, they tremble on the brink of doom; and well it is they should vanish from the earth."[118] Higham suggests that Roosevelt rose to power in a time when "nature" meant "virility," which "represented that masculine hardness and power that suddenly seemed an absolutely indispensable remedy for the artificiality and effeteness of the late nineteenth-century life." Terms that challenged such hypermasculine images—"sissy, pussyfoot"—became more commonplace in this period and were images eschewed by men.[119] Such a gender context, H. W. Brands suggests, sent Roosevelt to "the badlands of the Dakota Territory" to transform his "dandy" and "effete" image into one of power and strength.[120]

Similar gendered conceptions are still visible in the language of peace and war. Cynthia Enloe explains that "When war is seen as active, heroic, and masculine, then peace becomes merely the absence of all these stirring qualities."[121] Nira Yuval-Davis argues that women "have been constructed as naturally linked to peace" in the "western public imagination" since antiquity.[122] Referring to such constructions as the "myth" of war, Miriam Cooke details the "mystique of the unquestionable masculinity of soldiering, of the essential femininity of peace advocacy."[123] In the context of international politics, Tickner concludes, peace is "devalued" as a feminine construct while "a heroic kind of masculinity" functions to valorize war.[124]

During the Cold War, traditional gender conceptions re-emerged after women entered the workforce in support of America's World War II efforts. Elaine Tyler May asserts that the Cold War mentality resulted in a "domestic containment" for women that "hovered over the cultural landscape for two decades."[125] As presidents constructed notions of peace and war in the Cold War, feminine images of morality and peace merged, reflecting historical gender assumptions where women, Beasley notes, "were perceived as being morally superior."[126] Eisenhower's images of peace connoted nineteenth-century qualities of the "true woman," which re-appeared in the 1950s under the guise of what Betty Friedan called the "feminine mystique."[127] Eisenhower speaks of "honest," "just," and "true" peace in his April 16, 1953, "The Chance for Peace" speech, where "peace" is dependent upon such high morals as "truth" and "cooperative efforts."[128] In the "Atoms for Peace" speech of the same year, Eisenhower argues that in order to "move forward toward peace and happiness and well-being . . . we must not lack patience."[129] Johnson relies on a different feminine construct in his post-presidential book, *The Choices We Face*, when he asserts that "the maintenance of peace requires the continued *knitting* together of the three great power centers of the free world."[130] Equating knitting with matters of peace (and war) is not surprising given that historically, women's contributions to war involved knitting items for U.S. soldiers.[131] In *Beyond Peace*, Nixon provides peace with a religious foundation; in U.S. culture, women were historically viewed as the religious vanguards of the nation:[132] "the promise of peace means a better spiritual life . . . [as] faith guides the life of the nation." Such peace, Nixon concludes, "is like a delicate plant [that] has to be constantly tended and nurtured if it is to survive."[133] As Sara Riddick asserts, the construction of "morality" (i.e., peace) is expressed in "soft and feminine" terms and juxtaposed against the "realist . . . instrumentality" of war that is imbued with "hard" and "masculine" images.[134] Elaborating further, Pnina Werbner notes that women are often viewed as the "cultural carriers"[135] of the nation's "moral high ground . . . compassion, generosity and a sense of justice";[136] such perceived feminine images of peace provided a sense of maternal and ethical spirit to such presidential constructions of peace—constructions predicated on "the global reign of liberal democracy."[137]

Of course, as Barbara Welter noted, "Real women often felt they did not live up to the ideal of the True Womanhood," just as such presidential conceptions of an "ideal" peace seemed unrealizable in the Cold War context. After all, as Karlyn Kohrs Campbell explains, the perception was that the "public realm was competitive, driven by ambition," requiring "man's allegedly lustful, ruthless, competitive, amoral and ambitious" traits.[138] Such a political context, while viewed as an inappropriate place for women throughout U.S. history, also seemed uninviting for a feminine and idealized conception of peace. Nixon himself noted in *Beyond Peace* that an idyllic peace "invites danger. Utopian idealism has sometimes caused our foreign policy to swing dangerously between ideological crusades and shortsighted isolationism."[139] Reflecting other often-historical gendered terms, Kennedy promised in the "Cuban Missile Crisis" address that while the "goal" is "peace and freedom," the United States will "never choose . . . the path of surrender and submission."[140] Geoff Eley and Ronald Grigor Suny detail a phenomenon where feminine constructions in the context of nationalism are viewed in "positive term[s] of the national good"; in other crisis contexts, however, "the feminine" becomes a site of "threat" or fear, "orchestrating anxieties."[141]

Just as the early years of the Cold War helped reify more traditional conceptions of femininity, they likewise saw an intensification of traditional masculine expectations that rejected any hint of perceived sexual deviance. Van Gosse argues that "the character of state power in this period was . . . thoroughly associated with the restoration of patriarchal rule and stability, epitomized by the figure of Ike, and the containment of subversive sexual currents."[142] Concerns over being branded as "appeasers" to communism persisted after World War II, James T. Patterson remarks, as "Americans tended to glorify the 'manly' virtues of toughness. Those who were 'soft' ran the risk of being defined as deviant."[143] The biggest concern for many parents of the era, Stephen J. Whitfield maintains, was that "a son would become a "sissie,"[144] which helped propel presidents like Kennedy to create "martial sexual charm" or a "'hard' masculine mystique" to battle "the allure of communism."[145]

Such masculinist prescriptions in the Cold War focused attention on the identification of alleged homosexuals in the U.S. government—activities that were linked with the containment of communism. Charles E. Morris III explains that "there was an easy adoption of the homosexual contagion metaphor with partisan rhetoric to warrant oppressive practices during the McCarthy era."[146] John Wayne, for example, "the era's model of assertive masculinity," served on the Hollywood Committee for the Re-Election of Joseph McCarthy; for a man "to prove his heterosexuality," Bruce J. Schulman contends, "he had to eschew any effeminate behavior."[147] Such a hypermasculine context prompted an inquiry into the presence of "sex offenders" in the federal government, which culminated in a Senate report entitled "Employment of Homosexuals and Other Sex Perverts in Government."[148] In the final report, the Truman administration's Department of State—the agency most invested with matters of peace and diplomacy—represented the government agency that attracted the most attention, as 106 individuals were dismissed for alleged "sex perversion"—no other agency lost more than 19 individuals for similar charges in the investigation.[149] In relation to her research in the State Department, Carol Cohn contends that in "national security discourse . . . you learn that someone is being a wimp [or "a pussy"] if he perceives an international crisis as very dangerous and urges caution." Within the "defense community," Cohn concludes, "manliness is equated not only with the ability to win a war . . . it is also equated with the willingness . . . to threaten and use force."[150]

As conceptions of communism were clothed with a rhetoric of homosexuality, conceptions of liberalism assumed similarly coded connotations. Writing in the early days of the Cold War, well-known liberal Arthur M. Schlesinger Jr., suggested that totalitarianism (i.e., communism) "perverts politics into something secret . . . as homosexuality in a boys' school." He also talked of the "weakness of impotence" that inflicted "doughface progressivism," which constituted the "infiltration of contemporary progressivism by Communism," creating "a movement of 'democratic men with totalitarian principles.'"[151] Nixon furthered such conceptions of liberalism in his book *The Real War*, where he coined the term *trendies*, whom he defined as "overglamorized dilettantes who posture in the latest idea, [and] mount the fashionable protests." Nixon lamented that because "'liberalism' is in fashion," the media spotlighted these "antiwar, antinuclear, [and] antimilitary" celebrities. Nixon concluded that "in a less hazardous age we could afford to indulge the prancing of the trendies on the stage of public debate. But now our national survival depends on learning to distinguish between the meaningful and the meaningless."[152] Throughout the New Left and antiwar movements, the male membership "shared a widespread concern over the loss and recovery of manhood"[153]—images that continue to haunt liberals and any antiwar positions that they might assume. Certainly, the opposition to the Iraq war in 2003 was slow to mobilize in the U.S. Congress, explaining, perhaps, the ease with which

Bush was able to garner support for House Joint Resolution 114, the use-of-force resolution on Iraq.

Although expectations for hypermasculinity dominated the Cold War, the 1960s and 1970s also saw the rise of the *new man*. Rossinow uses the term to refer to Cuban revolutionaries in the 1950s;[154] Bruce J. Schulman details, though, how "new representations of maleness appeared" in the 1970s that challenged male aggression and championed a more feminine masculinity.[155] Simultaneously, male activists searched "for nonviolent masculine identities"[156]—identities that were perpetuated by certain presidents who relied on a less strident discourse of peace or human rights. In his inaugural address, President Jimmy Carter continued to call the United States a "strong nation," yet one that invoked "a quiet strength based not merely on the size of an arsenal but on the nobility of ideas."[157] In his State of the Union address of 1979, Carter asserted, "We have no desire to be the world's policeman. But America does want to be the world's peacemaker."[158] George H. W. Bush's focus on a "kinder, gentler nation" likewise exuded some of these "new man" qualities. He argued in his inaugural address that "America is never wholly herself unless she is engaged in high moral principle. . . . It is to make kinder the face of the Nation and gentler the face of the world."[159] Although Clinton acknowledged that the United States "will act . . . with force when necessary," he likewise argued that "our greatest strength is the power of our ideas."[160] Such images challenge, albeit tepidly, the confluence of militarism, masculinity, and the presidency.

Of course, such images of the new man were contested by other presidents. When Reagan entered office, he countered the diplomatic focus of the Nixon, Ford, and Carter administrations with "an aggressive, interventionist program around the globe . . . redeeming the president's pledge not merely to stand tall in the world but to stand tall *again*."[161] In his "Star Wars" speech of March 23, 1983, Reagan noted that when he took office in 1981, he was "appalled" by what he found: "American planes that couldn't fly and American ships that couldn't sail." In response to calls for cutting back defense spending, he blamed World War II on "democracies [that] neglected their defenses." In the end, he called forth "defensive technologies" that could render the Soviet's "nuclear weapons *impotent* and obsolete."[162] Goodnight explains that for Reagan, "All weapons deficits are

construed as signs of appeasement," which in the "nuclear age is attached
to an infinite risk."[163] Writing in 1980, Nixon noted that "even when you
are strong, it is bad strategy to let yourself appear weak." Nixon suggested
that the "Carter administration's mild reaction to previous Soviet moves"
may well have encouraged the Soviets to invade Afghanistan.[164] Cohn
quotes the vivid opinion of one defense expert regarding Carter's foreign
policies: "Under Jimmy Carter the United States is spreading its legs for
the Soviet Union."[165] Carter's failed actions in the Iranian hostage crisis,
Stephen Paul Miller contends, became "a symbol of American limitation"
and "humiliation."[166] George W. Bush also offered a hypermasculine persona that worked against his image of "compassionate conservatism."[167]
In his behind-the-scenes account of the Bush administration's response
to September 11, Bob Woodward cites Bush on Clinton's actions toward
Osama bin Laden and the threat of terrorism: "The antiseptic notion of
launching a cruise missile into some guy's . . . tent, really is a joke . . .
I mean, people viewed that as the impotent America . . . a flaccid, you
know, kind of technologically competent but not very tough country."[168]
Masculinist precedents may well explain Bush's landing on the USS
Abraham Lincoln by way of a Navy S-3B dressed in a flight suit, and his
response to counterinsurgent efforts in Iraq with the emboldened phrase
"Bring it on."[169] Susan Jeffords identifies "the discourse of war" as the
primary site for the "remasculization of American society."[170]

Challenging a presidential candidate's masculinity on matters of foreign policy also is still a viable campaign strategy. As Murray Edelman
reminds us, political candidates "who refuse to act chauvinistically are
likely to be defined as weak, ineffective, and vulnerable to attack."[171] In
1988, for example, democratic presidential candidate Michael Dukakis
appeared in an M1 tank to represent what *NBC Nightly News* suggested
was his "image toughening" on national security. In the same September
13, 1988, story, vice presidential candidate Dan Quayle declared that Dukakis "lost his top naval advisor last week. The rubber duck drowned in his
bathtub."[172] Later on, Dukakis's tank excursion became the centerpiece
of an attack ad, where the Bush campaign asserted that "America Can't
Afford That Risk," as images of Dukakis in the M1 tank rolled across the
screen. In the A&E series *The Living Room Campaign*, the producer of
the Republican ad, Roger Ailes, explained that Dukakis opposed most

military weaponry expenditures, which produced a "male gender gap" and the reason for Dukakis's appearance in the tank. Ailes suggested that the democratic candidate looked like "Rocky the flying squirrel" in the tank.[173]

In the 2004 presidential primary, candidates' posturing over military prowess was most evident, especially in the presidential campaigns of General Wesley Clark and Senator John Kerry. Of these two campaigns, conservative columnist George F. Will proclaimed in a *Washington Post* article entitled "The Politics of Manliness" that "Democrats who are serious about the candidates' electability understand that seriousness requires a retreat from the feminization of politics," in this case, issues related to children.[174] Such a military and thus manly centerpiece led Clark to talk of George Bush "*prancing* around on the deck of an aircraft carrier" in a flight suit, while Kerry spoke of President Bush "playing dress up" on the same aircraft carrier.[175] Much of the perceived power of both Clark and Kerry was their military status, which allowed Clark to be endorsed by George McGovern without weakening his image;[176] both candidates also promoted an antiwar response to Iraq while maintaining a strong militaristic image. The Bush administration's campaign tactics were clearly evident as the Republican Party produced an ad that suggested the Democratic Party was weak on defense: "Some are now attacking the President for attacking the terrorists. . . . Some have called for us to retreat, putting our national security in the hands of others. . . . Tell them to support the President's policy of preemptive self-defense."[177] The Bush administration's hypermasculine leadership image obviously prevailed. As *Newsday* reported during the 2004 presidential campaign, married women with children in particular "shifted to President George W. Bush because they think he will do a better job of protecting the nation from terrorism."[178]

Implications of Benevolent War and Imperial Peace

In part, this chapter situates the Bush administration's foreign policies in the idyllic beliefs of the United States—expansionism, exceptionalism, and militarism. As the morality of benevolence helped justify the colonialization (and eventual segregation) of African Americans, the removal of Native Americans, and the Americanization of immigrants, it was transformed into a rationale for U.S. interventionism around the globe, particularly in less empowered countries of color. From Cuba, to Puerto Rico, the Philippines, Korea, Vietnam, Grenada, Libya, and Iraq, the United States enhanced its superpower status through the "history of American expansion, not eastward against established European powers but westward and southward against vulnerable racial others."[179] Max Boot compares the "chaotic post–Cold War environment" to the "post-Napoleonic world, with the United States thrust willy-nilly into Britain's old role as globocop."[180] Such a "globocop" role combined with the events of September 11 to warrant a doctrine of preemption not without precedent in U.S. foreign policy discourse and actions.

Of course, the United States has faced formidable opposition in many of these places, explained, in part, by the postrealist context of international politics. Although postrealists often challenge the philosophies of realism and critique the idyllic moralities promulgated by U.S. presidents during times of war, they also believe it is only one narrative of many explanations for international relations. They equally hope to move beyond the assumption of the nation-state as the center of authority, recognizing that "power does not grow just from the barrel of a gun." As Beer maintains, "In the twenty-first century, international violence will continue, but the meaning of war will gradually evolve. It will become less physical . . . and more virtual" as national boundaries dissolve and take new shapes.[181] Such a vision views the enemy as less discernible, and war conditions are commonly related to "ethnic wars, which often overlap international borders, [and] are frequently the result of the artificial borders imposed by former colonial powers."[182] Postrealists also believe, Beer and Hariman contend, that "realist discourse replicates the dynamics of state legitimation," which has been used to "invent a tradition to legitimate contemporary forms of authority."[183] When the realist conception of the U.S. superpower status confronts a postrealist context where the enemy is less certain and more amorphous, problems result, which helps explain the foreign policy debacles of Vietnam, Lebanon, Somalia, and Iraq, inviting moments of rupture in the idealism of U.S. foreign policy rhetoric.

When U.S. exceptionalism and superpower status are challenged with failed military excursions and domestic attacks like Pearl Harbor and the September 11 attacks, we see the regeneration of a hegemonic masculinity in the performances of the presidency. American commitments to peace reflect imperialist reminders and exude a power that tempers any perceived feminine or weakened images of peace and its trappings—diplomacy, negotiation, and détente, which may help explain the Bush administration's repudiation of the United Nations in the pre-Iraqi war period.

The constitutive effect of such historical and ideological militarism and expansionism to U.S. national identity is visible in the perceptions of the American people.[184] DeConde believes that "presidential machismo could not thrive without the awe most Americans have for the presidency."[185] Mead also argues that "a significant element of American public opinion supports waging [war] at the highest possible level of intensity."[186] James K. Oliver reviews public opinion data from the 1970s through the 1990s, which shows the support for "an active U.S. role in the world."[187] Explaining the lure of battle, Chris Hedges asserts that "war is an enticing elixir. It gives us resolve, a cause. It allows us to be noble"[188]—to reaffirm the perception of American unity and to enhance the sense of U.S. moral benevolence. Evidencing the contestation involved in matters of war, especially the post–September 11 context, George P. Fletcher asserts: "We are engaged . . . in a quest . . . of grasping how we are simultaneously drawn and repelled by war, how we believe passionately that the government is doing the right thing to the point that we implicitly subscribe to emergency maneuvers that are arguably in violation of the Constitution."[189] Presidential discourse from Washington through Bush exemplifies the contestation over peace and war as part of the nation's discursive identity.

The moral anxiety over matters of peace and war also is associated with the events of recent memory. May explains that "the end of World War II brought a new sense of crisis. 'Peace' was ushered in by nuclear explosions. . . . It was not the kind of peace that brought confidence in a secure future."[190] Ivie details the endemic insecurity in another way, noting that the mission of expanding "the domain of liberal democracy" so as to "dispel international anarchy and tame the forces of chaos," necessitates an ongoing discursive focus on such conceptions of internal and external threats, exacerbating the "fear of domestic as well as foreign Others."[191] The events of September 11 only further exacerbate such feelings of fear. An enhanced military presence and a president who declares in the aftermath, "I will not yield; I will not rest; I will not relent in waging this struggle," offers for some a sense of reassurance in a time of unmatched anxiety, fulfilling the government's end of the social contract to keep its people safe. Also cathartic is a belief that "God is not neutral" in this battle,[192] and is the guiding force of this nation, perceived to be "destined." Finally, the masculinist character of the military and its commander-in-chief offer a sense of comfort for some as a dominant ideological force in U.S. nationalism. Holly Allen notes that "while most U.S. political institutions seek to protect the interests of the individual from interference from other individuals or by the state, the military does the opposite: it requires its members to risk their own personal interests for the sake of a national cause."[193] Such military sacrifice represents the ultimate contribution of the American people to the social contract.

Given the evolution of the country's historical and discursive commitments, which combine with the ongoing global turmoil, one can understand the allegiance to such historically rooted, patriarchal, and patriotic traditions that help unify the country around these empowering and shared beliefs. Yet such commitments come at a cost; they reify the idea that the "fraternal model of U.S. national community privileges heterosexual men, [and] it also makes strategic use of women and homosexuals."[194] The enemy is also often feminized and devalued, which may offer insight into such wartime atrocities as occurred at Abu Ghraib. While the nation may feel safer because of such preemptive acts, it is important to remember that this perceived sense of security comes about through the sacrificing of U.S. soldiers. Such feelings of security also often come at another expense—the death and destruction of thousands who reside in smaller nations of color and are the beneficiaries of American benevolence.

NOTES

1. John F. Kennedy, "Commencement Address at American University in Washington," *Public Papers of the Presidents of the United States: John F. Kennedy* (hereafter

Shawn J. Parry-Giles

cited as *PPPUS—Kennedy*), January 1 to November 22, 1963 (Washington, D.C.: Government Printing Office, 1964), 464.

2. Ronald Reagan, "Address to the Nation on Defense and National Security," *Public Papers of the Presidents of the United States: Ronald Reagan* (hereafter cited as *PP-PUS—Reagan*), Book 1, January 1 to July 1, 1983 (Washington, D.C.: Government Printing Office, 1984), 438.

3. The list of so-called aggressive actions on the part of the U.S. government is not intended to be exhaustive. See Fred I. Greenstein, *The Hidden-Hand Presidency: Eisenhower as Leader* (New York: Basic Books, 1982), 6; Rhodri Jeffreys-Jones, *The CIA and American Democracy* (New Haven: Yale University Press, 1989), 90–92; and Stephen F. Knott, *Secret and Sanctioned: Covert Operations and the American Presidency* (New York: Oxford University Press, 1996), 9.

4. Michael Beschloss demonstrates through the publication of the Johnson tapes that even President Lyndon Johnson was worried that North Vietnam did not fire the first shots in the Gulf of Tonkin. Beschloss concludes that "LBJ's instincts are excellent: the Pentagon will find no definite proof of a premeditated torpedo boat attack." See *Reaching for Glory: Lyndon Johnson's White House Tapes, 1964–1965* (New York: Touchstone Books, 2001), 37–38.

5. Ronald Reagan, "Address to the Nation on the United States Air Strike Against Libya," *PPPUS—Reagan*, Book 1, January 1 to June 27, 1986 (Washington, D.C.: Government Printing Office, 1988), 469.

6. George W. Bush, "State of the Union," January 28, 2003, accessed at http://frwebgate4.access.gpo.gov/cgi-bin/PDFgate.cgi?WAISdocID=467797115079+8+2+0&WAISaction=retrieve.

7. George W. Bush, "State of the Union," January 20, 2004, accessed at http://frwebgate4.access.gpo.gov/cgi-bin/PDFgate.cgi?WAISdocID=468024115114+4+2+0&WAISaction=retrieve.

8. John Kerry, "Making America Secure Again: Setting the Right Course for Foreign Policy," December 3, 2003, official campaign website, John Kerry for President, http://www.johnkerry.com/pressroom/speeches/spc_2003_1203.html. This text reflects the prepared manuscript rather than the delivered speech.

9. Wesley Clark, "New American Strategies for Security and Peace," October 23, 2003, official campaign website, Wesley Clark for President, http://www.clark04.com/speeches/008/.

10. Mary E. Stuckey, *The President as Interpreter-in-Chief* (Chatham, N.J.: Chatham House, 1991), 1.

11. John Collins and Ross Glover, eds., *Collateral Language: A User's Guide to America's New War* (New York: New York University Press, 2002), 9.

12. I assume an ideological and thus social constructionist understanding of gender that works against assumptions that gender differences are rooted in nature. By ideology, I draw upon Michael Calvin McGee's notion that "no present ideology can be divorced from past commitments," necessitating an evolutionary examination of ideological commitments and the ways in which contemporary generations live out, alter, and extend the ideologies of the past. See "The 'Ideograph': A Link between Rhetoric and Ideology," *Quarterly Journal of Speech* 66 (1980): 14.

13. Robin Tolmach Lakoff, *The Language War* (Berkeley and Los Angeles: University of California Press, 2000), 21.

14. J. Ann Tickner, *Gendering World Politics: Issues and Approaches in the Post–Cold War Era* (New York: Columbia University Press, 2001), 49, 56.

15. Thomas E. Cronin and Michael A. Genovese contend that when President George Washington "set a few precedents for unilateral executive action" with his issuance of the Neutrality Proclamation of 1793 without congressional consent, "Congress willingly conceded to Washington most of the executive powers he exercised, especially those in foreign policy matters." To lessen "monarchical fears," however, presidents often showed deference to Congress, with most assuming "only necessary executive powers." With such a "prudent" course, presidents were given latitude on international matters. See *The Paradoxes of the American Presidency* (New York: Oxford University Press, 1998), 69–70.

16. George Washington, "Farewell Address," *A Compilation of the Messages and Papers of the Presidents, 1789–1897*, vol. 1 (Washington, D.C.: Government Printing Office, 1896), 221, 224.

17. James Madison, "War Message to Congress," *Compilation of Messages and Papers*, 1: 502.

18. Forrest McDonald explains that in February of 1802, Congress empowered President Thomas Jefferson to use armed vessels to attack ships near Tripoli, an act that helped Jefferson fight piracy in Algiers and Morocco. See *The American Presidency: An Intellectual History* (Lawrence: University Press of Kansas, 1994), 264–265; and Max Boot, *The Savage Wars of Peace: Small Wars and the Rise of American Power* (New York: Basic Books, 2002).

19. Michael Hardt and Antonio Negri, *Empire* (Cambridge: Harvard University Press, 2000), 177–178. It is also important to understand that Monroe's secretary of state, John Quincy Adams, was the primary author of the Monroe Doctrine. See Anders

Stephanson, *Manifest Destiny: American Expansionism and the Empire of Right* (New York: Hill and Wang, 1995), 59.

20. James Monroe, "Seventh Annual Message," *Compilation of Messages and Papers*, 1:218 (emphasis added). Hardt and Negri characterize imperialism as imposing "hierarchical territorial boundaries, both to police the purity of its own identity and to exclude all that was other." In the process, imperialist countries establish a "territorial center of power" and rely more on "fixed boundaries or barriers." See *Empire*, xii.

21. Albert K. Weinberg, *Manifest Destiny: A Study of Nationalist Expansionism in American History* (Gloucester, Mass.: Peter Smith, 1958), x.

22. Charles L. Sanford explains that the ideology of manifest destiny is historically rooted in documents like Thomas Paine's *Common Sense* pamphlet of the revolutionary era. See *Manifest Destiny and the Imperialism Question* (New York: John Wiley and Sons, 1974), 26.

23. John L. O'Sullivan, "The Great Nation of Futurity," *United States Magazine and Democratic Review*, November 1839, 427. The essay most often credited with creating the phrase *manifest destiny* was published in 1845 by O'Sullivan, who wrote that those who opposed the annexation of Texas did so "for the avowed object of thwarting our policy and hampering our power, limiting our greatness and checking the fulfillment of our manifest destiny to overspread the continent allotted by Providence for the free development of our yearly multiplying millions." See John L. O'Sullivan, "Annexation," *United States Magazine and Democratic Review*, July 1845, 5.

24. Rogan Kersh, *Dreams of a More Perfect Union* (Ithaca, N.Y.: Cornell University Press, 2001), 116.

25. Vanessa B. Beasley, *You, the People: American National Identity in Presidential Rhetoric* (College Station: Texas A&M University Press, 2004), 5.

26. Walter Russell Mead, *Special Providence: American Foreign Policy and How It Changed the World* (New York: Routledge, 2002), 139.

27. Gordon S. Wood, *The Radicalism of the American Revolution* (New York: Vintage Books, 1991), 218.

28. Joseph Conforti, "David Brainerd and the Nineteenth Century Missionary Movement," *Journal of the Early Republic* 5 (1985): 321.

29. The United States followed Great Britain and abolished the slave trade—legislation that took effect in 1808. Just as Great Britain created Sierra Leone to help halt the slave trade, so too did the United States establish its own African

colony—Liberia—relocating some 13,000 free blacks there. Although attracting notable attention from the 1820s through the 1850s and beyond, the ACS, which often held its initial meetings in the House of Representatives, failed in its mission, in part because southerners like Andrew Jackson were fearful that a national policy on colonization could lead to a national policy on slavery. The impact of the ACS, though, outlived the organization's energy. See Paul Goodman, *Of One Blood: Abolitionism and the Origins of Racial Equality* (Berkeley and Los Angeles: University of California Press, 1998), 10–11, 15, 21–22; and Anthony W. Marx, *Making Race and Nation: A Comparison of the United States, South Africa, and Brazil* (New York: Cambridge University Press, 1998), 59. Note that Goodman argues that the American Colonization Society was established in 1816; Marx maintains that it began in 1817.

30. David Zarefsky explains that Lincoln supported Henry Clay's "policy of colonization . . . as late as 1862." See "Consistency and Change in Lincoln's Rhetoric about Equality," *Rhetoric and Public Affairs* 1 (1998): 29. The issue of colonization also entered the debate over the U.S. annexation of Texas, which represented another potential relocation site for free blacks. See Lyon Rathbun, "The Debate over Annexing Texas and the Emergence of Manifest Destiny," *Rhetoric and Public Affairs* 3 (2001): 467.

31. Robert Carr, *Black Nationalism in the New World: Reading the African American and the West Indian Experience* (Durham, N.C.: Duke University Press, 2002), 14.

32. John H. B. Latrobe, "The Christian Civilization of Africa," *American Colonization Society* (Washington City: Colonization Builders, 1877), 3, 10.

33. Kirt H. Wilson, *The Reconstruction Desegregation Debate: The Politics of Equality and the Rhetoric of Place, 1870–1875* (East Lansing: Michigan State University Press, 2002), 4.

34. Kersh, *Dreams*, 6, 116.

35. Wayne Fields, *Union of Words: A History of Presidential Eloquence* (New York: Free Press, 1996), 196–198.

36. Andrew Jackson, "Second Annual Message" to Congress, *A Compilation of the Messages and Papers of the Presidents*, vol. 3 (New York: Bureau of National Literature, 1897), 1082.

37. Kersh, *Dreams*, 115, 117.

38. Lucy Webb Hayes, "The Fifth Annual Meeting," Woman's Home Missionary Society, November 1, 1877, Papers of Rutherford B. Hayes, Series 9, Reel 297, Library of Congress, 87–89.

39. Theodore Roosevelt, *American Ideals and Other Essays, Social and Political* (Philadelphia: Gebbie and Company, 1903), 28.

40. Gary Gerstle, *American Crucible: Race and Nation in the Twentieth Century* (Princeton, N.J.: Princeton University Press, 2001), 8–9.

41. Frederick J. Turner, "The Significance of the Frontier in American History," in *American Historical Association Annual Report* (Washington, D.C.: Government Printing Office, 1894), 199–201, 210–211, 217.

42. Amy Kaplan, *The Anarchy of Empire in the Making of U.S. Culture* (Cambridge: Harvard University Press, 2002), 2.

43. Theodore Roosevelt, "The Strenuous Life," in *The Strenuous Life: Essays and Addresses* (New York: Century Company, 1901), 17–18.

44. Vincent L. Rafael calls President William McKinley's war in the Philippines "benevolent assimilation," which involved "making native inhabitants desire what colonial authority desired for them" while suggesting that the efforts were munificent and devoid of violence despite the death of over a hundred thousand Filipinos. See "White Love: Surveillance and Nationalist Resistance in the U.S. Colonization of the Philippines," in *Cultures of United States Imperialism*, ed. Amy Kaplan and Donald E. Pease (Durham, N.C.: Duke University Press, 1993), 186. The Filipinos wanted independence after the United States won control of the Southeast Asian country in the Treaty of Paris, signed on December 10, 1898, in the aftermath of the Spanish-American War. The United States eventually turned back the Filipino insurrection and took control over the country. The United States became involved in the Boxer Rebellion after "foreign . . . embassies" were seized in Peking, holding many foreigners, including Americans hostage. The hostages were eventually freed after the United States and other countries sent troops to battle the Boxers. See Boot, *Savage Wars of Peace*, 69–128.

45. Theodore Roosevelt, *Address of President Roosevelt at Chautauqua, New York, August 11, 1905* (Washington, D.C.: Government Printing Office, 1905), 16. Roosevelt fashioned the Roosevelt Corollary throughout his presidency and articulated it during his "Annual Message to Congress" on December 6, 1904, when the exigence of U.S. intervention in Latin America represented an important public issue. See "Message of the President of the United States Communicated to the Two Houses of Congress," Theodore Roosevelt Papers, Series 5C, Reel 426, Library of Congress, 1–40.

46. John Higham, "The Reorientation of America Culture of the 1890's," in *The Origins of Modern Consciousness*, ed. John Weiss (Detroit: Wayne State University Press, 1965), 26.

47. Roosevelt, *American Ideals*, 46–47.

48. Kersh, *Dreams*, 268.

49. Woodrow Wilson, "Address to a Joint Session of Congress," in *The Papers of Woodrow Wilson*, vol. 41, January 24–April 6, 1917, ed. Arthur S. Link (Princeton, N.J.: Princeton University Press, 1983), 521, 525.

50. Woodrow Wilson, "Address to a Joint Session of Congress," in *The Papers of Woodrow Wilson*, vol. 45, November 11, 1917–January 15, 1918, ed. Arthur S. Link (Princeton, N.J.: Princeton University Press, 1983), 536.

51. Alexander DeConde, *Presidential Machismo: Executive Authority, Military Intervention, and Foreign Relations* (Boston: Northeastern University Press, 2000), 290–291.

52. Franklin D. Roosevelt, "Fireside Chat on National Security," in *Public Papers and Addresses of Franklin D. Roosevelt* (hereafter cited as *PPA-FDR*), 1940 volume (New York: Macmillan, 1941), 636, 643–644.

53. Franklin D. Roosevelt, "Address to Congress on the State of the Union," *PPA-FDR*, 1942 volume (New York: Harper and Brothers, 1950), 34, 41–42.

54. McDonald, *The American Presidency*, 402.

55. Erwin C. Hargrove, *The President as Leader: Appealing to the Better Angels of Our Nature* (Lawrence: University Press of Kansas, 1998), 101, 107.

56. Benedict Anderson, *Imagined Communities* (London: Verso, 1983), 113.

57. Francis A. Beer and Robert Hariman, *Post-realism: The Rhetorical Turn in International Relations* (East Lansing: Michigan State University Press, 1996), 4–5.

58. Benjamin Frankel, ed., *Roots of Realism* (London: Frank Cass, 1996), iv.

59. Tickner, *Gendering World Politics*, 37–38.

60. John F. Kennedy, "Address in the Assembly Hall at the Paulskirche in Frankfurt," *PPPUS—Kennedy*, January 1 to November 22, 1963, 520.

61. Lyndon B. Johnson, "Remarks Upon Signing Joint Resolution of the Maintenance of Peace and Security in Southeast Asia," *Public Papers of the Presidents of the United States* (hereafter cited as *PPPUS—Johnson*), Book 2, July 1 to December 31, 1964 (Washington, D.C.: Government Printing Office, 1965), 947.

62. Lyndon B. Johnson, "Remarks in New York City Before the American Bar Association," *PPPUS—Johnson*, Book 2, July 1 to December 31, 1964, 952.

63. Richard Nixon, "State of the Union," *Public Papers of the Presidents of the United States—Richard Nixon* (hereafter cited as *PPPUS—Nixon*), 1972 (Washington, D.C.: Government Printing Office, 1974), 36.

64. Gerald R. Ford, "Address Before a Joint Session of the Congress Reporting on United States Foreign Policy," *Public Papers of the Presidents of the United States—Gerald*

R. Ford (hereafter cited as *PPPUS—Ford*), 1975 (Washington, D.C.: Government Printing Office, 1977), 465.

65. Jimmy Carter, "State of the Union," *Public Papers of the Presidents of the United States—Jimmy Carter* (hereafter cited as *PPPUS—Carter*), Book 1, January 1 to June 30, 1978 (Washington, D.C.: Government Printing Office, 1979), 95.

66. Jean Pickering and Suzanne Kehde, eds., *Narratives of Nostalgia, Gender, and Nationalism* (New York: New York University Press, 1997), 3.

67. Harry S. Truman, "Special Message to the Congress on Greece and Turkey: The Truman Doctrine," *Public Papers of the Presidents of the United States—Harry S. Truman* (hereafter cited as *PPPUS—Truman*), January 1 to December 31, 1947 (Washington, D.C.: Government Printing Office, 1963), 180.

68. Harry S. Truman, "Inaugural Address," *PPPUS—Truman*, January 1 to December 31, 1949 (Washington, D.C.: Government Printing Office, 1964), 113.

69. Lyndon B. Johnson, "Special Message to the Congress on the State of the Nation's Defenses," *PPPUS—Johnson*, 1965 (Washington, D.C.: Government Printing Office, 1966), 63.

70. Richard Nixon, "Address to the Nation on the Situation in Southeast Asia," *PPPUS—Nixon*, 1971 (Washington, D.C.: Government Printing Office, 1972), 525.

71. Ford, "Address Before a Joint Session of the Congress Reporting on United States Foreign Policy," 472.

72. George Bush, "Address Before a Joint Session of the Congress on the Cessation of the Persian Gulf Conflict," *Public Papers of the Presidents of the United States—George Bush* (hereafter cited as *PPPUS—Bush*), 1991 (Washington, D.C.: Government Printing Office, 1992), 222.

73. Bill Clinton, "Second Inaugural Address," *Public Papers of the Presidents of the United States—Bill Clinton* (hereafter cited as *PPPUS—Clinton*), Book 1, January 1 to June 30, 1997 (Washington, D.C.: Government Printing Office, 1998), 44.

74. George W. Bush, "State of the Union," 2004.

75. Robert L. Ivie, "Tragic Fear and the Rhetorical Presidency: Combating Evil in the Persian Gulf," in *Beyond the Rhetorical Presidency*, ed. Martin J. Medhurst (College Station: Texas A&M University Press, 1996), 176.

76. Michael Rogin, "'Make My Day!': Spectacle of Amnesia in Imperial Politics," in Kaplan and Pease, *Cultures of United States Imperialism*, 518–519.

77. John F. Kennedy, "Radio and Television Address to the American People: 'Nuclear Testing and Disarmament,'" *PPPUS—Kennedy*, January 1 to December 31, 1962 (Washington, D.C.: Government Printing Office, 1963), 190.

78. Robert L. Ivie, "Democratizing for Peace," *Rhetoric and Public Affairs* 4 (2001): 317–319.

79. Tickner, *Gendering World Politics*, 38.

80. "Notes for a General Policy Approach to the Lodge Project," July 1953, White House Office, NSC Staff: Papers, 1953–1961, PSB Central Files Series, Box 23, Dwight D. Eisenhower Presidential Library, 14–15. The Psychological Strategy Board was under the direction of the National Security Council and thus the president of the United States.

81. Lyndon Baines Johnson, *The Vantage Point: Perspectives of the Presidency, 1963–1969* (New York: Holt, Rinehart and Winston, 1971), 237.

82. Richard Nixon, "Address to the Nation on the Situation in Southeast Asia," *PPPUS—Nixon*, 1970 (Washington, D.C.: Government Printing Office, 1971), 410; Richard Nixon, "Second Inaugural Address," *PPPUS—Nixon*, 1973 (Washington, D.C.: Government Printing Office, 1975), 13.

83. Richard Nixon, *No More Vietnams* (New York: Arbor House, 1985), 10.

84. Jimmy Carter, "Farewell Address to the Nation," *PPPUS—Carter*, Book 3, September 29, 1980, to January 20, 1981 (Washington, D.C.: Government Printing Office, 1982), 2891.

85. Reagan, "Address to the Nation on Defense and National Security," 438.

86. Tickner, *Gendering World Politics*, 49.

87. John F. Kennedy, "Address Before the 18th General Assembly of the United Nations," *PPPUS—Kennedy*, January 1 to November 22, 1963, 695, 697.

88. See Lyndon B. Johnson, "Remarks on Foreign Affairs at the Associated Press Luncheon in New York City," *PPPUS—Johnson*, Book 1, November 22, 1963, to June 30, 1964 (Washington, D.C.: Government Printing Office, 1965), 495; Richard Nixon, "Inaugural Address," *PPPUS—Nixon*, 1969 (Washington, D.C.: Government Printing Office, 1971), 3; Carter, "State of the Union," 1978, 95; and Bill Clinton, "First Inaugural Address," *PPPUS—Clinton*, Book 1, January 20 to July 31, 1993 (Washington, D.C.: Government Printing Office, 1994), 1.

89. Nixon, "Inaugural Address," 1969, 4; and Nixon, "Address to the Nation on the Situation in Southeast Asia," 408.

90. Ronald Reagan, "Remarks at the Annual Convention of the National Association of Evangelicals in Orlando, Florida," *PPPUS—Reagan*, Book 1, January 1 to July 1, 1983, 363; and Reagan, "Address to the Nation on Defense and National Security," 437–438.

91. Clinton, "Second Inaugural Address," 45.

92. George W. Bush, "President Rallies Troops at MacDill Air Force Base in Tampa," accessed at http://frwebgate6.access.gpo.gov/cgi-bin/PDFgate.cgi?WAISdocID=47 095491911+0+2+0&WAISaction=retrieve.

93. Francis A. Beer, ed., "Language and the Meaning of War and Peace," in *Meanings of War and Peace* (College Station: Texas A&M University Press, 2001), 170.

94. Lyndon B. Johnson, "Inaugural Address," *PPPUS—Johnson*, Book 1, January 1 to May 31, 1965 (Washington, D.C.: Government Printing Office, 1966), 72.

95. Richard Nixon, "State of the Union," *PPPUS—Nixon*, 1970 (Washington, D.C.: Government Printing Office, 1971), 16.

96. Ronald Reagan, "Second Inaugural Address," *PPPUS—Reagan*, Book 1, January 1 to June 28, 1985 (Washington, D.C.: Government Printing Office, 1988), 58.

97. Bill Clinton, "Address to the Nation Announcing Military Strikes On Iraq," *PPPUS—Clinton*, Book 2, July 1 to December 31, 1998 (Washington, D.C.: Government Printing Office, 2000), 2184.

98. George W. Bush, "President Rallies Troops."

99. Rathbun, "Debate over Annexing Texas," 488. Rathbun's focus is on a nineteenth-century conception of manifest destiny.

100. Jimmy Carter, "State of the Union," *PPPUS—Carter*, Book 3, September 29, 1980 to January 20, 1981, 197.

101. Reagan, "Address to the Nation on the United States Air Strike Against Libya," 469.

102. George W. Bush, "State of the Union," 2003.

103. George W. Bush, "State of the Union," 2002, accessed at http://www.presidency.ucsb.edu/ws/index.php?pid=29644.

104. Etienne Balibar, *Politics and the Other Scene*, trans. Christine Jones, James Swenson, and Chris Turner (London: Verso, 2002), 61.

105. Otto Bauer, "The Nation," in *Mapping the Nation*, ed. Gopal Balakrishnan (London: Verso, 1996), 63.

106. Pickering and Kehde, *Narratives of Nostalgia*, 6.

107. Tickner, *Gendering World Politics*, 54.

108. George P. Fletcher, *Romantics at War: Glory and Guilt in the Age of Terrorism* (Princeton, N.J.: Princeton University Press, 2002), 13.

109. Carroll Smith-Rosenberg, "Political Camp or the Ambiguous Engendering of the American Republic," in *Gendered Nations: Nationalisms and Gender Order in the Long Nineteenth Century*, ed. Ida Blom, Karen Hagemann, and Catherine Hall (Oxford: Berg, 2000), 275.

110. R. W. Connell, *Masculinities* (Berkeley and Los Angeles: University of California Press, 1995), 68.

111. John Beynon, *Masculinities and Culture* (Buckingham, U.K.: Open University Press, 2002), 27–28, 33.

112. Ida Blom, "Gender and Nation in International Comparison," in Blom, Hagemann, and Hall, *Gendered Nations*, 17.

113. Smith-Rosenberg, "Political Camp," 275.

114. Linda K. Kerber, *Women of the Republic: Intellect and Ideology in Revolutionary America* (Chapel Hill: University of North Carolina Press, 1980), 229.

115. Nancy Hardesty, *Women Called to Witness: Evangelical Feminism in the Nineteenth Century*, 2nd ed. (Knoxville: University of Tennessee Press, 1999), 90. For additional insight into the impact of benevolence ideology, see Lori D. Ginzberg, *Women and the Work of Benevolence: Morality, Politics, and Class in the Nineteenth-Century United States* (New Haven: Yale University Press, 1990).

116. Kersh, *Dreams*, 28.

117. See Barbara Welter, "The Cult of True Womanhood: 1820–1860," *American Quarterly* 18 (1966): 151–174.

118. Roosevelt, *The Strenuous Life*, 3–4.

119. Higham, "Reorientation of American Culture," 27.

120. H. W. Brands, "Politics as Performance Art: The Body English of Theodore Roosevelt," in *The Presidency and Rhetorical Leadership*, ed. Leroy G. Dorsey (College Station: Texas A&M University Press, 2002), 116.

121. Cynthia Enloe, *The Morning After: Sexual Politics at the End of the Cold War* (Berkeley and Los Angeles: University of California Press, 1993), 64.

122. Nira Yuval-Davis, *Gender and Nation* (London: Sage, 1997), 94.

123. Miriam Cooke, "Wo-man, Retelling the War Myth," in *Gendering War Talk*, ed. Miriam Cooke and Angela Woollacott (Princeton, N.J.: Princeton University Press, 1993), 178.

124. Tickner, *Gendering World Politics*, 49.

125. Elaine Tyler May, *Homeward Bound: American Families in the Cold War Era* (New York: Basic Books, 1999), 79.

126. Beasley, *You, the People*, 126.

127. See Betty Friedan, *Feminine Mystique* (1963; New York: Laurel, 1983).

128. Dwight D. Eisenhower, "'The Chance for Peace' Delivered Before the American Society of Newspaper Editors," *Public Papers of the Presidents of the United States—Dwight D. Eisenhower* (hereafter cited as *PPPUS—Eisenhower*), 1953 (Washington,

D.C.: Government Printing Office, 1960), 179–188.

129. Dwight D. Eisenhower, "Address Before the General Assembly of the United Nations on Peaceful Uses of Atomic Energy," *PPPUS—Eisenhower*, 1953, 817.

130. Lyndon Baines Johnson, *The Choices We Face* (New York: Bantam Books, 1969), 14 (emphasis added).

131. See Dudley Harmon, "What is Mrs. Wilson Doing? The Part the President's Wife and His Daughters Have in the War," *Ladies Home Journal*, July 1918, 22, 44.

132. Glenna Matthews, *The Rise of Public Woman: Woman's Power and Woman's Place in the United States, 1630–1970* (New York: Oxford University Press, 1992), 55–56.

133. Richard Nixon, *Beyond Peace* (New York: Random House, 1994), 24, 35.

134. Sara Riddick, "Notes toward a Feminist Peace Politics," in Cooke and Woollacott, *Gendering War Talk*, 115–116.

135. Nira Yuval-Savis and Flora Anthias, eds., *Woman-Nation-State* (New York: St. Martin's Press, 1989), 9.

136. Pnina Werbner, "Political Motherhood and Feminisation of Citizenship: Women's Activisms and the Transformation of the Public Sphere," in *Woman, Citizenship, and Difference*, eds. Nira Yuval-Davis and Pnina Werbner (London: Zed Books, 1999), 241. See also Yuval-Davis, *Gender and Nation*, 94.

137. Ivie, "Democratizing for Peace," 315.

138. Welter, "The Cult of True Womanhood," 174; Karlyn Kohrs Campbell, *Man Cannot Speak for Her: A Critical Study of Early Feminist Rhetoric*, vol. 1 (New York: Praeger, 1989), 11.

139. Nixon, *Beyond Peace*, 191.

140. John F. Kennedy, "Radio and Television Report to the American People on the Soviet Arms Buildup in Cuba," *PPPUS—Kennedy*, January 1 to December 31, 1962, 809.

141. Geoff Eley and Ronald Grigor Suny, "Introduction: From the Moment of Social History to the Work of Cultural Representation," in *Becoming National: A Reader*, ed. Geoff Eley and Ronald Grigor Suny (New York: Oxford University Press, 1996), 26.

142. Van Gosse, *Where the Boys Are: Cuba, Cold War America, and the Making of a New Left* (London, Verso, 1993), 52.

143. James T. Patterson, *Grand Expectations: The United States, 1945–1974* (New York: Oxford University Press, 1996), 181.

144. Stephen J. Whitfield, *The Culture of the Cold War* (Baltimore: Johns Hopkins University Press, 1996), 43.

145. See Gosse, *Where the Boys Are*, 197; and Doug Rossinow, *The Politics of Authenticity: Liberalism, Christianity, and the New Left in America* (New York: Columbia University Press, 1998), 358 n. 33.

146. Charles E. Morris III, "'The Responsibility of the Critic': F. O. Matthiessen's Homosexual Palimpsest," *Quarterly Journal of Speech* 84 (1998): 270.

147. Bruce J. Schulman, *The Seventies: The Great Shift in American Culture, Society, and Politics* (New York: Free Press, 2001), 179.

148. John D'Emilio, "The Homosexual Menace: The Politics of Sexuality in Cold War America," in *Passion and Power: Sexuality in History*, ed. Kathy Peiss and Christina Simmons (Philadelphia: Temple University Press, 1989), 227.

149. U.S. Senate, "Employment of Homosexuals and Other Sex Perverts in Government," Committee on Expenditures in the Executive Departments, 81st Cong., 2nd sess., November 27, 1950, 25.

150. Carol Cohn, "Wars, Wimps, and Women: Talking Gender and Thinking War," in Cooke and Woollacott, *Gendering War Talk*, 234–236.

151. Arthur M. Schlesinger, Jr., *The Vital Center: The Politics of Freedom* (1949; New York: Da Capo, 1988), 38, 40–41, 151.

152. Richard Nixon, *The Real War* (New York: Warner Books, 1980), 242–243.

153. Rossinow, *The Politics of Authenticity*, 298.

154. For Rossinow, the "New Man" constituted those social activists that helped bring about the Cuban revolution in the 1950s. See *The Politics of Authenticity*, 223.

155. Schulman, *The Seventies*, 177–179.

156. Rossinow, *The Politics of Authenticity*, 229.

157. Jimmy Carter, "Inaugural Address," *PPPUS—Carter*, Book 2, June 25 to December 31, 1977 (Washington, D.C.: Government Printing Office, 1978), 3.

158. Jimmy Carter, "State of the Union" address, *PPPUS—Carter*, Book 1, January 1 to June 22, 1979 (Washington, D.C.: Government Printing Office, 1980), 106.

159. George Bush, "Inaugural Address," 1989, accessed at http://bushlibrary.tamu.edu/research/public_papers.php?id=1&year=&month=.

160. Clinton, "First Inaugural Address," 2.

161. Schulman, *The Seventies*, 221.

162. Reagan, "Address to the Nation on Defense and National Security," 440, 442–443 (emphasis added).

163. G. Thomas Goodnight, "Ronald Reagan's Re-formulation of the Rhetoric of War: Analysis of 'Zero Option,' 'Evil Empire,' and 'Star Wars' Addresses," *Quarterly Journal of Speech* 72 (1986): 396.

164. Nixon, *The Real War*, 255–256.

165. Cohn, "Wars, Wimps, and Women," 236.

166. Stephen Paul Miller, *The Seventies: Culture as Surveillance* (Durham, N.C.: Duke University Press, 1999), 7.

167. George W. Bush, "Remarks at a Rally on Inner-City Compassion in Cleveland, Ohio," July 1, 2002, accessed at http://frwebgate1.access.gpo.gov/cgi-bin/PDFgate. cgi?WAISdocID=471674327512+1+2+0&WAISaction=.

168. Bob Woodward, *Bush at War* (New York: Simon and Schuster, 2002), 38.

169. See "Commander in Chief Lands on USS Lincoln," *CNN.com/Inside Politics*, May 2, 2003, http://www.cnn.com/2003/ALLPOLITICS/05/01/bush.carrier.landing/; and James W. Pindell, "In NH, Democrats Criticize Bush's Language Over Iraq," *PoliticsNH.com*, July 4, 2003, New Hampshire's Online Political Network, http://www.politicsnh.com/archives/pindell/2003/July/7_4.shtml.

170. Susan Jeffords, *The Remasculinization of America: Gender and the Vietnam War* (Bloomington: Indiana University Press, 1989), 186.

171. Murray Edelman, *Constructing the Political Spectacle* (Chicago: University of Chicago Press, 1988), 61.

172. *NBC Nightly News*, September 13, 1988.

173. *Investigative Reports: The Living Room Campaign*, A&E Biography, 1988.

174. George F. Will, "The Politics of Manliness," *Washington Post*, January 29, 2004, A29.

175. The author attended a pancake breakfast in Keene, New Hampshire, where General Clark uttered the phrase on Sunday, January 18, 2004. He also repeated the phrase in a conversation with Clark in Newport, New Hampshire, later that same evening. See also Edward Wyatt, "The 2004 Campaign: The Stump Speech / General Wesley Clark; Rising above Politics, as High as Commander in Chief," *New York Times*, January 15, 2004, accessed at http://query.nytimes.com/gst/fullpage.html?res=9C06E1D61030F936A25752C0A9629C8B63; and John Kerry, "Iowa Jefferson Jackson Day Dinner," official website, John Kerry for President, November 15, 2003, http://www.johnkerry.com/pressroom/speeches/spc_2003_1115.html.

176. Kenneth O'Reilly talks of how the Nixon campaign sought to structure McGovern as the antiwar liberal who supported more extreme civil rights policies. See *Nixon's Piano: Presidents and Racial Politics from Washington to Clinton* (New York: Free Press, 1995), 324–325, 340–341.

177. See Mike Allen, "Bush Ad Criticizes Democrats on Defense: Doctrine of Preemption Is Touted as Effective," *Washington Post*, November 22, 2003, A03.

178. Philip A. Klinkner, "Deflating the 'Security Mom' Angle," *Newsday*, October 5, 2005, 1, online at Lexis Nexis Academic, November 18, 2004.

179. Rogin, "'Make My Day!'" 521.

180. Boot, *Savage Wars of Peace*, xx.

181. See Beer and Hariman, *Post-realism*, 6–10; and Beer, *War and Peace*, 84, 165, 167.

182. Tickner, *Gendering World Politics*, 41–42.

183. Beer and Hariman, *Post-realism*, 7–8.

184. James Jasinski explains how a "discursive constitution specifies the way textual practices structure or establish conditions of possibility, enabling *and* constraining subsequent thought and action in ways similar to the operation of rules in a game." See "A Constitutive Framework for Rhetorical Historiography: Toward an Understanding of the Discursive (Re)constitution of 'Constitution' in *The Federalist Papers*," in *Doing Rhetorical History: Concepts and Cases*, ed. Kathleen J. Turner (Tuscaloosa: University of Alabama Press, 1998), 75.

185. DeConde, *Presidential Machismo*, 5.

186. Mead, *Special Providence*, 220–221.

187. James K. Oliver, "The Foreign Policy Presidency after the Cold War: New Uncertainty and Old Problems," in *The Post–Cold War Presidency*, ed. Anthony J. Eksterowicz and Glenn P. Hastedt (Lanham, Md.: Rowman and Littlefield, 1999), 35–36.

188. Hedges, *War Is a Force*, 3.

189. Fletcher, *Romantics at War*, 9.

190. May, *Homeward Bound*, 78.

191. Ivie, "Democratizing for Peace," 309–310.

192. George W. Bush, "Address to a Joint Session of Congress and the American People, 2001," accessed at http://frwebgate4.access.gpo.gov/cgi-bin/PDFgate.cgi?WAISdoc ID=47228896910+2+2+0&WAISaction=retrieve.

193. Holly Allen, "Gender, Sexuality and the Military Model of U.S. National Community," in *Gender Ironies of Nationalism: Sexing the Nation*, ed. Tamar Mayer (London: Routledge, 2000), 310.

194. Ibid.

The Abu Ghraib Iconic Photographs: Constitutive Spectacles and the Gendering of Public Moralities

Rebecca Gill and Marouf A. Hasian Jr.

At Abu Ghraib, the normality of the abnormal was placed on spectacular display.
> —Michelle Brown, "'Setting the Conditions' for Abu Ghraib"

The horror of what is shown in the photographs cannot be separated from the horror that the photographs were taken—with the perpetrators posing, gloating, over their helpless captives.
> —Susan Sontag, "Regarding the Torture of Others"

The International Red Cross had been sending the US and UK authorities reports of abuses in military prisons in Iraq for months, and the reports were ignored. It wasn't that the authorities weren't getting any signals about what was going on: they simply admitted the crime only when (and because) they were faced with its disclosure in the media.
> —Slavoj Žižek, "Between Two Deaths"

The Iraqi campaign that is purportedly a major part of the larger "War on Terrorism" has now been waged for more than seven years. There is no shortage of citizens, politicians, and academics who have commented on the ethical dimensions of this conflict. For example, in the aftermath of the 2004 Abu Ghraib scandal, the 2005 Haditha shootings, and the 2006 rape and murder of a fourteen-year-old Iraqi girl and simultaneous murder of her family in Mahmudiyah, writers have looked into the "moral psychology" that animates individual or collective involvement in a host of wartime atrocities.[1] As various lawyers, historians, and diplomats debate the question of whether this is a "just" war that can be distinguished from other forms of conquest or intervention, other writers, photographers, and documentarians suture together disparate discursive and nondiscursive materials in the rhetorical wars that are fought for our hearts, minds, and remembrances of these contentious conflicts.

In some of these multifaceted debates lurk the public and academic discussions that we wage about the role that *visuality* plays in these moral, wartime struggles. When, for example, influential members of the American Bar Association saw some of the pictorial records from Abu Ghraib, they put together a resolution that stated that these and other wartime abuses provided "strong evidence" that the "nation's detention policies have lost their moral compass."[2] For creative writer Luc Sante the "jaunty insouciance," the display of "unabashed triumph of having inflicted misery upon other human beings," and the abandonment of some normative scruples meant that perhaps the digital camera would haunt the career of George W. Bush in the same way that the tape recorder had "sealed the fate of Richard Nixon."[3] Guy Adams, Danny Balfour, and George Reed went so far as to argue that the circulation of the Abu Ghraib photographs needed to be thought of as an example of "administrative evil," where systematic "moral inversion" had led to the acceptance of standardized cruelty.[4] Even Ruth Wedgwood—a staunch defender of Bush administration policies—was convinced that the "worthy ambitions of the war in Iraq" could not "mask the moral pain of the Abu Ghraib scandal."[5]

One of the problems in linking visual images to public morality in wartime, of course, is the subjective and intersubjective nature of public morality. As Celeste Condit has observed, the crafting of moral norms involves both individual and collective achievements, and this in turn means that various audiences need to see, feel, and *believe* that some wartime activities are immoral before they consider these conflicts to be unjust, unfair, or otherwise problematic.[6] Given the contingent nature of rationalizations for war, and the contestation that surrounds the circulation of photographic archives, the study of the rhetorical formation of public morality needs to take into account the ideological, ambivalent, and polysemic dimensions of even the most realistic of pictorial representations. To this end, we are convinced that what we call *constitutive spectacles* may help with the consciousness-raising that is needed in gauging the morality of problematic conflicts. By constitutive spectacles, we mean the visual wartime images (such as the Abu Ghraib photographs, the Haditha video,[7] and so on) that have served as constitutive rhetoric, and which have been particularly prevalent in the most recent conflict in Iraq.

In this chapter, we investigate the role that constitutive spectacles played in the moral framings of the 2004 Abu Ghraib scandal. We draw from McGee's differentiation of stable and vital myths to frame the debates that emerged from the Abu Ghraib photographs. According to McGee, stable myths perpetuate status quo assumptions and public collective identity, and vital myths represent a "new vision of the collective life" that challenge stable assumptions and collective identity.[8] It is our contention that for a short period of time, the public debates that swirled around some of these gendered visual displays had the potential to provide a new, vital myth of American morality and military values, but that the radical and unfocused questioning of some of the stable myths of America's political, military, and social cultures did not provide viewers with the types of visual registers that would stand the test of time. There were no shortage of outlets that were willing to print these shocking photographs, but in the battles that were fought over the framing of the public moralities inspired by these images, it would be the *defenders* of the stable myth(s) about the justness of the Iraq war and administration policies who often claimed the high moral ground for America. Rajiva correctly noted that the Abu Ghraib images "set the national and international media on fire,"[9] but there would nonetheless be considerable debate about what caused this fire and how to put it out.

To help us defend the heuristic value of studying the rhetorical crafting of iconic constitutive spectacles in wartime situations, we proffer three smaller subclaims: (1) the constitution of public moralities becomes more immediate when spectacular images are involved; (2) a rendering of rhetorical public moralities is incomplete without a consideration of gender and other signifying identities such as race and class; and (3) effective visual consciousness-raising depends on the successful "fixing" of photographic archives within dominant public moral frames.

This chapter unfolds in four sections. We first provide some theoretical grounding for the essay by explaining how visual spectacles are tied to the constitutive crafting of salient public morality. As a case study of sorts, we next introduce and give a brief overview of Operation Iraqi Freedom and the Abu Ghraib scandal, identifying key players and some of the key rhetorical templates that framed the moral debates that surrounded these images. Third, to expand our claim, we then provide a descriptive unpacking of these images so that we can examine the gendered nature of these images. It is here that we speculate about some of the reasons for the vacillating public interest in these images. Finally, in the concluding segment, we briefly take up the question of whether these visual registers can be effectively reappropriated by critics who are interested in helping with the constitutive reformation of other wartime public moralities. We contend that future commentators will need to assess how both stable and vital framings of Abu Ghraib provide fragments that can be sutured together to form novel moral arguments.

Iconic Photographs as Constitutive Moral Spectacles

On first impression, the bare photograph would appear to be the last place that one might look for the constitutive creation of individual and public moralities. This is because photographs often cannot provide viewers with a complete and concise narrative. Photographs deal in fragmented time, space, and limited information, where the "world becomes a series of unrelated, freestanding particles; and history, past and present, a set of anecdotes and *faits divers*."[10] We can attribute this, at least in part, to the confines of the photographic method, where a photograph only captures "what can be seen in a fraction of a second, most often 1/60th of a second or less,"[11] and involves compositional aspects such as cropping and lighting that are capable of deferring photographic meaning. Even changing technologies—not to mention motivations—can influence how one includes or alters these fragmentary photographic archives. This limits the claims that can be made about photographic realism, and in turn may indicate a "crisis of believability" in photography.[12]

However, because "the camera [also] makes reality atomic, manageable, and opaque,"[13] some have argued that the partiality and fragmentation of photographic "reality" serve a rhetorical function that allows the photograph to capture what is "real," to serve as a unified and complete "window" on the world's reality. According to Susan Sontag, "Photographs are valued because they give information. They tell one what there is; they make an *inventory*."[14] Filmmaker Errol Morris holds that

> photography because of its causal relationship to the world seems to give us the truth or something close to the truth. I am skeptical about this for many reasons. But even if photography doesn't give us truth on a silver-platter, it can make it harder for us to deny reality. It puts a leash on fantasy, confabulation and self-deception. It provides constraints, borders. It circumscribes our ability to lie—to ourselves and to others.[15]

Likewise, Cara Finnegan suggests that photographs offer some connection to a dynamic reality, and specifically that photographic representations are capable of "embody[ing] codes of power, domination, spectatorship, or surveillance." Moreover, photographs need to be spread in ways that build on "naturalistic" enthymemes if they hope to have any resonance in public controversies.[16]

With our recognition of photography's actual *inability* to capture reality, then, is the paradox that photographs claim to present a "true" picture of the world.[17] As such, the power of photographic re-presentations to serve as constitutive spectacles is limited to those images that are not only successful in gaining the attention of a public, but also—and perhaps most relevant to our chapter—those images that build on a "naturalistic" enthymeme, meaning that they resonate or "make sense" in a collective public that already exists. Obviously not all photographs have the potential or evocative power to become constitutive spectacles, because only a few key images prick our consciences, invite us to think about our moral compass, or find the contexts that provide meanings for these fragments. In other words, we have to be persuaded in some way that these epistemic markers have something to tell us about our ontological and axiological realities. Given the partial, contingent, and polysemic nature of these photographic images, collective consciousness and rhetorical effectivity depend on the discursive captioning, rhetorical framing, and political contextualization of these artifacts.

Part of the process of crafting public moralities therefore depends on the ways that fragmentary shards such as photographs, captions, and commentary are sutured together around constitutive spectacles, where the personal becomes political through the collective process of identity formation. When audiences begin to *think* that they are seeing the same morality or immorality, the same upholding or violation of national or international norms, or the same framing of wartime activities, then these mass-mediated representations can become some of the vehicles for consciousness-raising. McGee provided a similar argument about the ontological existence of some mythic "people" when he emphasized that publics simply needed to *believe* that they were processing information in similar ways. For McGee, "'the people' . . . are not objectively real in the sense that they exist as a collective entity in nature; rather, they are a fiction dreamed by an advocate and infused with an artificial, rhetorical reality by the *agreement* of an audience to participate in a collective fantasy."[18]

Robert Hariman and John Lucaites have furthered exploration into the constitutive effects of photographs and images during war and crises by arguing that *iconic* images—those that enjoy extensive recognition; are commonly viewed as representative of a particular, noteworthy, event; cause emotional responses or identifications; and are replicated in various media or genres—can work to construct a public identity.[19] Hariman and Lucaites argue that in order for a public to be constituted by visual images, its members must be interpellated; they must "see themselves in the collective representations that are the materials of public culture."[20] This is especially relevant regarding national and international images, where a perceptual "civic identity" is constituted within a public realm. The recursive nature of the photographic process, therefore, means that to the degree that individualized strangers in the public sphere are brought together through shared spectatorship, they may come to believe that they share similar attitudes toward some pictorial representations. Thus, visual texts may indeed be potentially polysemic, but the normative frames that surround particular visual images invite publics to believe that they "all *seem* to see the same thing."[21] In the case of Abu Ghraib, then, we hold that the images were the catalyst for the constitutive development of human relationships and public collectivities. Yet, this collective process of identity formation through iconic images, and the resulting potential for consciousness-raising, necessarily pivots on whether the images can be understood as *spectacle*.

SPECTACLE AND COLLECTIVE IDENTITY

Guy Debord's theoretically rich notion of spectacle refers not to events or images themselves, but more specifically to the *illusion of a collective identity* or group-ness that is formed as a result of spectacular images and events. Spectacle is "a social relationship between people that is mediated by images,"[22] according to Debord, and yet is also a "product of real activity."[23] Thus, while spectacle is real in the sense that activity has occurred, it is nonetheless ultimately an appearance or representation of social order, wherein "the specialized role played by the spectacle is that of spokesman for all other activities, a sort of diplomatic representative of hierarchical society at its own court, and the source of the only discourse which that society allows itself to hear."[24] This theorizing deviates from other versions of spectacle that argue for spectacle as a literal "public gathering of people who have come to witness some event and are self-consciously present to each other as well as to whatever it is that has brought them together."[25] In this second view, spectacle is the large, colorful, or dynamic public display that stimulates the human visual senses. As John MacAloon explains, "Spectacles give primacy to visual sensory and symbolic codes; they are things to be seen."[26]

These two versions of spectacle are useful for our purposes, for they describe the impact of the Abu Ghraib photographs on collective identity. Though the images were not spectacular in the sense that all citizens were physically present at Abu Ghraib to witness the event, they are spectacular in that they are "things to be seen," and are, for many, artifacts that stimulate the visual senses. However, the images, it seems to us, serve to operate more along the lines of Debord's spectacle; they promote hierarchical power and dominant ideology while causing viewers to feel as though there is a collective sense of support or outrage (whichever side one identifies with) for what the images depict. Importantly, spectacle is no longer something to interact with (through providing commentary, participation, or aid in the case of crises), but has d/evolved into only *something to be witnessed.* In each version of spectacle, individuals as audience members are a necessary part of spectacle in the sense that the spectacular relationship needs to be collectively created and embraced. Yet, with Debord's theory, the notion that individuals do not need to be present to witness a spectacle implies a decreased level of accountability on the part of the audience.

Debord's theory suggests that spectacle is a means by which dominant regimes retain and circulate controlling discourses and practices: "By means of the spectacle the ruling order discourses endlessly upon itself in an uninterrupted monologue of self-praise. The spectacle is the self-portrait of power in the age of power's totalitarian rule over the conditions of existence."[27] The mechanism of spectacle can be found in mass-mediated and technologized relationships that alienate individuals from one another. In this sense, each spectator is linked to the spectacle (through viewing it on television, in papers, and other media), but *not* to each other. Thus, Debord's spectacle requires that audiences witness spectacle atomistically and look to other commentators to direct the "proper" interpretation of the event or image. This simultaneously retains and reinforces an oppressive power dynamic, since separated peoples are passive peoples and are not as capable of seizing the means and positions of power. Tony Schirato and Jennifer Webb explain:

> Debord . . . sees in this same process the outward evidence of the alien-
> ation of individuals from the community, and from themselves: spec-
> tacle should be understood first as the site of power, and read in terms
> of the division of society into classes which has necessarily brought
> about the separation (the alienation) of the people from power. The
> effect of spectacle is thus simultaneously the production of the many as

passive observers, and the institution of the few as those "sacred" and privileged subjects able—in the sense of "permitted" and "capable"—to accomplish what everyone else cannot.[28]

Yet despite the consequence of spectacle's alienating capabilities, we contend that spectacle can nonetheless be constitutive of a moral public identity. As with photographs, we may all think we're seeing the same thing and so we feel, even if temporarily, that we're united under a shared moral umbrella. Such an effect is ultimately important because it stimulates curiosity and discussion. As Barbara Biesecker, drawing from Foucault, reminds us, oppressive power operates on the same grid as resistive power,[29] and so while a collective identity may only offer false consciousness for Debord, it stands to reason that the feeling of shared moral identity has the *potential*, at least, to push back against the stable status quo, leading to resistive and vital discussion, activities, and collective identity. Drawing from Mark Danner's journalistic account of the events at Abu Ghraib, Carol Payne and Amy Lynford support this line of theorizing, writing that "the notorious snapshots made by American military personnel at the Iraqi prison at Abu Ghraib exemplify the photographic spectacle in contemporary media. In depicting military brutality, these images buttressed American authority; yet they have also motivated searing critiques and widespread outrage."[30] As we will argue, the Abu Ghraib images "project and naturalize dominant authority,"[31] but they also, through the ostensibly shared act of witnessing, may instigate the perceptual formation of "a people"—a collective, rhetorical, and public identity—who agree to be defined as such for the time being.[32]

Constitutive spectacles therefore provide select opportunities for audiences to think about how these images are tied to their individual and collective belief systems. We contend that this is especially important during times of war and civil strife because of the morally motivated beliefs and decisions that are inextricably linked to these times and events. If, as Condit has argued, "Collective discourse [is] the source of an active public morality,"[33] then we need to track those visualities that become the markers that "indicate shared commitments and prescribe what each person as a member of a collectivity is obligated to do within the collectivity."[34] In the arena of public argument, where Condit locates her discussion, arguments often index the "greater good" and self-sacrifice, as well as what is "right" or "good" in certain beliefs and behaviors. She writes, "The moral element is necessarily engendered by the process of public argument. Needs and desires of others are the foundation of the morality expressed in the general moral concept of the categorical imperative 'thou shalt not' . . ."[35] In terms of these "greater good" arguments for what is "right" and "just," war and wartime are spaces and activities with enormous moral implications, both in war-waging and war-fighting.[36] When it comes to the rhetorical constitution of publics in wartime, the morality or immorality of war is already on the table, always-already implicated in public discussions.

Particularly, we need to understand that photographs can be interesting as stand-alone images in and of themselves, but that it is when they are adopted into these larger public specular frames surrounding just war arguments and policies that they are most powerful as motivating factors for collective moral identity and motivations. While photographs have traditionally been valued as in support of the written word, theorists have begun to posit the "new sense of information that has been constructed around the photographic image."[37] This type of theorizing influences the way that we think about the facts and norms associated with wartime. The alleged realism of these photographic images may influence the way that various publics negotiate moral meaning and competing hierarchies of values in wartime. This alleged realism can influence our notions of authenticity, censorship, and the truthfulness of the ideological campaigns that are waged during major international conflicts. As one reporter comments from his experiences with covering war, "War forms its own culture . . . it is peddled by mythmakers—historians, war correspondents, filmmakers, novelists, and the state."[38] It is perhaps this mythic quality of war that ensures that "even with its destruction and carnage [war] can give us what we long for in life. It can give us purpose, meaning, a reason for living."[39]

Given the polysemic and polyvalent nature of photographic images, it is imperative that scholars who are interested in the power of the spectacular treat governmental officials as only *some* of the social agents who are involved in the purveying of visual information about war. Advances in digital photography have altered the directional flows of wartime information, and now ordinary soldiers may foil the plans of administration officials who may want to serve as informational and moral gatekeepers.[40] Moreover, the fact that many of these Abu Ghraib photographs were taken by members of the lower echelons of the military hierarchy may help explain why human rights accounts and military reports of the abuses at Abu Ghraib went largely unheeded until the photographs surfaced to "prove" what was occurring.[41] This indicates that with regard to the Abu Ghraib scandal, we cannot ignore the role that the photographs played in exposing the torture and sparking major domestic and international debate, because we are convinced that in our scopophilic world, the word tells us only part of the story when it comes to moralizing and national identity formation.

GENDERING SPECTACLE

We also claim, however, that in considering spectacle, we often cannot fully grasp how a moral public is constituted without also considering how *gender* is sutured into fragments such as photographs and commentaries. The Abu Ghraib photographs caused a scandal not only because of the action perceived to be happening in the images, but in particular because of the gender(ed) displays of the Military Police (MPs) and detainees—how the MPs and detainees were framed against the backdrop of a hegemonically masculine military. In essence, Abu Ghraib was gendered not only for what was said about the sexed bodies of those featured in the photographs, but also for what was not said. Marita Gronnvoll explains that while the gender, sexual bodies, and capacity of the women soldiers at Abu Ghraib was largely debated and contested in official and public commentary, the "male soldiers remain[ed] invisible as representatives of men," thereby holding women soldiers in the military accountable in ways that men soldiers were not held accountable.[42] Such a move is not new.

In general, our discursive landscape is already filled with numerous political arguments about the problematic nature of women's presence on the battlefield, suggesting that "yesterday's discourses," in Maurice Charland's terms,[43] have already constructed an American public and their opinions about women in combat; women's place in the U.S. military has

always been seen as abnormal, since publics struggle to reconcile the notion of "woman" with the notion of "soldier."[44] The Abu Ghraib images reinvigorated these debates about women in combat, therefore holding great
potential to either revolutionize or entrench gendered notions of martial
bodies with "today's discourse." Indeed, our rhetorical histories are filled
with claims about women soldiers who have threatened home and family,
or who have put male soldiers at risk during times of war. Some have
gone so far as to argue that the gendering of the military increases the risk
of sexual promiscuity, or the acceptance of lesbianism.[45] Such arguments
against women in the military ultimately protect the masculinity of male
soldiers, and while some scholars have suggested that traditional gender
roles in the military are changing,[46] others have confirmed the existence of
deeply entrenched gender assumptions.[47] For example, Howard and Prividera report that in the 2003 Pfc. Jessica Lynch media hype, media worked
to differentiate between Lynch's femininity and her (military) masculinity
by emphasizing her civilian identity, her traditional feminine good looks,
and her status as a victim in need of rescue.[48]

The gendering of war therefore complicates matters for any critic of
official policies because those who want to deploy these photographic
archives have to deal with what Laura Sjoberg has called the "militarized
femininity" of the Iraqi conflict, where the presence and absence of gendered commentary speaks volumes about how publics and government
officials will think about sanctioned violence, deviant behavior, and even
torture.[49] Critics not only have to deal with a host of patriotic rhetorics—
they now must also figure out ways of persuading audiences who have
preconceived notions of masculine and feminine ways of fighting just or
moral wars.

In terms of spectacle, the ways in which a collective identity is formed
around gendered norms, assumptions, and performances becomes an
important factor. More than simply acknowledging the biological sex of
individuals in a visual spectacle, we must look to how femininity and masculinity are rhetorically deployed in the construction of a public identity.
One of the key questions therefore involves issues related to what the
American public *thought* they were seeing in the Abu Ghraib images vis-à-
vis gender. Given the immediate impact of the images and the vehemence
with which some parties debated the "meaning" of the images, it becomes
important to question how the images were being translated and to what

end. First, we provide some context leading up to the events at Abu Ghraib and give an overview of the unfolding of events.

Operation Iraqi Freedom and the Photography of Abu Ghraib

Following the 2001 attacks on the World Trade Center in New York City and the Pentagon in Washington, D.C., President George W. Bush declared a War on Terrorism, which he aligned with previous struggles to secure freedom and which he justified as a morally "right" war, using just war rationalizations.[50] The War on Terrorism physically commenced in October 2001 with Operation Enduring Freedom, a war in Afghanistan intended to destroy al-Qaeda and capture Osama bin Laden. United States efforts in Afghanistan were soon matched by Operation Iraqi Freedom in 2003, a war in Iraq that sought to continue the War on Terrorism while also "liberating" the Iraqi people. Bush declared that the United States was

> once again engaged in a real war that is testing our nation's resolve. While there are important distinctions, today's war on terror is like the Cold War. It is an ideological struggle with an enemy that despises freedom and pursues totalitarian aims. Like the Cold War, our adversary is dismissive of free peoples, claiming that men and women who live in liberty are weak and decadent—and they lack the resolve to defend our way of life. Like the Cold War, America is once again answering history's call with confidence—and like the Cold War, freedom will prevail.[51]

Dominant rhetorics of the war were therefore initially steeped in abstract arguments about freedom, democracy, and nobility, minimizing the reality that human life would be lost and economies and communities destroyed in the act of warring.[52] Kenneth Zagacki argues that Bush's war rhetoric embodied prophetic dualist ideals, which "[hold] that Americans are morally and spiritually superior and destined to spread 'good' around the globe."[53] In this, the Bush administration drew on and maintained a stable myth of U.S. benevolence and American exceptionalism, arguing that "once again" the United States was performing good deeds in world affairs.

However, almost immediately after the commencing of hostilities in Iraq on March 20, 2003, we saw the beginning of a series of key visual and mediated events that affected the United States, Iraq and Afghanistan, and the international community in various ways, including the largely media-hyped capture and rescue of Pfc. Jessica Lynch, the toppling of Saddam Hussein's iron statue, the friendly-fire killing of Arizona Cardinals football star Pat Tillman, the Haditha massacre, and the scandal at Abu Ghraib. Abu Ghraib's particular impact in the United States and worldwide was due to a series of photographs that depicted U.S. soldiers smiling and giving the "thumbs up" as they harassed, abused, and tortured the Iraqi detainees of Abu Ghraib prison,[54] including photographs of detainees being threatened with vicious dogs and gruesome images of dead or wounded inmates.

On April 28, 2004, CBS's 60 *Minutes II* publicly aired the first set of photographs of the Abu Ghraib abuses,[55] which touched off a firestorm of public debate and demands for rhetorical justification. The images of Abu Ghraib, and the circulation of these photographs, can be used as illustrative proof that early reports of abuse could no longer be dismissed. It was not until a CD of the photographs surfaced at the Army's Criminal Investigation Division (anonymously submitted by Specialist Joseph Darby) in December of 2003 that reports of the abuse were taken seriously by government officials, and so the photographs are testament to the salience of visual images as "proof" of a particular reality; they made it "harder to deny reality."[56] The significance of the images cannot be minimized, argues Seymour Hersh, since "in the absence of photographs the complaints had little traction."[57] Reports detailing the unimaginable abuses and tortures had previously surfaced in the *Washington Post* as early as January of 2004,[58] and the abuses had been ongoing for at least eight months when then-Secretary of Defense Donald Rumsfeld was notified, and in turn, notified President Bush.[59] Thus, previous discursive materials produced by Human Rights Watch, the Red Cross, the ACLU, and other organizations did reach some audiences around the world, but their tales of immorality seemed to have fallen on deaf ears until the photographs surfaced.

The photographs, released (or leaked) to the public in small batches, initially totaled at least 1,800 images and videos, some of which have been viewed by the U.S. Congress.[60] They feature Staff Sergeant Ivan L. Frederick II, Specialist Charles A. Graner, Sergeant Javal Davis, Specialist Megan Ambhul, Specialist Sabrina Harman, Private Jeremy Sivits, and Private Lynndie England ostensibly engaging in "cruelty toward prisoners, maltreatment, assault, and indecent acts."[61] According to one commentator:

> The photos . . . were riveting—a hooded figure in a ragged black poncho balanced uneasily on a box, an off-kilter Halloween Christ with bare feet and palms plaintively open, electric wires running from the hands like the strings of a marionette; an American girl with a cigarette dangling from the corner of her mouth in one photo and an impish grin in another as she points derisively at the genitals of a naked, hooded, Iraqi man and signals thumbs up; smiling soldiers behind naked men posed in a tangled human pyramid; hooded, stripped prisoners simulating fellatio and sodomy; an unmuzzled dog snarling at a cowering, naked prisoner. CBS news claimed it had dozens, even worse.[62]

Quickly, the Abu Ghraib photographs became known as iconic images representative of American intervention in foreign countries, despite the fact that only a small percentage of the images were initially released. These images, nonetheless, represented the complete set of images, a representation that was bolstered by insider commentary that suggested the unpublished images were worse than the published images.[63] Despite the fact that the Abu Ghraib images generically fit better into the category of "snapshot" photographs (private, familial, and amateur), they soon took on the status of iconic images in that they were widely recognized; represented the events at Abu Ghraib and the war in Iraq as windows on a reality that existed outside of the official gaze; evinced emotional reactions leading to public reaction and outrage; and were replicated not only in formal print media and news reporting but also in cartoons and throughout the Web on both official and unofficial sites (where they are even mocked and imitated). It is partly due to the snapshot qualities of the Abu Ghraib photographs that they became iconic images of the war in Iraq, given the odd juxtaposition of amateur photographs and ostensible military procedures which induced "irony or some other moment of reflection."[64] Iconic photographs such as these therefore catalyzed a constitutive spectacular public identity by implicating U.S. citizens in such events and calling them to account both for the photographs themselves and for the actions depicted therein.[65]

Worries about the potential effect of these images galvanized the efforts of those who thought that their circulation served the cause of the insurgents, and for several months a host of human rights groups waged a running battle with officials who tried to control the dissemination of these photographs. At the same time that Bush administrators asked for censorship and self-censorship, outlets in Australia and other places were only partially successful as they tried to tell viewers about the existence of several different batches of Abu Ghraib pictures. But like the fragmentary nature of the photographs themselves, the early specular framing of these images did not always provide viewers with coherent and consistent explanations of how to think about them. As audiences tried to comprehend the moral grounding of these images, they were told that the photographs showed that the U.S. soldiers from the 372nd Military Police Brigade assigned to Abu Ghraib were involved in acts that included humiliation, physical abuse, and emotional stress. Questions quickly arose, however, that underscored the vacillating meanings of these photographs, as both defenders and critics of the Iraqi War struggled to "explain" or "justify" this behavior. Rarely did observers question the *authenticity* of the images or the identities of the participants reported in news coverage, and so the focus of attention was on deciphering what exactly was going on in the photographs, and whether superior officers had known about or sanctioned any of this behavior.

The battles over the morality of these activities soon turned into public debates about the rectitude of America's fighting forces and the methods that were used to carry out what the Bush administration had tried to sell as a just war. These visual archives thus became a part of a much more complex debate about U.S. martial dominance and use of coercive interrogation methods, the visibility and accountability of the CIA and other empowered forces, the secrecy that swirled around official and unofficial policy regarding torture, the relevance of Geneva Convention articles for the war in Iraq, and whether these photographs accurately represented American military and public morality.

Military officials not only attempted to control the initial seizure of the Abu Ghraib images, they also waged legal and cultural campaigns with those who argued that these types of trophies were circulating throughout the military ranks in many countries, both before and after the exposure of the photographs. When Lynndie England was interviewed by Germany's *Stern* magazine in March 2008, she alleged that these tactics were widespread, and that although she herself was only in "five or six pictures" that were circulated by the media, the control tactics that were used by her squad had also been used by the unit that came before her.[66] England also implied that when Graner showed some of the military interrogators these photographs, they approved of this picture taking because it provided evidence of the effective softening up of the detainees before interrogation.

Interestingly enough, one could argue that the gendering of these images during these early years set the tone for some of the later domestication of the images. The intense and immediate focus on the images of women soldiers (to the near exclusion of male soldiers) as perpetrators of abuse almost instantly made the public debate about gender, both explicitly and implicitly.[67] Media attention to Pvt. Lynndie England and comparisons to Pfc. Jessica Lynch raised broad questions about women in combat, but also scrutinized England herself for her in/appropriate performance of femininity and masculinity. The photographic depictions and ensuing images of England all seemed to serve as evidence that Lynndie England failed both as a woman, since she did not measure up to traditional feminine standards of beauty and behavior, and as a soldier, since she was neither a man nor the kind of honorable military figure publics would like to see. Gender, in fact, represented an implicit way in which to construct many of those featured in the photographs in that public figures and commentators on both sides of the fence spoke of the "feminization"[68] of both detainees and soldiers. As we discuss, the feminization of the persons and activities in the images at least partially allowed the images to eventually be swept under the rug.

After 2004, most of the moralizing about the Abu Ghraib photographs seemed to coalesce around one of two contradictory rhetorical frames: (1) *either* these pictures were viewed as evidence of atypical, deviant, sexual behavior on the part of a few "bad apples," thus maintaining the sanctity and "American values" of the U.S. military; (2) *or* they became a part of crafted narratives that assumed that this was a generalizable and officially sanctioned military behavior, thereby damning the U.S. military and negatively implicating American public morality. These debates about culpability at Abu Ghraib mutated into controversies about other acts of similar immoralities, ranging from the circulation of harmful images during times of war to the immunity of President Bush and Donald Rumsfeld.

The first line of argument upheld a stable myth, siding with official government rhetoric that only a few bad apples[69] were to blame for what happened at Abu Ghraib, and that the U.S. military was otherwise doing an effective job in Iraq. Such a perspective is found, for example, in Bush's post–Abu Ghraib rhetoric,[70] and it attempted to protect the U.S. military from widespread scrutiny in at least two arenas. First, the stable myth sought to deflect blame from the Bush administration and other higher-ups, using scapegoating tactics to contain the scandal within the actions of a few "wild" reservists. Second, such scapegoating sought to maintain the sanctity and stability of military masculinity by emphasizing those involved as having deviated from traditional (masculine) military bodies and behavior. This rhetorical move attempted to control threats to the dominant hegemonic masculinity of the U.S. military, which have historically been intensely monitored to avoid a certain kind of military undermining.[71] The effects have been to increase adherence to the "proper" body and behavior of the American soldier, which promotes and rewards patriarchal white, heterosexual, middle-class maleness.[72]

The second rhetorical frame, however, offered a vital myth by calling into question the U.S. military chain-of-command, and by extension, the U.S. military itself, suspecting that these abuses were sanctioned by superiors and were widespread, and using evidence and rumors of similar abuse at Guantánamo Bay and in Afghanistan as evidence. This vital myth challenged the stable myth of martial hegemony and suggested that U.S. military masculinity was not as admirable or desirable as previously believed. Moreover, this perspective often went the extra mile to turn the lens on the American public, arguing that "*the photographs are us*"[73] in that they reflected American behavior and values as instituted within our military training; if the images questioned the U.S. military, then we must all—according to this frame—question our own role in creating and contributing to American and military discourse, for the images served as "Americana: the quintessential, familiar and recognisable stuff of US identity."[74]

The allegations that these Abu Ghraib acts were somehow representative of the moral nature of American identity formation was a constant refrain from this camp. Slavoj Žižek commented that "in the photos of the humiliated Iraqi prisoners, what we get is, precisely, an insight into 'American values.'"[75] In this sense, the photographs offered a window perhaps not onto "reality," but onto an undercurrent of an American cultural narrative; one that emerged in the juxtapositioning of foreign penal policy with domestic penal policy.[76] What gave these images a special power as iconic images is that they were "unconsciously made. . . . These images seemed to have welled up out of our own unconscious, showing us what we knew, but didn't know that we knew."[77]

As we reviewed permutations of the stable myth and the vital myth framing of these affairs, we wondered about how various observers were thinking about the photographic material and coming up with these linkages. Given the fragmentary nature of both photographic images and the fragility of collective identity formation, we believed that we needed to temporarily step away from these contextualizations and think about the visuality of these images; what caused publics to defend/justify or condemn/self-reflect these images? If Lynndie England and the other reservists had to deal with the constant circulation of just a few iconic images, then what was in those pictures that warranted this type of attention?

Rereading the Abu Ghraib Photographs to Understand Potential Moral Problematics

At this juncture, we revisit the Abu Ghraib photographs to unpack their composition for clues as to how they were being read by the American and international public and eventually reconstituted through explanations and justifications. This work is important, since the Abu Ghraib photographs have been and likely will continue to be used as "evidence in ongoing debates about the causes, nature, outcome, and consequences

of war. Used in this way, images reproduce and transform ideologies such
as nationalism and patriarchy that conventionally support war."[78] For our
purposes, we draw from some of the most infamous photos, including
the Lynndie England "leash" photograph and the "pointer" photograph;
the hooded prisoner standing on a box, wires attached to his extremities,
which was featured on the front pages and covers of newspapers and
newsweeklies; the series of "thumbs up" and "pyramid" photographs; and
the images of prisoners being threatened with dogs.[79]

Taken as a whole, these images share similar compositional aspects in
terms of color, lighting, and staging. Backgrounds and settings are often
stark and muted: beige or tan walls with dirty and peeling paint; hall-
ways or wide-open spaces extending back or framing the action; exposed
infrastructure; prison doors symmetrically set into the walls; harsh light
washing out the background; and crude, makeshift walls and screens. An
initial reading of the setting identifies the space as a prison or some sort
of industrial space. It may be odd to American viewers, therefore, to see
women in this setting in the first place. It may also be curious that the
behavior of the soldiers and detainees does not reflect what we might
expect from a prison setting—"prisoners" are seen out of their cells, and
chaotic and complex scenes are presented that deny the expected order
and control in a prison.

It is likely that for most images, the viewer's eye hones in on the
human figures and their actions or positions. Bodies become a major
marker in these photos because it is through clothing, body type and
color, postures and positioning, and facial expressions that the human
figures are usually demarcated into the two distinct groups of "soldiers"
and "prisoners." First, viewers surmise who the soldiers are because of
their clothing, which is mostly long-sleeve or short-sleeve tan or black
shirts, camouflage pants, and combat boots, with some soldiers and dog
handlers dressed more heavily in combat vests. Interestingly, we do not
see official military insignias or military personnel wearing formal dress
uniforms, though they occasionally use occupational gear such as dog-
handling or medical gloves. The individuals likely more readily identified
as prisoners, on the other hand, are most often naked, sometimes covering their genitals with their hands. Seldom are they clothed/covered, with
the notable exceptions of a prisoner wearing an orange jumpsuit and the

hooded prisoner standing on a box, covered by a black, tattered cloth. Boxy black or green hoods over prisoners' heads are common. When the Iraqi men are clothed or covered, they nonetheless remain differentiated from the soldiers in that their clothing is atypical and evokes powerlessness or imprisonment (e.g., American audiences will likely identify an orange jumpsuit as a prisoner's uniform).

While the soldiers' bodies are always covered or concealed in some way, observers are in many pictures able to view the thin, naked bodies of the Iraqi detainees. Because of their nakedness, it is clear that the Iraqis are male; in many images, their full bodies, chests, and genitalia are exposed, even though their faces are often covered by the hoods. Among the images made public early on, only a few feature women detainees, including one with a woman flashing her breasts to the camera but otherwise being clothed. In many images, we can surmise that the MPs are raced white, based on what we can see of their skin color and features. On the other hand, in some pictures we notice that the detainees are brown-skinned, and that their body hair is dark. This is particularly apparent in the images where the soldiers are close to the prisoners, highlighting the contrasting skin tones. Yet, the lighting and resolution of the photography does not always distinguish between the race of military police and detainees, and viewers may draw from discursive captions and reports of the ethnicity of the soldiers and prisoners to "fill in" the corresponding "appropriate" color. The contrast of bodies of color becomes a factor in reading the images, in that it implicitly challenges the U.S. military for its claim of benevolence toward "others" who are not "like us." Thus, the bodies of the detainees in the photographs represent an imperialist "othering" or feminizing of wartime enemies, as evidenced in the white soldiers' dominating treatment of brown prisoner bodies.

In terms of physical space, the soldiers tend to occupy wider or higher spaces and their postures and gestures (standing upright, feet firmly on the ground, pointing and giving thumbs up, etc.) indicate that the soldiers have control over how they move and position their bodies, whereas the positions and postures of the prisoners insinuate submission and discomfort. Prisoners are at times in "human pyramids," sitting on each other, or lined up, often simulating masturbation or oral sex. For example, the leash photograph features England center stage, standing up, and looking down upon a naked Iraqi man on the floor. The Iraqi man is in an awkward and contorted position, and his body is cropped out of the picture at the waist; the photograph does not even afford him his whole body. The same is true for other images—the detainees often occupy lower planes, or their bodies are contorted and look uncomfortable, as in the pyramid pictures, and soldiers pose in the background, standing up, and commanding the space in the image. Moreover, the "props" that are present in the photographs, such as the leash, hoods, robes, and electrical wires corroborate the power and positioning of the soldiers, as they are used *on* the prisoners, instead of used *by* the prisoners, thereby further objectifying the detainees. In addition, the use of props and body positioning can be read by some members of the public as implying not only power, but also a sexualized domination/submission dimension of power. In the case of Lynndie England, for example, perhaps what disturbed many viewers was the possibility that they were being confronted with an image of "a young woman leading a naked man around on a leash in classic dominatrix imagery,"[80] a sexualized image that seems to have little to do with official interrogation procedures or administration policies.

This treatment ultimately invokes a history of imperialist photography that purposefully featured white domination over ostensibly subhuman bodies. Abu Ghraib was not the first time that audiences were confronted with realistic evidence of the machinations of imperialism or the depravity of some human beings. Janina Struk has explained that "atrocity photographs" have been around for a long time,[81] and the Abu Ghraib images remind us of the abusive activities associated with the "Belgians of the Congo, the French in Algeria," the "practicing of torture and sexual humiliation on despised recalcitrant natives."[82] Moreover, the Abu Ghraib photographs recall a U.S. history filled with tales of civil rights abuses, including, for example, the "lynching photographs" taken between the 1880s and 1930s of white Americans posing with the dead bodies of black men and women.[83]

Bodily comportment and positioning therefore is particularly salient in terms of publics trying to make sense of these images. The bodies and body parts of the Iraqi men are displayed in ways that make it difficult to read their bodies as anything other than tortured and submissive. And where the bodies of the detainees are on display, their facial expressions are often obscured, or the detainees seem expressionless. In several photographs, the inmates are hooded or their faces are turned away from the camera, which has the effect of masking and denying their identity; at times, their bodies are the camera's object and their heads are cropped out of the image. When we do see their faces, their expressions suggest that they are decidedly not "mugging" for the camera, in contrast to the smiles and direct eye contact of the soldiers. Rather, they present blank expressions that are difficult to read. Other prisoners indicate extreme fear, as in the case of detainees being threatened with dogs.

On the other hand, the facial expressions of the soldiers involved in the images reveal that they are performing for the camera—they are "hamming it up." Lynndie England and Specialist Sabrina Harman are featured in several photographs, smiling and giving the thumbs-up for added emphasis (a notable exception is England's almost bored, nonsmiling expression in the leash photograph). The smiling of these women soldiers confuses the viewer, who may expect women to smile when on display,[84] but who might also expect a more staid and serious militaristic (read: masculine) expression in the carrying out of orders. Moreover, some may want to initially believe that the images are part of some sort of military-sanctioned training program or information-gathering, and so these images belie the possibility that these could be "official" photographs because of the informality and congeniality of the smiles and the poses. Overall, viewers do not usually see the faces of male soldiers in the images, save for Specialist Charles Graner, labeled the "ringleader" of the MP group. Like England and Harman, Graner also smiles for the camera and gives the thumbs-up, as when, for example, England and Graner stand behind a pyramid of Iraqi bodies, looking as though they were tourists enjoying a Disneyland vacation, as one commentator described it.[85] Most often, however, the faces of male soldiers are turned away from the camera or are obscured by activity or distance; they do not "pose" for the photograph in the same way that England, Harman, and Graner do.

What is little discussed about these images is that several iterations exist for some photographs, and that others have been cropped in their published versions, lending even more opportunity for multiple interpretations. In the case of the leash photograph, the most popular image circulating shows only the Iraqi detainee and Lynndie England, but when we turn to other archives, we discover that "at least four other military intelligence soldiers appear in the same picture."[86] Likewise, a photograph of Iraqi bodies stacked on top of each other also shows, in the uncropped version, "other soldiers at the scene, some not even paying attention."[87] As some of the eleven defendants in legal actions prepared for the Abu Ghraib trials, they were interviewed by members of the press who helped widen the scope of moral culpability and give context to what was seen and not seen in the photographs.

Along these lines, Lynndie England was quoted as saying that she did not think that these few soldiers had "thought of this on their own," and allegations were made that these young subalterns were simply following the orders of the "MI" (military intelligence officers) and the "OGAs" (other governmental agencies). During one of her early interviews with reporters, England explained that during the fall of 2003, "something would come up," an "MI or OGA" would come in during the night shift and tell those present that "so-and-so needs this," and that when the officials came back in a few hours or days, they expected that the prisoners had been "softened up and [made] weak for interrogation."[88] One of England's lawyers, Rick Hernandez, argued that the abuses were a "systematic problem" because everyone was learning that "these military intelligence tactics" were being "used at places my client has never seen."[89] The inference here was that England was just one of many soldiers or prisoners who were influenced or directed by superior officers, and that the redacted images failed to present a more "accurate" window onto reality that may more clearly implicate higher-ups.

The cropping of the images, along with the nature of photographs to begin with, therefore presents only a partial version of what was going on at Abu Ghraib, and yet American publics expectedly focused on who and what was depicted in the published images. In terms of the actions and positions that we see in these images, Staff Sergeant Chip Frederick, who had a hand in staging and taking some of the pictures and who was sentenced for his role in the Abu Ghraib abuse,[90] suggested after the fact that the soldiers were, indeed, aiding military interrogation efforts, corroborating the claim that these were officially sanctioned procedures and therefore diffusing, to some degree, the outrage over the procedures and images. Frederick wrote home about the procedures:

Military Intelligence has encouraged and told us "Great Job." They usually don't allow others to watch them interrogate. But since they like the
way I run the prison, they have made an exception. . . . We help getting
[the POWs] to talk with the way we handle them. . . . We've had a very
high rate with our style of getting them to break. They usually end up
breaking within hours.[91]

These types of commentaries turned the reservists in these images into
collaborators, unthinking soldiers who did the bidding of the CIA interrogators or other unnamed abusers. Therefore, it became possible for
audiences to read both the prisoners and the soldiers in the images as
submissive and feminized. Indeed, if the soldiers possessed the power
not to perform these acts, then surely—as one line of argumentation
claimed—they would have *refused* to engage in this particular kind of
"softening up."

The ways that the individuals featured in the images are interpreted
and debated offer us clues to how the public at least initially reacted to
the images. Given the large official and public outcry in both the United
States and internationally, it stands to reason that these bodies, especially those of the Abu Ghraib inmates, could be viewed as "monuments"
to American morality and behavior. In this suggestion, we borrow from
Bryan C. Taylor's use of Shakespeare's *Richard III,* in the famous scene
where Richard mulls over the end of the war and speaks of "our bruised
arms hung up for monuments."[92] In his discussion, Taylor takes "arms" to
indicate weaponry and discusses *nuclear arms* as monuments.[93] For our
purposes, we appropriate "arms" synechdocally to refer to the bruised
and battered *bodies* of war. In this sense, then, the prisoners' contorted,
stressed, and bruised bodies may, for some viewers, have taken on the
quality of monuments and testaments to the morality of American martial
behavior.

The implications of the bodies of the U.S. soldiers and Iraqi men for
gender constructions and the military, moreover, cannot be ignored. Our
point here is to draw attention to how these bodies are read as gendered
in certain ways, though we do not belabor this point because others have
analyzed the images for what they say (and don't say) about militarized
gender.[94] However, it is still worth discussing, especially in the case of

Lynndie England, who, like Jessica Lynch before her, became the poster child for women in the military.[95] Not surprisingly, public discussions about gender focused mainly on the women soldiers in the images, lending credence to the assumption that women are gendered whereas men are gender-neutral.

Lynndie England and Sabrina Harman, the women most often depicted in the images and discussed in public and media circles, are identifiable in the photos as women by virtue of their slight frames and traditionally feminine characteristics, even as they also deviate from these characteristics. England, for example, has a slight frame and a small waist, and we can see the shadow of her breasts in the leash photograph. But her dark hair is cut short with no particular style to it. The overall result is that she looks androgynous, or rather, boyish. Harman, on the other hand, is more traditionally feminine, with blonde hair pulled back from her face with a few loose wisps of hair. Harman more resembles the iconic Jessica Lynch for her small stature and femininity, and the media focus on England over Harman as the deviant dominatrix suggested that publics perhaps warily recalled the "Barbie Rambo" and the ensuing media spin, and were more forgiving of a traditionally feminine woman in general. In other words, it may be that Harman was let off easily because of her obvious femininity, whereas England was so condemned in the press because she dared deviate from submissive, traditional femininity. Throughout the fall of 2004, millions of people around the world read that Lynndie England seemed to be "having a good time" as she pointed at the genitals of some of the Iraqi detainees, or stood behind a human pyramid of prisoners.[96] One witness, Jeremy Sivits, recalled how England stepped on prisoners' fingers and toes, and how these abusers ignored the warnings that came from a noncommissioned officer who told them to "knock it off."[97] Harman, on the other hand, was seldom constructed as acting against the detainees, whereas England's leash-holding and finger-pointing were seen as an indication that she was actually performing questionable acts.

Indeed, despite the fact that the photographs featured seven of the eleven court-martialed Abu Ghraib defendants (and then some) at some point, public discourse quickly focused on England, who was portrayed as a lower-class young soldier from a "West Virginia trailer park," a camera ham who played while her captives were "tortured." One critic commented on the power of England's presence in the photographs:

> The first Abu Ghraib image I saw was the one with Lynndie England holding that man on a leash, humanity irrelevant, physical, fallen by his cage. If nothing else, the world of images performs magic on the world of images. For me, a thousand images of abject humanity were sucked up and expunged by this one.[98]

One wonders, of course, whether this specific outrage can be channeled into effective—and more general—moral condemnation.

As well as being the poster child for scapegoating by the Bush administration, England is symbolic of the larger debate surrounding gender and warfare, as, in the photographs, "it remains disturbingly hard to separate the obvious repulsiveness of what she is doing from the fact a woman is doing it."[99] Moreover, those involved in the Abu Ghraib photos and some superior officers called to court-martial were feminized through the process of scapegoating as unable to appropriately perform and embody martial duties and values. For England, though she is feminized in her role as a naïve small-town girl, as a soldier in the U.S. Army she can still claim some semblance of power and masculinity in relation to the Iraqi inmates whom she is humiliating in the photographs. Some critics point to the outrage over England's transgressions as evidence that America expected martial women to be on better behavior, and yet "it seems unfair to expect your basic idiotic female to behave any differently from your basic idiotic male."[100] For some, the photographs may indicate that women are ultimately deviant,[101] and when left to their own devices (because the cropped pictures suggest that she is acting alone) and given power, cannot make appropriate choices.

In comparison to the female soldiers, the male soldiers tended not to be as visible or attended to in the images, even though they likely are present in the *majority* of the thousands of images. As Gronnvoll points out, this may be because their bodies are assumed to be "appropriate" bodies for war activities, and they therefore go unquestioned for their presence. The assumption that men "belong" in the images is backed up by the fact that Charles Graner is really the only male discussed in the media; the other male soldiers, identifiable by their larger-framed bodies and traditionally male facial characteristics, become part of the background in the photographs (as evidenced by some particularly telling photos that depict detainees in stress and fear positions while multiple male soldiers are more or less "milling about"). In a similar twist, the male detainees also quickly faded into the background of the photographs. By virtue of being male and also seemingly lacking power and discernable identities, mainstream public discussion focused mostly on the actions and identities of the soldiers, as though it was impossible to imagine that the detainees may have had actions or any recourse to speak of. This may have the effect of further relegating the Iraqi detainees to merely being objects in an orchestrated display.

The scapegoating of Lynndie England extended to the whole crew of Abu Ghraib perpetrators, and the scapegoating served to feminize the soldiers (who had feminized the Iraqi prisoners) so as to protect traditional masculine military values. If the soldiers were made to be seen as specially incompetent cases, then the military itself could retain its hegemonic control as righteous and discerning in its use of "appropriate" power. In an interesting twist, the Abu Ghraib soldiers responded by claiming that they were, indeed, not competent, and therefore, could not have orchestrated months of abuse and torture by themselves. The defendants in these photographs were characterized in some public critiques as trusting of masculine political and military figures, and therefore, exploited by those higher up the chain of command. In England's case, she had been "used by Private Graner [and] didn't realize it at the time."[102] And according to the lawyer for Sergeant Javal Davis, "Some of the last words my client heard before being deployed in Iraq was President Bush saying, 'This is a war on terror. The Geneva conventions don't and will not apply.'" Davis's lawyer defended him by saying:

> My client never trained as a corrections officer or in military intelligence acquisition. He was asked consistently on a daily basis to soften up detainees to save the lives of US soldiers. Hooding, keeping prisoners naked, the use of dogs—these techniques were all approved by the authorities. *Where does the grey line end? How does he know how to differentiate between these things?*[103]

These reservists could be configured, therefore, as small fry, mere cogs in the complex machinery of modern warfare. This point is made more salient when we consider the nature of photography, for again, even though these images *seem* to show an incontrovertible reality, they only capture moments in time and cannot possibly visually depict all of the players in the abuse, regardless of who they are. And yet, even though they represent only moments in time, the sheer volume of images and the intensity of the action seem to have been enough to convince viewers that something had occurred that needed interpretation and understanding. On the one hand, some of the critics of the war may have had inflated hopes about the lasting effectivity of these photographic shards. A very typical discourse advanced at the time claimed that no amount of whitewashing could explain away the graphic realities of the Abu Ghraib horrors. For example, Neil Mackay, an investigative reporter for the *London Sunday Herald,* argued that fourteen key pictures "lost the war," and pinpointed Lynndie England as a key figure in recording images that "would do Saddam proud."[104] However, other commentators diminished the potential for these images to promote consciousness-raising, and viewed the soldiers' behavior as just one more manifestation of the war's brutality. Under this interpretation, the Abu Ghraib abuse is ultimately blameless since the logics of military occupation created the stresses and conditions that encouraged the abuse of the insurgents.[105]

These images therefore provide several clues to how to read the action and events at Abu Ghraib, and yet we must also understand them within the interpretations presented in the media and in official documents. It is our contention that the public commentaries about Lynndie England and the taking of the Abu Ghraib photographs may have *once* had the potential to be a part of larger spectacular constitutive rhetorics that were radical in nature and presented a competing vital myth of U.S. public morality, but that they had to compete with more moderate, stable, and mainstream interpretations of these same images that could themselves be linked to a host of other issues. We review and further unpack these dominant readings of the Abu Ghraib images next.

THE CONSTITUTION OF A STABLE PUBLIC MORALITY

The stable myth of U.S. martial morality perpetuated the "justness" of the war in Iraq and maintained the Abu Ghraib defendants as a "few bad apples." In addition, this myth sought to gain empathy for the military and American public, which had been duped by these few immoral agents. Detractors of Bush administration policies may have configured Lynndie England as the typical chauvinistic coalition trooper, but in many of the Anglo-American commentaries it was the members of the American military, writ large—and not just the Iraqi detainees—who were characterized as the penultimate *victims* of this tragedy. "The photographic depictions of the U.S. military personnel that the public has seen," argued Donald Rumsfeld, "have offended and outraged everyone in the Department of Defense."[106] While the defense secretary admitted that there were "other photos that depict incidents of physical violence toward prisoners" that could only "be described as blatantly sadistic, cruel and inhuman," he took solace from the fact that "the responsible chain of command was relieved and replaced."[107]

Given the volatile nature of this controversy, America's military leaders needed to find a way of dissociating themselves from the actions of England and the other few bad apples, while preserving the orchard that brought the world American virility and honor. Lynndie England became a condensation symbol for all of the Abu Ghraib abuses committed by the U.S. armed forces serving in Iraq. "For a while," argued Richard Cohen, "there was no more famous face in all the world than this Army reservist's."[108] The object of contempt in thousands of chat rooms and blog sites, England became a symbolic container of information for what supposedly happened when troops forgot about the importance of honor, or when subalterns disobeyed the basic rules that were a part of the U.S. military command structure.

All of these pictures could have been used as evidence of systematic abuse in the Abu Ghraib prison, and many critics did try to use them as indicators that Americans had squandered their moral capital, but these strategies would only have been effective if audiences were willing to admit that the Iraq intervention may have involved violations of international law. At the same time, the Abu Ghraib photographs transmigrated into legal debates, including discussions of just how far up the chain of command one has to go in order to find the "real" American position on acceptable behavior in Iraq. After all, as Hersh explains, this type of "dehumanization is unacceptable in any culture."[109] Yet this statement only gains traction if one believes that this dehumanization could be linked to American prison culture, typical martial behavior, or systematic violations of the Geneva Conventions.

Of course parts of these processes of containment and disassociation depended on the policing of the arguments and positions that would be deemed relevant in key legal forums, including court-martial proceedings. Given the fact that only a few bad apples were thought to be involved in the Abu Ghraib scandals, was it not safe to assume that only a few American soldiers were being interpolated into this netherworld of "dark tourism"?[110] How many witnesses or bystanders are truly culpable when only the night shift crew knew about Graner's or England's activities? When Colonel Denise Arn (the presiding officer at one of England's early hearings) was asked to approve a list of some 160 additional witnesses, she approved only one—a former army reservist who claimed that he had specific knowledge that some military interrogators had indeed abused prisoners.

All told, these and other rhetorical tactics attempted to alleviate the moral or legal responsibility of America's military leaders, and they ensured that only the members of the "lower" ranks could be held culpable in these situations. This in turn created the perception that perhaps these acts had been perpetrated by soldiers who had not yet imbibed the American rules of engagement. Furthermore, in terms of witnessing a spectacle, this framing offered a reassuring "Nothing to see here, folks" to those individuals who did not want to believe that the Abu Ghraib images also implicated American morals and American citizens who arguably had nothing to do with the scandal. Those who operate from this type of American framework could then argue that U.S. honor and valor provided the self-restraint that allowed Americans to view themselves as chivalrous and "humane" civilizers.

THE CONSTITUTION OF A VITAL PUBLIC MORALITY

As we noted above, some critics did suggest that Americans needed to take a close look at themselves in the mirrors that were provided by these images, which might encourage American introspection and consciousness-raising. Intellectual circles that included Susan Sontag, Slavoj Žižek, Barbara Ehrenreich, and Bill Maher reread the images and offered critiques of the dominant framing as controlling and minimizing the interpretive potential of the photographs. The questions raised in these circles centered around the cultural connection to American culture and morality, writ large.

For some pundits, the graphic rhetorical power of the most famous Abu Ghraib photographs created rare opportunities for U.S. introspection and moral expurgation. If laypersons or decision makers were going talk about the masculine abuse of power and the feminization of Iraq, then why not extend some of these claims and look at the domestic abuses that might be taking place within the walls of America's prisons? The controversial Bill Maher was convinced that American citizens could now at least begin thinking about domestic penal reform, and he argued that the entire country needed to understand why some two million Americans were being held as prisoners. Maher, who did not accept the popular rationales that viewed the events at Abu Ghraib as an isolated example of prankster abuse, magnified the circle of culprits who might be blameworthy, stating, "You can make fun of Lynndie England all you want, but when it comes to prisons, we are all holding the leash."[111]

Along similar lines, Žižek claimed in the *London Review of Books* that the Abu Ghraib photographs represent the *unknown knowns* of American culture and morality—"the disavowed beliefs, suppositions, and obscene practices we pretend not to know about, although they form the flipside of public morality."[112] Žižek instigates questioning of domestic American culture:

> Anyone acquainted with the U.S. way of life will have recognised in the photographs the obscene underside of U.S. popular culture. . . . This, then, was not simply a case of American arrogance towards a Third World people. The Iraqi prisoners were effectively being initiated into American

culture: they were getting a taste of the obscenity that counterpoints the public values of personal dignity, democracy and freedom.[113]

Susan Sontag, writing in the *New York Times Magazine,* also looks into the theme of American exceptionalism that threads throughout much of the dominant Bush administration rhetoric. It is telling, she argues, that Rumsfeld and others refused to label the photographed acts as "torture." Indeed, Rumsfeld took pains to differentiate between abuse and torture, arguing that "my impression is that what has been charged thus far is abuse, which I believe technically is different from torture, and therefore I'm not going to address the 'torture' word."[114] To deny the use of the word *torture*, however, effectively shuts down the potential for the U.S. public to name and reflect on the events at Abu Ghraib. Sontag recognizes that "to acknowledge that Americans torture their prisoners would contradict everything this administration has invited the public to believe about the virtue of American intentions and America's right, flowing from that virtue, to undertake unilateral action on the world stage."[115]

This rhetorical exclusion of *torture*, as well as the previously discussed scapegoating and feminizing of those purportedly involved, is criticized by those who would like to entertain a new construction of the American military, one that would force a rethinking of American domestic and international policy and morality. This "alternative" reading of the images contends that Abu Ghraib is not just a case of a "cellblock that had gone wild,"[116] but, rather, was about atrocities that had been approved by many members of an extended chain of command. Indeed, even the selective publication of very circumspect Pentagon reports implicates hundreds of intelligence officers and military officials in the abuses at Abu Ghraib.[117] As Sontag averred shortly before her death, the "Bush administration and its defenders have chiefly sought to limit a public relations disaster—the dissemination of the photographs—rather than deal with the complex crimes of leadership and of policy revealed by the pictures."[118] This critique, however, misses some of the nuances that come from the rhetorical reappropriation of these photographs. Supporters of the stable myth could argue that these administrators did indeed deal with crimes of leadership and policy—through the court-martial trials of England and the other involved parties.

Importantly, within the broader context of our digital age, the Abu Ghraib images have increasing implications for public morality. If we are to acknowledge that "war is hell," then we must also be willing to interrogate how digital imaging will alleviate or contribute to the stress of war, and in what ways. This is a necessarily collective endeavor:

> To live is to be photographed, to have a record of one's life, and therefore to go on with one's life oblivious, or claiming to be oblivious, to the camera's nonstop attentions. But to live is also to pose. To act is to share in the community of actions recorded as images. The expression of satisfaction at the acts of torture being inflicted on helpless, trussed, naked victims is only part of the story. There is the deep satisfaction of being photographed, to which one is now more inclined to respond not with a stiff, direct gaze (as in former times) but with glee. The events are in part designed to be photographed. The grin is a grin for the camera. There would be something missing if, after stacking the naked men, you couldn't take a picture of them.[119]

The American public, therefore, is called by the vital myth to respond to the progress of photographic technology in addition to (or because of) the "discovery" of wartime torture. If we are to be continually photographed and captioned, then what does this indicate for our public and personal identities and moralities? Horrible atrocities against others have occurred both in the United States and internationally, and yet they have not seemed as "real" to the public as they do now that viewers are able to glimpse a semblance of photographic reality. Does this mean that we will therefore put our best "moralities" on display in war and other times when the cameras are present, but jettison those moralities when we are out of the camera's field of vision?

Public intellectuals like Žižek and Sontag were able to put forth powerful arguments about how the images could or should be read in order to craft a truly revolutionary American morality. Others reflected on their own moralities and theories, as was the case with some feminists and supporters of women in the military. England's actions caught feminists and supporters of women in the military off guard, as they were called to question a variety of assumptions about gender differences. Indeed, critic Barbara Ehrenreich writes about her own struggles in coming to terms with "feminism's assumptions," and reminds herself and us that "a uterus is not a substitute for a conscience."[120] Ultimately, as she reviewed these images, she called for a "tough new kind of feminism with no illusions. Women do not change institutions simply by assimilating into them, only by consciously deciding to fight for change. We need a feminism that teaches a woman to say no . . . to the military or corporate hierarchy in which she finds herself."[121]

Those urging a radical, vital myth of American morality, therefore, sought to open the door for a collective reflection about the Abu Ghraib events, and the meaning behind the taking and distribution of the images. This reflection would ostensibly also extend to a critique of the Iraq war itself. Given this radical questioning, however, we should not be surprised to find that the more that *critics* of the Bush administration complained about the scapegoating of Lynndie England and the rest of the Abu Ghraib defendants, the more *defenders* of these same policies underscored the importance of staying in Iraq, and harped on the exceptional nature of American values. Moreover, they rallied around the generals or Bush administrators who may have written controversial memos, arguing that there was a difference between accepting "responsibility" and engaging in acts that involved legal "culpability." As the details about Abu Ghraib and, subsequently, Guantánamo Bay, became more public, definitions of torture and the classification of terrorists with regard to the Geneva Conventions were debated, with the Bush administration inducing a "cultural amnesia"[122] regarding these issues.

The shifting of blame in these public arenas only confirms the hegemonic martial values that inform this scandal, which, in turn, influence public understandings of what "really" happened at Abu Ghraib. For example, the published, redacted photographs indicate that it was only these several actors who were involved in this abuse. This photographic proof, therefore, is held up as what *really* happened at Abu Ghraib—a constitutive rhetorical strategy with which it is difficult to contend. Even Sontag seems to accept that the images will not make the important statement that is so necessary, that they eventually will be swept under the rug:

So now the pictures will continue to "assault" us—as many Americans are bound to feel. Will people get used to them? Some Americans are already saying they have seen enough. . . . Already the backlash has begun. Americans are being warned against indulging in an orgy of self-condemnation. The continuing publication of the pictures is being taken by many Americans as suggesting that we do not have the right to defend ourselves: after all, they (the terrorists) started it. They— Osama bin Laden? Saddam Hussein? What's the difference?—attacked us first.[123]

Constitutive Spectacles, the Crafting of Moralities, and the Reappropriation of the Abu Ghraib Images

At this point in time, half a decade after the Abu Ghraib images were made public and sparked a national and international firestorm of debate, talk about Abu Ghraib has quieted. For several years it has appeared as though many Americans have accepted the rationalizations that were contained in the "bad apples" narratives. The ACLU, *Salon,* and a few other organizations sought to publicize the existence of a "new" batch of pictures from Abu Ghraib that put on display the infamous "iceman" who purportedly died during CIA interrogations and other grisly photos, but the stories that have pathologized or otherwise explained away these behaviors seemed to have gained in resonance.

Though many high-ranking officers were identified as culpable in the scandal, only eleven soldiers were ultimately court-martialed and convicted, none of whom were ranked higher than staff sergeant. The twelfth soldier and only *officer* court-martialed was acquitted of responsibility for the events at Abu Ghraib.[124] And as of August 2007, there were no more trials pending regarding Abu Ghraib, indicating that the case is essentially closed. Though at this time, the media occasionally offers updates for the court-martialed MPs and their superiors, there is little lasting discussion about American *public morality* that the photographs originally incited. Rather, the debate that is ongoing seems to be confined only to finger-pointing and continues to assign moral culpability, rather than addressing what an American public can *learn* from Abu Ghraib.

Dozens of investigative reports survive in cyberspace, apparently destined to become digital relics in the chronicling of one campaign in the protracted war against terrorism.

We set out in this essay to discuss how visual images can be deployed in times of war by various interested parties to construct the morality or immorality of the particular war effort. As we see, these iconic snapshot photographs and the rhetorical context of the Abu Ghraib scandal worked to provide publics with various immediate and salient representations of the realities and moralities associated with American activities in Iraq. On the surface, therefore, the majority of commentaries on the Abu Ghraib scandal—fueled by the publishing of photographs that showed what was "really" happening in Iraq—might be viewed as material that provides antiwar critics with positive proof of the problematic nature of this conflict.

What is clear in this case is that the Abu Ghraib constitutive spectacles at one time hailed an American public by offering a new, *vital myth* about American public morality. Meanings ascribed to what was depicted in the photographs challenged stable myths about American beneficence and martial goodness, lifting the veil of false consciousness operating in the American public and allowing rhetorics to emerge that offered new and various ideological commitments. As Charland explains,

> Various contradictory subject positions can simultaneously exist within a culture: we can live within many texts. These contradictions place a strain upon identification with a given subject position and render possible a subject's rearticulation. Successful new constitutive rhetorics offer new subject positions that resolve, or at least contain, experienced contradictions.[125]

Unfortunately, the vital myth of American morality that could have caused an American public to sincerely reflect on and perhaps alter our involvement in international conflicts and domestic policy, was subsumed by a more staid, traditional, and dominant rhetoric that maintained the hegemony of American military policy and procedures. Thus, the vital myth as a whole failed in introducing a new moral identity to the American public.

Ultimately, defenders of Bush administration policies or pundits who write about the desirability of this second U.S.-Iraqi conflict appropriated these pictures for use in narratives that contained or domesticated antiwar criticism. Some of the permutations of these narratives included ideological fragments that invite us to value a hegemonic, masculine military, so that we could join the ranks of those who fear the feminization of U.S. soldiers, or the existence of diverse gender roles. These gendered ideologies were tied to military policies supporting the feminization of prisoners and scapegoating of small-town soldiers. Wartime "abuse" thus became an individuated act carried out by those who violate American martial or cultural norms, an activity that does not go unrecognized or unpunished, and that is kept rhetorically distinct from notions of the "real" and collective American public. Ultimately, the Bush administration rhetoric was the more successful of the competing rhetorics in constituting U.S. wartime identity and morals, in part because it provides audiences with a *coherent* constitutive rhetoric.

Such an outcome may have been predicted by Debord, who would argue that the ubiquity of mediated spectacle causes passivity among potential audience members, such that vital myths eventually lose traction. As spectacle, the Abu Ghraib images presented possibilities for new collective moralities and resistance against official just war discourse and American exceptionalism, but if spectacle is ultimately about the (re) circulation of discourse sanctioned by particular regimes of power, then it stands to reason that introducing and maintaining a vital myth of collective morality is an uphill battle to begin with.

Condit suggests that morality is a collective craft, stating that "To recognize morality as a collective craft is also to call ourselves to account for our participation in the ebb and flow of human morality."[126] While we certainly see the struggle for a collective morality in the constitution of the American public, it is not as clear in the Abu Ghraib case that a "strong moral code that demands human equality has gained currency," as Condit suggests.[127] Though moral dilemmas were inherent in all of the Abu Ghraib rhetorics, the successful constitutive rhetoric ultimately allowed issues of morality to quietly seep away and, therefore, to remain relatively absent, in the American public identity.

When we look at the Abu Ghraib torture photographs, they nonetheless look back at us, which at least keeps the door open for a vital myth to be resurrected. They show us a presidential administration high on its ability to exact imperialist force on cultures labeled as "other." They show us a culture at odds with itself about the punishment of criminals and others who cannot adequately "follow the rules" of society. They show us an ongoing struggle with deeply running gender ideologies entwined with historical events and current decision making. They show us that we are comfortable with allowing our lower-class and minority citizens to fight our wars for us, while our upper-class (white) citizens make the decisions that will ensure that they are not held accountable for such decisions.

On our more optimistic days we hope that the photographs of England, Graner, and some of the other Abu Ghraib reservists will one day be tethered together with the additional photographs and video coming out of Haditha and other places. It seems to us that the rhetorical use and reuse of the Abu Ghraib images—perhaps in political campaigns—is capable of opening up space to revisit the issue of public morality, especially as the captioning and context of the images work to rearticulate how the images are interpreted. Indeed, though the vital myth failed as a whole, we hope that it did at least make significant, albeit brief, strides toward a more reflective public and perhaps set a particular consciousness-raising in motion. Indeed, select individuals and groups are continuing the investigation into Abu Ghraib, such as is seen with the recent documentary *The Ghosts of Abu Ghraib*,[128] as well as Errol Morris's recent documentary.[129] We are also heartened by the potential for a paradigm shift that has been presented by the Obama administration. Though recently, even Obama has declared that he is not willing to release the remaining Abu Ghraib photos.[130] And yet, under President Obama, Guantánamo Bay detention camp, itself criticized for inhumane treatment and torture of prisoners, is slated to close by the end of 2009.[131] Recent media outlets have also reported on the reopening of Abu Ghraib as the Baghdad Central Prison under Iraqi authority, where officials are purportedly focusing on prisoner rehabilitation and have promised humane treatment and conditions for prisoners.[132]

We tentatively side with Sontag, then, who claims that "in our digital hall of mirrors, the pictures aren't going to go away. Yes, it seems that one picture is worth a thousand words. And even if our leaders choose not to look at them, there will be thousands more snapshots and videos."[133] We thus consider the current "fixing" of the images to be only a moment in the larger debate about morality in times of war, and we look forward to a time when these images are resurrected as vital myths that are wholly successful in the (re)constitution of a more honest, reflexive public morality.

NOTES

1. See, for example, John M. Doris and Dominic Murphy, "From My Lai to Abu Ghraib: The Moral Psychology of Atrocity," *Midwest Studies in Philosophy* 31 (2007): 25–55.

2. Bill Rankin and Bill Torpy, "Lawyers Slam Iraq Prison Abuse," *Atlanta Journal-Constitution,* August 10, 2004, A3.

3. Luc Sante, "Tourists and Torture," *New York Times,* May 11, 2004, pars. 3, 8, http://proquest.umi.com.

4. Guy B. Adams, Danny L. Balfour, and George E. Reed, "Abu Ghraib, Administrative Evil, and Moral Inversion: The Value of 'Putting Cruelty First,'" *Public Administration Review* 66 (2006): 680–693.

5. Ruth Wedgwood, "The Steps We Can Take to Prevent Another Abu Ghraib," *Washington Post,* May 23, 2004, B5.

6. Celeste Michelle Condit, "Crafting Virtue: The Rhetorical Construction of Public Morality," *Quarterly Journal of Speech* 73 (1987): 79–97.

7. "Evidence" for the 2005 shootings at Haditha, Iraq, was in the form of a videotape that was sent to *Time* magazine, which broke the story; Bobby Gosh, "On Scene: Picking Up the Pieces in Haditha," *Time,* May 29, 2006, http://www.time.com/time/world/article/0,8599,1198977,00.html.

8. Michael C. McGee, "In Search of 'The People': A Rhetorical Alternative," *Quarterly Journal of Speech* 61 (1975): 245.

9. Lila Rajiva, *The Language of Empire: Abu Ghraib and the American Media* (New York: Monthly Review Press, 2005), 11.

10. Susan Sontag, *On Photography* (New York: Dell, 1977), 23.

11. David Finn, *How to Look at Photographs: Reflections on the Art of Seeing* (New York: Harry N. Abrams, 1994), 32.

12. David Levi Strauss, *Between the Eyes: Essays on Photography and Politics* (New York: Aperture, 2003), 71.

13. Sontag, *On Photography,* 23.

14. Ibid., 22, emphasis added.

15. Errol Morris, "Not Every Picture Tells a Story," *New York Times*, November 20, 2004, par. 1, http://www.nytimes.com/2004/11/20/opinion/20morris.html.

16. Cara A. Finnegan, "The Naturalistic Enthymeme and Visual Argument: Photographic Representation in the 'Skull Controversy,'" *Argumentation and Advocacy* 37 (2001): 134.

17. Strauss, *Between the Eyes*.

18. McGee, "In Search of 'The People,'" 240, emphasis added.

19. Robert Hariman and John Louis Lucaites, "Public Identity and Collective Memory in U.S. Iconic Photography: The Image of 'Accidental Napalm,'" *Critical Studies in Media Communication* 20 (2003): 35–66.

20. Ibid., 36.

21. Ibid., emphasis in original.

22. Guy Debord, *The Society of the Spectacle*, trans. Donald Nicholson-Smith (New York: Zone Books, 1995), 12.

23. Ibid., 14.

24. Ibid., 19.

25. S. Michael Halloran, "Text and Experience in a Historical Pageant: Toward a Rhetoric of Spectacle," *Rhetoric Society Quarterly* 31 (2001): 5.

26. John J. MacAloon, "Olympic Games and the Theory of Spectacle in Modern Societies," in *Rite, Drama, Festival, Spectacle: Rehearsals toward a Theory of Cultural Performance*, ed. John J. MacAloon (Philadelphia: Institute for the Study of Human Issues, 1984), 243.

27. Debord, *Society of Spectacle*, 19.

28. Tony Schirato and Jennifer Webb, "The Media as Spectacle: September 11 as Soap Opera," *Journal for Cultural Research* 8 (2004): 412–413.

29. Barbara Biesecker, "Michel Foucault and the Question of Rhetoric," *Philosophy and Rhetoric* 25 (1992): 351–364.

30. Carol Payne and Amy Lyford, "An Excerpt from 'The Secret Road to Abu Ghraib' with an Introduction by Carol Payne and Amy Lyford," *Visual Resources* 21 (2005): 194.

31. Ibid., 193–194.

32. McGee, "In Search of 'The People.'"

33. Condit, "Crafting Virtue," 79.

34. Ibid., 82.

35. Ibid., 83.

36. Laura Sjoberg, *Gender, Justice, and the Wars in Iraq: A Feminist Reformulation of*

Just War Theory (Lanham, Md.: Lexington Books, 2006).

37. Sontag, *On Photography*, 22.

38. Chris Hedges, *War Is a Force That Gives Us Meaning* (New York: Public Affairs, 2002), 3.

39. Ibid.

40. Susan Sontag, "Regarding the Torture of Others," *New York Times Magazine*, May 23, 2004.

41. Seymour M. Hersh, *Chain of Command: The Road from 9/11 to Abu Ghraib* (New York: Harper Perennial, 2005), 18.

42. Marita Gronnvoll, "Gender (In)visibility at Abu Ghraib," *Rhetoric & Public Affairs* 10 (2007): 394.

43. Maurice Charland, "Constitutive Rhetoric: The Case of the *Peuple Québécois*," *Quarterly Journal of Speech* 73 (1987): 133–150.

44. Leisa D. Meyer, *Creating GI Jane: Sexuality and Power in the Women's Army Corps during World War II* (New York: Columbia University Press, 1996), 3.

45. Meyer, *Creating GI Jane*.

46. Clyde Wilcox, "Race, Gender, and Support for Women in the Military," *Social Science Quarterly* 73 (1992): 311–323.

47. John W. Howard III and Laura C. Prividera, "Rescuing Patriarchy or Saving 'Jessica Lynch': The Rhetorical Construction of the American Woman Soldier," *Women and Language* 27 (2004): 89–97.

48. Ibid.

49. Laura Sjoberg, "Agency, Militarized Femininity and Enemy Others," *International Feminist Journal of Politics* 9 (2007): 82–101.

50. Kenneth S. Zagacki, "Constitutive Rhetoric Reconsidered: Constitutive Paradoxes in G. W. Bush's Iraq War Speeches," *Western Journal of Communication* 71 (2007): 272–293.

51. U.S. Office of the Press Secretary, "President Bush Discusses Global War on Terror," (transcript), April 10, 2006, http://merln.ndu.edu/archivepdf/iraq/WH/20060410-1.pdf.

52. Sjoberg, *Gender, Justice*.

53. Zagacki, "Constitutive Rhetoric Reconsidered," 273.

54. Several accounts suggest that all of the detainees of Abu Ghraib were Iraqi; among these accounts are Hersh, *Chain of Command*; Donald H. Rumsfeld, "Testimony of Secretary of Defense Donald H. Rumsfeld," U.S. Department of Defense, May 7, 2004, http://www.defenselink.mil/speeches/speech.aspx?speechid=118.

55. Ibid.; Rajiva, *The Language of Empire*.

56. Morris, "Not Every Picture."

57. Hersh, *Chain of Command*, 18.

58. Mark Danner, "The Logic of Torture," in Meron Benvenisti et al., *Abu Ghraib: The Politics of Torture* (Berkeley, Calif.: North Atlantic Books, 2004), 17–46.

59. Hersh, *Chain of Command*.

60. Dan Glaister and Julian Borger, "1,800 New Pictures Add to US Disgust," *The Guardian*, May 13, 2004, http://www.guardian.co.uk/world/2004/may/13/iraq.usa.

61. Hersh, *Chain of Command*, 23.

62. Rajiva, *The Language of Empire*, 11.

63. For example, after viewing the photographs, Senator Ron Wyden (D-Ore.) remarked to reporters, "I expected that these pictures would be very hard on the stomach lining and it was significantly worse than anything I had anticipated. Take the worst case and multiply it several times over." Quoted in Glaister and Borger, "1,800 New Pictures," par. 3.

64. Robert Hariman and John Louis Lucaites, "Ritualizing Modernity's Gamble: The Iconic Photographs of the Hindenburg and Challenger Explosions," *Visual Communication Quarterly* 11 (2004): 12.

65. For example, Errol Morris's latest Abu Ghraib project suggests that when we see people smiling in pictures, we want to smile back. Thus, the images of U.S. soldiers smiling and giving the thumbs-up causes viewers to want to respond in kind, despite the graphic horror depicted in the images. Errol Morris, "The Most Curious Thing," *New York Times*, May 19, 2008, http://morris.blogs.nytimes.com/2008/05/19/the-most-curious-thing/index.html?ref=opinion.

66. Lynndie England, "Rumsfeld Knew," interview with Michael Streck and Jan-Christoph Wiechmann, March 17, 2008, http://www.stern.de/politik/ausland/614356.html.

67. Gronnvoll, "Gender (In)visibility."

68. Feminization is the construct whereby characteristics traditionally associated with females and often devalued in society are assigned to humans of either sex, to organizations, to sociopolitical constructions, and so on. See Kathy E. Ferguson, *The Feminist Case against Bureaucracy* (Philadelphia: Temple University Press, 1984).

69. Michelle Brown, "'Setting the Conditions' for Abu Ghraib: The Prison Nation Abroad," *American Quarterly* 57 (2005): 973–997.

70. Zagacki, "Constitutive Rhetoric Reconsidered."

71. Meyer, *Creating GI Jane*.

72. Michael Kimmel, *Manhood in America: A Cultural History* (New York: Free Press, 1996).

73. Sontag, "Regarding the Torture," par. 7, emphasis added.

74. Jonathan Jones, "All the Lonely People," *The Guardian*, May 19, 2004, par. 1, http://arts.guardian.co.uk/critic/feature/0,,1219957,00.html.

75. Slavoj Žižek, "Between Two Deaths: The Culture of Torture," *London Review of Books*, June 3, 2004, par. 9, http://www.lrb.co.uk/v26/n11/zize01_.html.

76. Brown, "Setting the Conditions."

77. David Levi Strauss, "Breakdown in the Gray Room: Recent Turns in the Image War," in Benvenisti et al., *Abu Ghraib*, 98.

78. Bryan C. Taylor, "'Our Bruised Arms Hung Up as Monuments,'" *Critical Studies in Media Communication* 20 (2003): 6.

79. These images and others can be viewed at http://en.wikipedia.org/wiki/Image:Abu-ghraib-leash.jpg; and http://www.salon.com/news/abu_ghraib/2006/03/14/introduction/index.html.

80. Sontag, "Regarding the Torture," par. 9.

81. Janina Struk, *Photographing the Holocaust: Interpretations of the Evidence* (New York: I. B. Tauris, 2005), 5.

82. Sontag, "Regarding the Torture," par. 7.

83. Sontag, "Regarding the Torture."

84. Julia T. Wood, *Gendered Lives: Communication, Gender, and Culture* (Boston: Wadsworth, 2007).

85. Strauss, "Breakdown in the Gray Room."

86. Luke Harding, "Actions of a Few, or a Policy from the Top?" *The Guardian*, May 17, 2004, http://www.guardian.co.uk/international/story/0,,1218248,00.html.

87. Sontag, "Regarding the Torture," par. 23.

88. Quoted in Dan Rather, "The Pictures: Lynndie England," *CBS News*, May 12, 2004, par. 8, http://www.cbsnews.com/stories/2004/05/12/60II/main617121.shtml.

89. Rick Hernandez, quoted in Renee Montagne and Ari Shapiro, "Military Hearing for Private First Class Lynndie England," *NPR Radio*, August 4, 2004, par. 6, http://web.lexis-nexis.com.

90. CBS Broadcasting, "Abu Ghraib Guard Gets 8 Years," October 21, 2004, http://www.cbsnews.com/stories/2004/08/08/iraq/main634647.shtml.

91. Staff Sergeant Chip Frederick, quoted in Neil Mackay, "The Pictures That Lost the War," *London Sunday Herald*, May 2, 2004, pars. 22–24, http://www.sundayherald.com/search/display.var.1032546.0.the_pictures_that_lost_the_war.php.

92. William Shakespeare, *Richard III*, http://www.shakespeare-literature.com/Richard_III/1.html.

93. Taylor, "Our Bruised Arms."

94. Gronnvoll, "Gender (In)visibility."

95. Carol Mason, "The Hillbilly Defense: Culturally Mediating U.S. Terror at Home and Abroad," *NWSA Journal* 17 (2006): 39–63.

96. Catherine Elsworth, "England 'Enjoyed' Abuse of Prisoners," *London Daily News*, August 31, 2004, http://web.lexis-nexis.com.

97. Jeremy Sivits, quoted in "Ex-Soldier Testifies in Abuse Hearings," *New York Times*, August 31, 2004, http://web.lexis-nexis.com.

98. Charles Stein, "Abu Ghraib and the Magic of Images," in Benvenisti et al., *Abu Ghraib*, 114.

99. Marina Hyde, "This Week," *The Guardian*, May 8, 2004, http://www.guardian.co.uk/comment/story/0,,1212159,00.html, par. 5.

100. Ibid., par. 9.

101. Sondra M. Archimedes, "Female Deviance in the Twenty-first Century: From Martha Stewart to Lynndie England," in *Gendered Pathologies: The Female Body and Biomedical Discourse in the Nineteenth-Century English Novel* (New York: Routledge, 2005), 157–162.

102. *Guardian Ulimited*, "Abu Ghraib Soldier Sentenced to Three Years in Jail," September 28, 2005, http://www.guardian.co.uk/international/story/0,,1580000,00.html, par. 9.

103. Jonathan Steele, "Top Brass Called to Torture Hearings," *The Guardian*, June 22, 2004, par. 7, 16, emphasis added, http://www.guardian.co.uk/international/story/0,,1244457,00.html.

104. Mackay, "Pictures That Lost War," par. 1.

105. Mark Danner, "Torture and Truth," *New York Review of Books*, June 10, 2004.

106. Defense Secretary Donald Rumsfeld, "Text of Rumsfeld Opening Statement," May 7, 2004, *CBS News.com*, par. 9, http://www.cbsnews.com/stories/2004/05/07/iraq/printable616250.shtml.

107. Ibid., pars. 25, 11.

108. Richard Cohen, "Victimizer and Victim," *Washington Post*, May 6, 2005, par. 3, http://web.lexis.nexis.com/universe.

109. Hersh, *Chain of Command*, 23.

110. John Lennon and Malcolm Foley, *Dark Tourism: The Attraction of Death and Disaster* (New York: Continuum, 2002).

111. Bill Maher, "New Rules," *HBO: Real Time with Bill Maher*, August 6, 2004, par. 6, http://www.hbo.com/billmaher/new_rules/20040806.html.

112. Žižek, "Between Two Deaths," par. 9.

113. Ibid., pars. 3, 5, 6.

114. Donald Rumsfeld, quoted in Sontag, "Regarding the Torture," par. 2.

115. Sontag, "Regarding the Torture."

116. Senator Joseph Lieberman, quoted in Glaister and Borger, "1,800 New Pictures," par. 8.

117. For example, The Taguba Report, an official military inquiry conducted by Maj. Gen. Antonio Taguba, can be found at: http://www.npr.org/iraq/2004/prison_abuse_report.pdf.

118. Sontag, "Regarding the Torture," par. 2.

119. Sontag, "Regarding the Torture."

120. Barbara Ehrenreich, "Feminism's Assumptions Upended," in Benvenisti et al., *Abu Ghraib*, 69.

121. Ibid., 70.

122. James Hedges and Marouf Hasian, Jr., "Campaign Posturing, Military Decision Making, and Administrative Amnesias," *Rhetoric & Public Affairs* 8 (2005): 694–698.

123. Sontag, "Regarding the Torture," par. 21.

124. Reuters, "General Clears Army Officer of Crime in Abu Ghraib Case," *New York Times,* January 11, 2008, http://www.nytimes.com/2008/01/11/washington/11abuse.html?ex=1357707600&en=b9e2c727e5c5afa8&ei=5090&partner=rssuserland&emc=rss&pagewanted=all.

125. Charland, "Constitutive Rhetoric," 142.

126. Condit, "Crafting Virtue," 94.

127. Ibid., 92.

128. *Ghosts of Abu Ghraib,* directed by Rory Kennedy, 2007 (Brooklyn, N.Y.: Moxie Firecracker Films).

129. See Morris, "The Most Curious Thing."

130. Jeff Zeleny and Thom Shanker, "Obama Moves to Bar Release of Detainee Abuse Photos," New York Times, May 13, 2009, http://www.nytimes.com/2009/05/14/us/politics/14photos.html

131. The executive order to this effect, signed by President Obama, can be found at: http://www.whitehouse.gov/the_press_office/ClosureOfGuantanamoDetention-Facilities/.

132. Sam Dagher, "With New Name and Mission, the Infamous Abu Ghraib Prison is to Reopen," *New York Times,* February 20, 2009, http://www.nytimes.com/2009/02/21/world/middleeast/21abughraib.html?ref=todayspaper.

133. Sontag, "Regarding the Torture," par. 27.

Public Address and Public Morality

Shawn J. Parry-Giles and Trevor Parry-Giles

For centuries, human beings have pondered just how to reach a reasonable, valid judgment about the morality of actions and behaviors. At the same time, those same humans have used public communication to express those judgments, have rhetorically beckoned audiences to share and identify with moral judgments and ethical conclusions. In many ways, humans have always adhered, as Richard Weaver articulated in response to the general semanticists, to the "ancient belief that a divine element is present in language" and that deeply imbedded in the human mind is "the feeling that to have power of language is to have control over things."[1] This volume grapples with the inherent relationships and tensions that characterize the connections between rhetoric and morality. When public actors enact moral codes, when orators give expression to ethical judgments, rhetorical critics step in to assess and evaluate, and the critics gathered here have surveyed a wide range of public articulations about morality. From their readings come many insights into the nature of both historical and contemporary articulations of moral judgment.

In her vision of a rhetorically crafted virtue, penned in 1987, Celeste Michelle Condit concluded that "'morality' is constructed by collectivities through their public discourse in a process of reflexive reproduction that utilizes the capacity of discourse simultaneously to create, extend, and apply moral concepts."[2] Her optimistic approach to a rhetorical morality argues that "as with all crafts, the rhetorical construction of morality fulfills the human urge for goodness, creativity, and perfection."[3] In this volume, Condit maintains her optimism, even as she calls for public address scholars to embrace again a concern for ethics and morality. Concerned as she is about the erosion of moral discourse that gave rise to the photographs of prisoner abuse at Abu Ghraib, we still must attend to public address, Condit says, because "we need to think of public speeches as nexus points where popular discourses are amplified, reworked, redirected, and deployed to produce concentrated change." We are asked, via Condit's analysis, to believe as she does that "if we have a chance of raising ourselves out of the muck of our worst potentials it is through the tool of language, and that the careful, critical study of human discourse is essential to enacting our better rather than worse potentials." Public address is the means by which public morality is voiced, and the criticism of public address allows for the betterment of human morality.

Vanessa B. Beasley moves us to think more specifically about the role of a particular type of public address, presidential oratory, in the articulation of a particular type of moral judgment, national identity and civil rights. In her book *You, the People: American National Identity in Presidential Rhetoric*, Beasley details the relationship between presidential rhetoric and national identity, speaking to the ethical tensions that often emerge in the expressions of nationalism, from the feelings of "connectedness where there otherwise might be none" to the "undeniably evil side" of nationalistic fervor. The national "we," she suggests, can be so powerful as a moral call that "it is compelling enough for people to willingly sacrifice both their livelihoods and their lives in its name."[4] Beasley's chapter in this volume takes a more specific approach, exploring how President George H. W. Bush's oratory regarding civil rights and particular legislation during the early 1990s articulated an individualistic notion of civil rights, removing a sense of pluralistic "group talk" from U.S. presidential discourse. Beasley significantly notes the moral consequences of these rhetorical choices, asking, "How can the United States, one of the world's largest functioning diverse and culturally pluralistic democracies, survive as such without a way of talking about its own pluralities in terms of their own needs, histories, and obligations to each other?" Calling this a "curious predicament," Beasley attends carefully to the profound moral implications of Bush's rhetoric for an increasingly diverse community.

Martin J. Medhurst departs somewhat from his customary focus on presidential rhetoric to consider, in some detail, the contentious and divisive debate over same-sex marriage in the United States. At the same time, Medhurst uses his criticism of that debate, as he does with much of his criticism, to comment on the moral and the ethical, to reveal the rhetorical articulations of moral codes and the problematics that attend to those articulations. With the same-sex marriage debate, Medhurst highlights the perils of language use and narrative emplotment in the expression of public moral argument. His analysis leads Medhurst to some imminently ethical conclusions that concern rhetoric and public moral argument generally as much as they do the same-sex marriage debate. Public moral argument, Medhurst proposes, must be characterized by mutual respect, by a willingness to forego demonization of one's opponents. It must proceed with the agreement that one's opponents may have genuine beliefs and good arguments to offer, and it must be willing to admit error. Ultimately, in Medhurst's normative vision of public moral argument, democracy may finally depend on the ability to compromise, to set aside certainty and demagoguery for the sake of a broader, more culturally accepted solution.

Much of public moral argument in the United States occurs within contexts of war or in situations where advocates compete over the extension or restriction of civil rights. Martin Luther King Jr.'s Riverside Church address of April 1967 operates at the nexus of both war and civil rights. James Jasinski and John M. Murphy recognize the uniqueness of King's rhetorical situation, arguing that King faced a popular president who had helped advance civil rights legislation and that King divided himself from much of the civil rights leadership in opposing the Vietnam War. King is able in this speech, Jasinski and Murphy contend, to interanimate "two traditions of American dissent, civic republicanism and the jeremiad." As a result, they argue, King manifested a compelling refiguration of public moral argument: "To craft an effective ethical response to the powerful imperatives of presidential war rhetoric asks such character work of dissidents. An end to war means an end to the communal identity that sustained the slaughter and a refiguration of the community in light of such experiences."

As he highlights the U.S. Treasury Department's World War II war bonds propaganda program, James J. Kimble speaks to the capacity of institutional public address to constitute a public in a time of war and the moral consequences of this constitutive discourse. Kimble reminds us that "when rhetors constitute audiences, their moral values are on display . . . [and] when the text in question emerges from a government agency— and when it takes on the form of widespread domestic propaganda in a context of war—such ethical assessments are all the more vital." Noting that such rhetoric "becomes rather intriguing" when considered morally in the context of the "just war" that World War II became, Kimble invites a consequentialist approach to the assessment of the government's ethics in its propaganda attempts to unify the nation. "What if the home front had *not* been united, potentially causing morale to crumble, production to plummet, and public resistance to the war to crescendo?" Kimble asks.

Employing an ideologically driven critique of presidential war discourse, and covering presidents from George Washington to George W. Bush, Shawn J. Parry-Giles argues that presidents have maintained a symbiotic and contested relationship between war and peace. Through a masculinized presidency, they have manipulated questions of war and peace to demonstrate American exceptionalism, preemptive conflict, and acts of aggression. "Such a discourse helps form the foundation of moral responsibility integral to the social contract," Parry-Giles suggests, "as the government acts to secure its people with an all-empowered military force; the role of the American people in turn is to unify around such military efforts." Echoing the consequentialism at the base of Kimble's analysis, Parry-Giles notes that "given the evolution of the country's historical and discursive commitments, which combine with the ongoing global turmoil, one can understand the allegiance to such historically rooted, patriarchal, and patriotic traditions that help unify the country around these empowering and shared beliefs." But, she cautions, such rhetoric comes with a cost that complicates its morality—a gendered sense of the presidency and war and peace that may justify atrocity and discrimination and the perpetuation of war to the detriment of the "beneficiaries of American benevolence."

This volume began with Celeste Condit's discussion of the Abu Ghraib photographs and what they tell us about the state of U.S. public moral argument. The volume concludes with Rebecca Gill and Marouf A. Hasian Jr.'s discussion of the same photographs, with a focus on the role "that *visuality* plays in these moral, wartime struggles." Gill and Hasian call attention to the way that these photographs work as "constitutive spectacles," proposing that "the study of the rhetorical formation of public morality needs to take into account the ideological, ambivalent, and polysemic dimensions of even the most realistic of pictorial representations." Even though the furor about the Abu Ghraib photos has quelled, in their immediate context they "hailed an American public by offering a new, *vital myth* about American public morality. What was depicted in the photographs challenged stable myths about American beneficence and martial goodness, lifting the veil of false consciousness operating in the American public and allowing vital myths to emerge that offered new and various ideological commitments."

The essays in this volume reveal, quite compellingly, how situated public address figures in the crafting of public morality and how such crafting is difficult, tenuous, and often confusing. These authors point to the range of problematics that attend to the investigation of public morality as it is expressed rhetorically, from tensions about language and narrative to concerns about gender, ideology, and visuality. They reveal how public morality is shaped in times of great social tension and stress. Wars, periods of social disruption, and eras of contentious public debate are all times when public morality emerges from public address. From gay rights to civil rights, from the Revolutionary War to the war in Iraq, whatever the context, the rhetoric in those times addressed to those contexts has profoundly ethical ramifications for the society.

The studies here also point to future directions for the investigations of the relationship between public address and public morality. The critics who offer their insights in this volume embrace the role of the rhetorical critic as a moral actor. Not shy about putting forth their ethical judgments, these critics recognize that those judgments are the stuff of rhetorical criticism, and their conclusions speak both to the moral dimensions of the rhetoric scrutinized and to the morality of rhetoric itself. As they embrace their roles as ethical, moral actors, these critics also invite our continued analysis of the moral role of rhetoric and the rhetorical critic. In short, how do we make the moral judgments that we make as rhetorical critics? What is the basis of our ethical judgment?

Each of the chapters here engages in some way in a process of normative ethics, asking and judging important questions about public morality and how that morality is crafted. Do we, in the assessment of public morality and the discourse that expresses it, employ a deontological standard of judgment, assessing ethics by the nature of the act, by its rightness or wrongness? This ethical position invites judgments of acts rooted in their divinity, or their adherence to duty, or their inherent morality. Moreover, how does rhetoric function deontologically? For centuries, the rhetorical act itself was seen suspiciously, and a deontological approach to public morality as expressed rhetorically reignites persistent anxieties about rhetoric's capacity to accurately, powerfully, and honestly craft public morality.

Or do we take a consequentialist approach to ethics, with its focus on outcomes and consequences rather than inherent goodness or rightness of a particular act? Such an approach, of course, immediately occasions questions of definition, highlighting the inherently rhetorical process of crafting public morality. When reaching ethical judgments, rhetoric defines the acts and their consequences. As such, there is almost a second-order consequentialism involved in the rhetorical construction of public morality. On the first level is the manner of the rhetorical construction and definition of ethical consequence, while on the second level is the consequentialist judgment of the rhetorical act itself as a moral performance. Rhetoric, thus, both crafts and performs public morality, and its consequences are automatically entailed by a consequentialist stance toward normative ethics.

Or do we investigate, via rhetorical discourse, the "virtue ethics" at work in specific contexts and situations, where instead of assessing a particular act or its consequences, the discourse offers a moral judgment about the character of the agent engaged in ethical or unethical conduct?

Traditionally, rhetoric and rhetorical criticism has been speaker centered, investigating the "first persona" and the "ethos" of each rhetorical moment. Dangerously, such an approach, as Condit points out, may individuate ethical judgment, ignoring important social factors or structural, material realities in the assessment of public morality.[5] At the same time, a focus on virtue ethics engages the fact that public morality and the rhetoric that defines and expresses it are intensely human processes, performed by humans, affecting humans, and with meaningful human consequences.

From the language that expresses it, to the visual rhetorics that image it, to the rhetorical genres that give it form, public morality, as the authors in *Public Address and Moral Judgment* reveal, is a rhetorical enactment. Situated examples of public address, where advocates present their cases and advance their positions before audiences that are live, or mediated, or both, have profound ethical and moral meanings for the community in which they are situated. Embracing the moral judgments produced in such rhetoric, and engaging seriously the ethical tensions that such public address expresses, is the telos of this book, and the very nature of rhetorical inquiry. Our contributions here will, we hope, further an ongoing and flourishing line of critical inquiry that seeks to offer meaning and judgment about the crafting of public morality, the advancement of public moral argument, and the maintenance of a publicly moral community.

NOTES

1. Quoted in Richard L. Johannesen, Rennard Strickland, and Ralph L. Eubanks, eds., *Language Is Sermonic: Richard M. Weaver on the Nature of Rhetoric* (Baton Rouge: Louisiana State University Press, 1985), 33.
2. Celeste Michelle Condit, "Crafting Virtue: The Rhetorical Construction of Public Morality," *Quarterly Journal of Speech* 73 (1987): 93.
3. Ibid., 94.
4. Vanessa B. Beasley, *You, the People: American National Identity in Presidential Rhetoric* (College Station: Texas A&M University Press, 2004), 4.
5. Condit, "Crafting Virtue."

Contributors

◼◼
◼◼

VANESSA B. BEASLEY is an associate professor in the Department of Communication Studies at Vanderbilt University. She is the author of *You, the People: American National Identity in Presidential Rhetoric* (2004) and the editor of *Who Belongs in America: Presidents, Rhetoric and Immigration* (2006). Beasley serves as the book review editor of *Rhetoric & Public Affairs* and the editor for the Presidential Rhetoric book series for Texas A&M University Press.

CELESTE MICHELLE CONDIT is a professor in the Department of Speech Communication at the University of Georgia. She is the author or co-author of *Decoding Abortion Rhetoric: Communicating Social Change* (1990), *Crafting Equality: America's Anglo-African Word* (1993), and *The Meanings of the Gene: Public Debates about Human Heredity* (1999). A former co-editor of *Critical Studies in Media Communication* and *Wom-*

en's Studies in Communication, Condit is also a National Communication
Association Distinguished Scholar.

REBECCA GILL is a doctoral candidate in the Department of Communica-
tion at the University of Utah. Her research has appeared in the *Journal of
Applied Communication Research, Organization,* the *Electronic Journal of
Communication,* and *Management Communication Quarterly.* She is the
recipient of a Graduate Research Fellowship and the Steffenson-Cannon
Scholarship from the University of Utah Graduate School.

MAROUF A. HASIAN JR. is a professor in the Department of Communica-
tion at the University of Utah. He is the author of five books, including
The Rhetoric of Eugenics in Anglo-American Thought (1996), *In the Name
of Necessity: Military Tribunals and the Loss of American Civil Liberties*
(2005), and *Rhetorical Vectors of Memory in National and International
Holocaust Trials* (2006). Among other awards, Hasian has received the
National Communication Association's Golden Anniversary Monograph
Award.

JAMES JASINSKI is a professor and chair of the Department of Commu-
nication Studies at the University of Puget Sound. He is the author of
Sourcebook on Rhetoric: Key Concepts in Contemporary Rhetorical Studies
(2001) and numerous articles and book chapters. His work has appeared
in the *Quarterly Journal of Speech,* the *Western Journal of Communication,*
Rhetoric Society Quarterly, and *Critical Studies in Mass Communication.*
Among other awards, Jasinski has received the Marie Hochmuth Nichols
Award from the National Communication Association's Public Address
Division.

JAMES J. KIMBLE is an assistant professor in the Department of Communication at Seton Hall University. He is the author of *Mobilizing the
Home Front: War Bonds and Domestic Propaganda* (2006). His research
has appeared in the *Quarterly Journal of Speech, Rhetoric & Public Affairs,*
and the *Southern Communication Journal.* He is the recipient of the National Communication Association's Karl Wallace Memorial Award and
the Gerald R. Miller Outstanding Doctoral Dissertation Award.

Martin J. Medhurst is a Distinguished Professor of Rhetoric and Communication at Baylor University where he is also a professor in the Department of Political Science. He is the author or editor of fourteen books, including *Eisenhower's War of Words: Rhetoric and Leadership* (1994), *The Rhetorical Presidency of George H.W. Bush* (2006), and *Words of a Century: The Top 100 American Speeches, 1900–1999* (2008). Medhurst is the editor of *Rhetoric & Public Affairs* and the recipient of numerous awards, including the National Communication Association's Distinguished Scholar Award.

John M. Murphy is an associate professor in the Department of Communication at the University of Illinois. His research has appeared in the *Quarterly Journal of Speech*, *Rhetoric & Public Affairs*, *Presidential Studies Quarterly*, and elsewhere. A former book review editor of the *Quarterly Journal of Speech*, Murphy is also a recipient of the National Communication Association's Golden Anniversary Monograph Award and the NCA Public Address Division's Wrage-Baskerville Award.

Shawn J. Parry-Giles is a professor and the director of graduate studies in the Department of Communication at the University of Maryland. She is the author, co-author, or editor of five books, including *The Rhetorical Presidency, Propaganda, and the Cold War, 1945–1955* (2002), *The Prime-Time Presidency: The West Wing and U.S. Nationalism* (2006), and *The Handbook on Rhetoric and Public Address* (forthcoming). Parry-Giles is also a co-director of the Voices of Democracy: The U.S. Oratory Project, funded by the National Endowment for the Humanities and the co-editor of *Voices of Democracy*.

Trevor Parry-Giles is an associate professor in the Department of Communication at the University of Maryland where he is also an affiliated scholar with the Center for American Politics and Citizenship. He is the author or co-author of three books, including *The Prime-Time Presidency: The West Wing and U.S. Nationalism* (2006) and *The Character of Justice: Rhetoric, Law, and Politics in the Supreme Court Confirmation Process* (2006).